RHAPSODY FOR AN OBSESSIVE LOVE

BOOKS BY DUNCAN MCLAREN

Personal Delivery

Red Marauder

The Strangled Cry of the Writer-in-Residence

Stay Here and Make Art (with Bill Drummond)

Per Hüttner

Laura Ford: Armour Boys

George MacDonald 1824–1905

Looking for Enid

DUNCAN MCLAREN ALSO WRITES

www.duncanmclaren.co.uk

www.enidblyton.me.uk

www.strangebundle.co.uk

www.nobsonnewtown.co.uk

www.scenesfromthepassion.co.uk

www.patisback.co.uk

www.evelynwaugh.org.uk

Evelyn!

RHAPSODY FOR AN OBSESSIVE LOVE

DUNCAN McLAREN

Harbour

First published as a paperback original by
Harbour in 2015
Harbour Books (East) Ltd, PO Box 10594
Chelmsford, Essex CM1 9PB
info@harbourbooks.co.uk

Copyright © Duncan McLaren 2015
a continuation of the copyright information
is to be found on page 292–3

Duncan McLaren has asserted his moral right under
the Copyright, Designs and Patents Act, 1988, to be
identified as the author of this work

A CIP record for this book is available
from the British Library

ISBN 978 1905128280

Typeset in Great Britain by Antony Gray
Printed and bound in Finland by Bookwell

TO
KATHRYN CLAYTON
IN HOMAGE AND AFFECTION

CONTENTS

'Well, in *our* country,' said Evelyn, still panting a little, 'you'd generally get to somewhere else – if you ran very fast for a long time, as we've been doing.'

'A slow sort of country!' said She-Evelyn. 'Now, *here*, you see, it takes all the running *you* can do, to keep in the same place. If you want to get somewhere else, you must run at least twice as fast as that.'

★

'If I wasn't real,' Evelyn said – half laughing through his tears, it all seemed so ridiculous – 'I shouldn't be able to cry.'

'I hope you don't suppose those are real tears?' She-Evelyn interrupted in a tone of great contempt.

Evelyn Through the Looking Glass

PRELUDE

English Gothic

1

A recollection: it's 1975 and I'm a seventeen-year-old lying on the carpeted floor in the lounge of my parents' house in suburbia reading a paperback edition of *Decline and Fall*. It's that time in the day – between my getting home from the local secondary school and my father's getting home from work – that is completely given over to self-indulgence. Some homework as well? After all, I'm studying A levels. Possibly, but that's not what I remember filling this period. Evelyn Waugh novels and David Bowie records are what I remember. The Maths, Physics and Geography have dissolved without trace.

The Bowie influence came first. A young man could love himself that much? But, a year or two later, the Penguin editions of the Waugh novels were also having a big impact on my evolving psyche. The books were somehow as relaxed, self-absorbed and fulfilling as Bowie's music was. Who was this Evelyn Waugh? (In its own way, a name to rival Ziggy Stardust's.) The period covers of the books typically featured a single figure, long-legged and languid, with a deadpan expression on his face, against an exotic environment. How cool were those covers! It wasn't until much later that I discovered that Evelyn was – at about five-foot-seven – a small pugnacious man, ill-at-ease with his physical appearance, constantly at odds with the world but just as constantly transforming uncomfortable experience into exquisite fiction.

I've still got my diary from way back then. By and large it makes for embarrassing reading. Luckily, it is also studded with what could loosely be described as facts. Two entries from spring and summer, before and after mock A levels, read as follows:

15 March 1975
Really like Bowie's single 'Young Americans'. I keep singing: 'Gee, my life's a funny thing, Am I still too young?'

21 July 1975
Reading a terrifically funny book by Evelyn Waugh. *SCOOP*.

Most of the July entry was written with a black pen, but for the single word SCOOP, I switched to brown felt-tip. Perhaps, unconsciously, I was establishing a link between the shapeless brown bean-bag I was resting on as I read the novel, and the stylish brown armchair on which a man was featured sitting on the front of the Penguin edition of the book. His elegant brogues rested on a leopard-skin rug. He looked as cool as Bowie did on the cover of *Space Oddity* when it was reissued, where the singer appears wearing a sparkly jump-suit and long pink boots.

I've still got those Penguin paperbacks, just as I've still got the vinyl records and their handsome sleeves. In 1975 I read the *Sword of Honour* trilogy, *Scoop, Put Out More Flags* and *Black Mischief*. And in 1976, while in my last year at school, I read *Brideshead Revisited, The Loved One* and *The Ordeal of Gilbert Pinfold*. But the book that made most impact was the one I read first, and kept coming back to, namely *Decline and Fall*. I just could not believe how funny it was. And I felt connected to the intelligence behind the novel. I've now got some idea why.

Waugh was in his mid-twenties when he wrote the masterly black comedy in 1927–8. Apart from his time at Oxford, the main things he'd experienced were being a pupil at one public school and teaching at another. When I read the book, I was slowly getting round to the prospect of going up to university to read Geography (though literature, art and music were my only interests). And here was a book that began with its undergraduate hero, Paul Pennyfeather, coming home to his rooms in college. Suddenly a giant was standing in his way, shouting to the rest of a drunken rabble: 'Here's an awful man

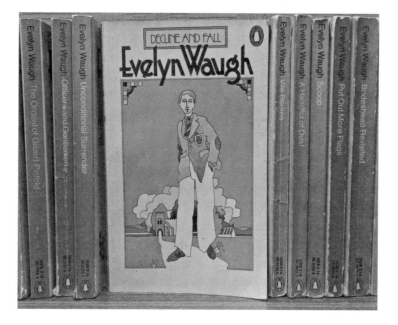

wearing the Boller tie.' Minutes later, the members of the Bollinger Club, in their collective outrage, had stripped Paul of his clothes. The next day he was sent down from Oxford for indecent behaviour. 'Ran the length of the quadrangle without his trousers on,' reported one senior member of the college to another. '*Without trousers?*' said the other, ostensibly shocked, though they both understood exactly what had gone on. (The upper classes must have their fun.) So, poor Paul Pennyfeather found himself chucked out of his élite station in life, and had no choice but to teach at a third-rate public school. Was that the sort of fall from grace that was going to happen to me, especially if I insisted on carrying on with a course of study that wasn't right for me? Was I destined to teach Geography at an inner city comprehensive? And if life was to serve up this kind of humbling experience was I going to be able to take it on the chin like *blasé* Paul? I can imagine generations of bright young boy readers responding positively to *Decline and Fall*, simply through identifying with the main character.

Almost as important a character in the novel is Captain Grimes.

Wooden-legged Grimes is one of Pennyfeather's two fellow masters at Llanabba Castle. He is a paedophile, although that's never explicitly stated. What Grimes tells Paul is that he's been 'in the soup' several times in the past. At Llanabba Castle, the apple of Grimes's perverted eye is a 'pretty boy' called Clutterbuck. His father owns the local brewery and at one point in the story, Grimes, as a reward for taking a special interest in the boy, is, ironically, offered a job at the brewery as a professional beer taster, with a decent salary, all expenses paid and a company car. 'God's own job,' is how Grimes puts it, in a passage I remember laughing aloud at. Partly this was because I myself was discovering the joys of alcohol at the time. Indeed, I lived for the Friday- or Saturday-night pub crawl that a group of us embarked on every weekend. That and the period of leisure between school and evening meal were the only times that I felt free of convention.

What I found most exciting about Waugh's writing concerning Grimes was its seeming amorality. A posed amorality was rife within the group of friends I associated with in the sixth form. One subject of occasional in-jokes among us was seal-culling. My chum Colin and I were all for it. Of course, we were not. But the fact that seal-culling went on in barbarous parts of the world, and that various moral guardians – the press, teachers, and the more earnest of our fellow pupils – felt the need to state the obvious – over and over again – was simply too boring to put up with. It was the cliché that wanted knocking on the head, not the seal pup. Grimes was a confirmed seal-clubber. That's to say he was a child molester. So what? – beyond the obvious fact that this would have been terrible for the children concerned.

Now I'm uncomfortable with such an attitude. And all I can say in defence of my seventeen-year-old self is that the sexual abuse of children was not a topic that had been much discussed by the mid-seventies and I knew of no one who had been a victim of it. Which I suppose may also be the defence for Evelyn Waugh writing about such a character in 1928. More important to both of us, writer and reader, was that Grimes was an irrepressible life force. Whatever fate threw at him, Grimes would bounce back from. Waugh's Pennyfeather and I admired the resilient sense of identity that Grimes possessed. And we were eager to learn how we could develop our own.

Of course, I am not the only reader to have noticed the sparks that lit up *Decline and Fall*. The work was admired from the word go. When its first ten thousand words had been written towards the end of 1927, Waugh's chum from Oxford, Anthony Powell, laughed aloud over the handwritten pages. Asked later whether he had thought the book would be a success, Powell replied that he hadn't, because it was just too funny in an absolutely original way. When the manuscript had grown to about fifty pages, Dudley Carew, an acolyte of Waugh's from public-school days, was the one to get the benefit of a private reading. In Carew's own book published several years after Waugh's death, *A Fragment of Friendship*, Carew refers to the reading as perhaps the most precious of all his memories of Evelyn. 'A happiness, a hilarity sustained him that night, and I was back giving him my unstinted admiration as I had at Lancing. It was marvellously funny and he knew that it was. As was his habit in those old innocent days, he roared with laughter at his own comic invention.' And the person to whom *Decline and Fall* was eventually dedicated 'in homage and affection', Harold Acton, who'd been such a dominant intellectual influence on Waugh at Oxford, had this to say in his *Memoirs of an Aesthete*. 'All his friskiness bubbled into the pages of *Decline and Fall*. It was as if he'd been rolling in the early morning dew, so light, so fresh, so mischievous were the sentences that rippled off his pen.'

Which reminds me. In 1983 there was a three-part television biopic made about Waugh on the back of the success of the 1981 Granada TV adaptation of *Brideshead Revisited*. I've watched it again lately. It features, among other things, several of Evelyn's peers reading from Waugh's books. In each case, the books are the same Penguin editions that I read in the mid-seventies, so I guess those style classics were around for a while. Harold Acton, smartly suited, sitting in the grounds of the magnificent villa he inherited in the countryside near Florence, reads from *Decline and Fall*'s Prelude. His rich, full, fruity voice brings to life the section that focuses on the two senior members of Paul Pennyfeather's college on the night of the Bollinger binge.

Craftily keeping out of view in the deanery, the dons are excitedly wondering what sort of mischief the Bollinger boys are going to carry out that night, and how much of a windfall in fines the college will be enjoying the next day.

At another point in the biopic, Anthony Powell, sitting in front of a bookcase in what I understood to be his personal library, dressed in jacket and tie, bends the paperback back on itself and reads the section that immediately follows in the Prelude, in *his* rich, full, plummy voice. This passage introduces Paul Pennyfeather in terms that make it clear that Evelyn Waugh is referring to himself. That is, like Waugh, Pennyfeather attended a small public school on the South Downs, where he had edited the magazine and been president of the debating society, and had, as his report said, 'exercised a wholesome influence for good' in the house of which he was head boy. The reading ends just before the drunken Lumsden of Strathdrummond, proud member of the Bollinger Club, sways across his path like a druidicial rocking-stone, precursor of experience.

So there's me, aged seventeen in 1975, having experienced very little of life. And there's Harold Acton and Anthony Powell, both aged about eighty in 1983, having experienced a great deal. And what did we have in common? We could each have put our hands on Penguin paperback copies of *Decline and Fall*, a working knowledge of which we regarded as one of our most treasured possessions.

It's marvellous that the director of the *Arena* programme was able to get the co-operation of these contemporaries of Waugh. And timely as well. Harold Acton died in 1994 at the age of ninety. Anthony Powell died in 2000 at the age of ninety-four. They were born into the upper class, with silver spoons full of all the right kinds of nutrition glistening in their mouths. Evelyn, making his own way through life, relying on his middle-class professional wits, was a different case, and he died . . .

But I'm getting ahead of myself. There is to be no talk here of Evelyn Waugh's dying. Back to *Decline and Fall*. Back to Grimes the irresistible life-force. Apparently, in the original manuscript, Grimes's attraction to boys is made explicit. Such explicitness could never have survived into the published work of 1928, which instead relies on innuendo. Luckily for candour, in the first and only volume of Waugh's autobiography, *A Little Learning*, published in 1964, Waugh states that he based Grimes on a master who worked with him at a school in North Wales. That is also clear from the now published *Diaries*, which give the man's name as Dick Young. In an entry in the *Diaries* for May 1925, Waugh wrote that Young had told him that he'd already lost several jobs in public schools, usually for sodomy with a pupil in his charge, but once for being drunk six nights in a row. Despite this, Young assured Waugh, his career as a schoolmaster had gone from strength to strength, with better and better jobs falling into his lap. Why did Waugh not report his fellow teacher to his headmaster or other school authority? Surely he accepted that as teachers they were jointly responsible for the welfare of their pupils.

It gets worse. The *Diaries* themselves don't contain one specially revealing account. *A Little Learning* of forty years later does. After a hectic holiday on the slopes of Mount Snowdon, which Evelyn and a second fellow master reckoned no one could possibly have enjoyed, Young begged to differ. *He'd* enjoyed it all right. 'What was there to enjoy?' asked Waugh. 'Knox Minor,' was the answer. Young went on to describe how he had felt the games become too boisterous. So he'd taken Knox Minor behind some rocks for his own safety. There he'd 'removed the boy's boot and stocking, opened his own trousers, put the boy's dear little foot in there and experienced a most satisfying emission'.

I suppose it shows what a miserable human being Evelyn Waugh was in those days, straight out of education himself, with no fixed sexual identity of his own. He did nothing to ensure that the children that he was responsible for were made safe from the influence of Dick Young. Instead, he stored away both the man's words and his sense of entitlement and used them, albeit in a brilliant way, a few years later when he sat down to make light of his experience as a schoolmaster.

And poor traumatised Knox Minor's reaction? Well, Waugh doesn't record that in 1925, and nor does he in 1964. So I'll have a stab at it right now, albeit with my own sweetly bemused and innocent self of 1975 in mind:

> *'Gee, my life's a funny thing.*
> *Do I love Dick Young?'*

2

Yesterday I came close to convincing myself that I would like to embark on a project centring on Evelyn Waugh's life and works. But before doing so I should answer a question: Does the world need another book about Evelyn Waugh?

Christopher Sykes, who'd known Waugh and been a friend of his since the 1930s, wrote a tactful official biography in 1974. That was just before the scandalous *Diaries of Evelyn Waugh* came out in 1976, which were followed by *The Letters of Evelyn Waugh* in 1980. *Brideshead Revisited* was made into a sublime serial a year later, and it was pretty obvious that, notwithstanding the fine *Arena* programme made for BBC2 in 1983, a large-scale critical analysis written by a respected academic was going to be needed for the reading public. Step forward, Martin Stannard, Lecturer in English at the University of Leicester, who'd already published essays and reviews about Waugh. A five-hundred-pager covering 'The Early Years' appeared in 1986, and to complete a thousand pages, 'No Abiding City' appeared six years later. *The Yorkshire Post*'s reviewer said of the first volume: 'Stannard's work is so thorough that, if the final volume is anywhere near as good, there may be no need for further biographies.' Selina Hastings disagreed, explaining in the Foreword of her 1994 book, *Evelyn Waugh: a biography*, 'With every major writer there is room for at least three biographies, the third being a more general account, but drawing on primary sources and on original research.' Her stated aim was 'to give as close an impression as possible of what it was like to know Evelyn Waugh, even something of what it was like to be Evelyn Waugh'. The good news for my own ambition is that in this latter aim she doesn't – indeed can't – succeed. Both Stannard and Hastings stand well back from their subject, trying to get a balanced and objective view, as good biographers traditionally have done. Me? Every time I get close enough to Evelyn, I intend to shake hands with the man. I want to see his owl-like eyes staring back into mine; I want to feel his hot, whisky-laden breath on my face.

Is reading Stannard or Hastings (or Paula Byrne, who has more recently published *Mad World*, an analysis of the origins of *Brideshead*) a bit like reading one of Waugh's novels? No, it is not. For a start, there are no laughs. Why the hell not? – Waugh was a funny writer. I want to celebrate his sense of humour, in part by running with the baton of some of his jokes. That's the kind of tribute Evelyn is crying out for. So, I'm going to picture him as he lived his life, in the way that Waugh pictured Paul Pennyfeather. Do I actually mean that? I suppose I'll have to wait and see how the relationship of me as narrator and Evelyn as subject pans out in practice.

Maybe that would be enough by way of a new approach to Waugh studies. But whether I like it or not, there's another thing I'm bringing to the biographers' table. I'm interested in different kinds of creativity, and much of my published writing engages with the work of contemporary artists. For the last twenty years or so the graduates of art schools have been very good at thinking outside the various boxes society would try to place them in. And I feel that, over the years, I've picked up something of the habit myself.

In 2004 I was a passenger on a bus trip to France. The party was organised by Naomi Pepys and Katherine G. The artists raised the money for fifty individuals to do the journey in a yellow coach that had IN REMEMBRANCE OF THINGS PAST emblazoned down one side of it, and WE ARE NOT AFRAID OF MARCEL PROUST down the other. It turned heads did that luxury coach, whether it was swishing down the motorway towards the Dover end of the Channel Tunnel, or parked in the middle of the French *campagne*.

The artists' programme involved taking the party to Illiers, the real-life equivalent of Combray, where Proust's book's narrator spends his summers as a child. Then the coach went on to the original of

Balbec on the Normandy coast where adolescent Marcel falls in love with the teasing Albertine. The trip culminated in Paris, with the coach illegally parked on the Boulevard Haussmann, where, in a cork-lined room, Proust spent most of his last years writing and rewriting his monster autobiographical novel sequence.

Part of the idea was to see whether visiting these sites added to an appreciation of the books or simply detracted from them. For the majority of us, the visits added truckloads. That is, if you believe – from inclination and experience – that biography adds to your appreciation of an author's fiction, then the case for studying the actual places – the buildings and localities – where an author lived his or her one-and-only life is already made.

En route, a video made by Naomi Pepys and Katherine G was played to us on the coach's overhead monitors. I remember one scene clearly. Naomi was seen standing outside a country house in Gloucestershire, quoting what Evelyn Waugh had to say to Nancy Mitford in 1948 about Marcel Proust:

> 'Darling Nancy . . . I am reading Proust for the first time – in English, of course – and am surprised to find him a mental defective. No one warned me of that. He has absolutely no sense of time. He can't remember anyone's age. In the same summer as Gilberte gives him a marble & Françoise takes him to the public lavatory in the Champs Elysées, Bloch takes him to a brothel. And as for the jokes – the boredom of Bloch and Cottard.'

Then Katherine was shown standing on a smart Parisian boulevard, reading Nancy Mitford's reply: 'Darling Evelyn, I am sad to think of you reading Proust in English – there is not one joke in all the 16 of Scott-Moncrieff's volumes. In French one laughs from the stomach, as when reading you.'

The whole trip allowed passengers to engage with Proust in a fresh way. That seems clear to me. But I'm glad I don't have to explain it to Alexander Waugh, Evelyn's grandson. In 2004 he published *Fathers and Sons*, which adds to our understanding of Evelyn Waugh by explaining how relationships with his father and his brother impacted on his developing psyche. The book is informed by many privately held documents. It's hard on Evelyn at times, but broadly admiring of his life's work. In many ways, *Fathers and Sons* represents the culmination of the Waugh family's engagement with English literature over the last hundred years.

All too easily, I can bring to mind an exchange at a forthcoming meeting of the Evelyn Waugh Society. Alexander, author of *Time and God* as well as the book on his male progenitors, is looking at me through owl-like eyes that I recognise as inherited from his famous grandparent:

Alexander: 'Let me get this straight. You have written widely about contemporary art and you feel this qualifies you to organise a coach trip between the main sites of my grandfather's life?'

Me: 'Not exactly. In order to add to the list of significant books about Evelyn Waugh, someone who has had a profound impact on me and many other readers, I feel I must take advantage of whatever literary skills I have, along with my art-world experience.'

Alexander (thoughtfully): 'The best of both worlds, eh?'

Me: 'The best of both worlds. Oh, and I rather hope there'll be as much going on creatively as there will be of a critical and analytical nature.'

But I've lost his full attention. He's glancing towards a group of family members. I can tell he's on the point of pulling the plug on our promising exchange. Time for a bit of lateral action.

Me (pointing towards a lecturer in English at the University of Texas in Austin, where so much archival material relating to Evelyn Waugh has ended up in storage): '*There's an awful man wearing the Boller tie.*'

Suddenly Alexander is wide-eyed again, as he appears in a photograph adorning the back of *Fathers and Sons*. In the picture, wise old Evelyn is holding his chubby grandson in one hand and a fat cigar in the other. Right now it is me that's holding the fat cigar, in my mind's eye, as I sway from side to side like a druidical rocking-stone. As for the now adult and distinguished Waugh minor, is he wondering what I'm going to say next? For the moment, that's all I could hope for.

UNDERHILL

Hampstead Walls Do Not a Prison Make

This morning I've done what Evelyn must have done hundreds of times. I've taken a Northern Line train from the centre of London and disembarked at Golders Green. From there I've walked south, along a straight road rising towards the top of Hampstead and the Heath. But just before getting to the summit of the hill I've found my destination, a house called Underhill when it was built by Evelyn's father in 1907. A house soon joined by many others, so that it was designated 145 North End Road by the Post Office.

Evelyn was just three years old when the family moved here, so to most intents and purposes it was his starting point. It was still the nearest thing to a home for him when his parents sold the house thirty years later. The blue plaque that shines out from the white wall states Evelyn's overall dates but it does not attempt to specify the years that he actually lived in this house. That would be hard to do without misleading people.

There is a For Sale sign in the narrow front garden, which is other-wise dominated by a tall hedge. The house is split into flats these days, and I don't expect I'll have any difficulty in taking a look around the exterior. Down hill of the house there is a wide drive connected with some kind of a car business. I wander along the company's drive and soon have the view of the north-west corner of the house that crops up in some of the Waugh literature. The picture I'm thinking of shows a large suburban house, with Arthur in a white straw hat sitting on a garden seat alongside his elder son, Alec. Arthur's wife stands supportively behind the seat. Evelyn is nowhere in sight. Did he take the photograph? Alec looks about ten in the picture so Evelyn would

have been just five-years-old, and, no, the photograph is not credited to him. Perhaps Evelyn was sheltering behind the seat, protected by his mother's skirts, in the knowledge that Alec was Arthur's favourite. That was certainly the case: a capable, athletic boy, much older than Evelyn, Alec enjoyed the most intimate friendship with his father. Arthur Waugh was bullied and beaten by his own father and would seem to have used his first son as a means of revisiting childhood, ensuring it was happy the second time around. By the time Evelyn came along, there simply wasn't room for a third person, so completely had father and first son bonded. When Evelyn asked his mother which of her two sons *she* loved most, her answer was that she loved them both equally. 'Then I am lacking in love,' deduced the earnest little boy.

Both Alec and Evelyn became writers, at least partly because they shared the most literary of upbringings. Arthur was managing director of the publishing firm Chapman and Hall: he loved books and respected the people who wrote them. He read poetry at the table before meals. After meals he read to his family in the large ground-floor 'book-room' – theatrical speeches from Dickens being a favourite. And he read to the boys in their bedroom prior to their going to sleep. By the time Alec was nine, he knew much of Shakespeare by heart and had acted the part of Hamlet.

But it's Evelyn I'm concerned with, and he too showed an early interest in his future profession. In the piece of juvenilia called 'Fidon's Confetion', a father of two boys, Tom and Ralfe, is stabbed at the beginning of the story by a pair of villains who have been playing cards with the older brother. One of the killers accuses the older brother, Ralfe, of the murder, but the younger brother, Tom, finds out from the second killer, Fidon, that it was the card players who killed their father in order to get revenge for something that had happened in the past. The fast-paced story proceeds with Tom being handed a written confession by Fidon. Brave Tom has to fight hard to keep it from falling into the clutches of the second murderer, so that he can present it to the court during Ralfe's trial. Which he does, with the desired effect of gaining his brother's freedom. Surely a great story as far as young Evelyn was concerned: the father that does not love the younger son gets what he deserves – stabbed in the heart. While the older son that the younger son so desperately wants to impress, surely *is* impressed by his brother's resourceful and selfless behaviour.

In reality, when Evelyn was eight and Alec thirteen, the older brother was sent to Sherborne School and the rapport between father and first son reached a new level of intensity. Arthur wrote fulsomely to Alec every day and got almost as frequent replies. After work on Friday during term, the besotted father would travel the hundred and fifity miles to set up a home-from-home in a Sherborne hotel for the weekend. Alec excelled in two things: cricket and English literature. Both parents avidly followed every step of his progress in these pursuits. One of the Waugh biographies contains details of a letter written by the boys' mother, to Alec, expressing the delight – nay, ecstasy – that his cricketing prowess has engendered in his parents' hearts. At Underhill, the talk at the table, when not about books and authors, was of Alec and Sherborne. Come the end of each term, Arthur would put up a banner over the grandfather clock in the hall proclaiming: WELCOME HOME THE HEIR OF UNDERHILL. That is, until the occasion Evelyn piped up with: 'And when Alec has inherited the house and everything in it, what will there be for me?'

There's a story that Evelyn wrote when he was in his early thirties – still regularly returning to his parents' home – called 'Winner Takes All'. As with 'Fidon's Confetion' the story is about two brothers, the younger called Tom, a name that Evelyn clearly liked for its unambiguous masculinity. The story proceeds quickly in numbered sections each about as long as the sections in the earlier story. I have a copy of Evelyn's *Complete Stories* in the small pack I'm carrying on my back today and have already gone through 'Winner Takes All' with a blue highlighter. So let me quickly remind myself how the story goes, even as I stand in the drive of whatever garage business operates from 143 North End Road:

One. Gervase Peregrine Mountjoy St Eustace is born in an expensive London nursing home. Two years later another child is born in a shoddy modern house on the east coast. Mrs Kent-Cumberland would have preferred a daughter on this second occasion. Mrs who? Well, Evelyn's mother was called 'K', short for Katie, but had been christened Catherine, possibly giving the K-C of Kent-Cumberland.

Two. Both brothers grow up accepting the fact of Gervase's primary importance just as each accepts the elder's superiority of knowledge and physique. They grow up in a house called Tomb Hill. Not Underhill. No, no, never Underhill.

Three. At the age of seven, Tom desperately wants a model car to pedal about the garden for Christmas (just as Evelyn had wanted a bike at that age). An uncle obliges, but Mrs Kent-Cumberland thinks there must have been a mistake with the labels, which she switches round, giving the expensive car to Gervase and landing Tom with yet another book. (At Underhill, Alec got the bike that Evelyn had asked his father for, while Evelyn had to settle instead for a box of theatrical face paints.)

Four. In 1915 the boys' father is killed. (There doesn't seem to be much room for live fathers in young Evelyn's stories.) Thereafter Mrs Kent-Cumberland would crush Gervase – not Tom – to her body and say, '*My poor fatherless boy.*'

Five. When Gervase's cast-off clothes cease to fit Tom, and when the 'extra' expense of carpentry lessons and mid-morning milk are refused the younger brother, Mrs Kent-Cumberland blames 'Death Duties'. (One has to say that Evelyn is piling it on by now, tongue-in-cheek.)

Six. Gervase goes to Eton but Tom has to settle for a lesser public school. (Upon publication of Alec's book *The Loom of Youth*, exposing the prevalence of homosexuality at an unnamed English public school, Sherborne disowned both Alec and his father, who'd also gone there. This meant there was no chance of Evelyn's following in their footsteps to the WONDERFUL SCHOOL that he'd heard so much about.)

Seven. Gervase goes up to Oxford, but it isn't thought to be worth the expense of sending Tom to university as well. (Evelyn is too committed to the structure of his story by this time to bother about the fact that it was *he* who went to Oxford while Alec missed out on the hallowed place because of the war. However, it's Christ Church that Gervase attends, the college that Evelyn always acknowledged as the *crème de la crème* of colleges, decidedly superior to his own.) So Tom stays back at Tomb Hill, cataloguing the library. In doing so, he comes across a manuscript written by an ancestor. Mrs Kent-Cumberland takes charge of both it and Tom's consequent essay. Why? She is sure that Gervase will be interested in the work and may even think it worth showing to a publisher. Ho-ho!

Eight. Tom gets a job in the motor business in Wolverhampton (I can picture Evelyn sniggering to himself as he looked up how to spell the name of such a beyond-the-pale Midlands town). Meanwhile, *The Journal of an English Cavalry Officer during the Peninsular War*, edited with notes and biographical introduction by Gervase Kent-Cumberland, appears to respectful reviews in the weekend papers. Parts Nine to Twelve continue in the same vein, with Gervase getting

Tom's girl and the fortune that comes with her. The concluding sentence of the brilliantly controlled but not exactly big-hearted little story is that 'everyone is content'.

I close the thick paperback and put it back into my pack. In so doing I notice that someone from the garage is taking an interest in my presence on the drive of this Wolverhamptonesque car boutique. He, secure in his world, is staring at me, in search of Waugh's world. I almost go over and chat with him about the relative advantages of our mutual positions. Instead, I amble back towards the North End Road and take a seat adjacent to the hedge at the front of the house not far from a bus stop. Fine, I might be waiting for a bus up to the Heath or all the way into town. As Evelyn no doubt did on many occasions.

Did Waugh mean 'Winner Takes All' to be a critique of his own family? Yes, of course. But did he mean it to be a criticism of his mother in particular? I don't think so. She played an undramatic but important supportive role in his childhood. Rather, I think he was disguising his disdain for his father's favouritism. But to be fair to old Arthur, on occasion he did try to be an even-handed father. Arthur Waugh dedicated a book of his called *Reticence in Literature* to Alec. The dedication was a public declaration of filial love. But five years later, though he reported to Alec that he sorely wanted to dedicate the new book to him also, the dedication of *Tradition and Change* went to Evelyn. However, the piece is so flaccid and equivocal that when Evelyn came to make his own first effort to write a novel, as a school-boy, he triumphantly and sarcastically dedicated it to himself, taking a swipe at the whole bookish environment in which he'd been raised.

I cross the street so as to get a perspective on the house frontage. It's a busy road so I have to wait a full minute before being able to get across, and then I have to jog. The ground floor of Underhill was dominated by what was called the 'book-room'. This was Arthur Waugh's territory, being used as a library and as a meeting place for his literary salon. Arthur's cronies would gather there and be entertained by their wordy and theatrical host. Evelyn stayed clear of that room for the most part, especially as he got older. Evelyn's day nursery was on the first floor at the back of the house overlooking the garden. But the night nursery, Evelyn's bedroom, was on the second floor at the front of the house and I'm staring at its distinctive window now.

I recognise the upturned-bowl shape from the cover of another book I have in my portable library, this one still protected by the padded envelope in which it arrived at my door. *Evelyn Waugh: Part One of a Literary Biography* covers the years 1903–24 and was written by John Howard Wilson. It was published in the States a few years ago by a combined university press. I tried and failed to trace a copy on the Internet, either in Britain or the States. But its author is the professor that runs the Evelyn Waugh Society, and I've been communicating with him about Waugh. He graciously accepted my offer of a copy of my book about Enid Blyton in exchange for a copy of his book, which I've now read. It's meticulously argued, but a meticulous argument cannot hope to bring Evelyn back to life. And that's the task I've set myself.

The window I'm looking at appears in a sketch on the cover of Wilson's book, a sketch that Evelyn made of the interior of his bed-room for his diary of 10 June 1912, when he was coming up to nine years old. The picture is extraordinary and appears again, with anno-tations by young Evelyn and with notes by Wilson, as the frontis-piece of the book. The distinctive semi-circular window is in the back-ground and locates it absolutely as the second floor of 145 North End Road, overlooking the busy road. In the foreground is Evelyn lying on his back on a table in the middle of his appendectomy. The operation actually took place in the kitchen on the ground floor. But as Evelyn was put to sleep in his bedroom and awoke there after the operation, he's quite reasonably taken the liberty of locating the whole scene in the night nursery. There are three figures standing over him. The first is placing a cone over his nose, the action that put him to sleep. A middle figure is triumphantly holding aloft a pair of scissors in one hand and what looks like a sword, but can be taken to be a surgical knife, in his other hand. The operation would appear to have been a success as far as this surgeon is concerned. A third figure is standing over Evelyn's lower body. John Howard Wilson suggests that it looks as if the boy is about to be castrated. Alexander Waugh has suggested in *Fathers and Sons* that it looks as if this figure is about to knock a chisel into the boy's penis. These gruesome interpretations of the drawing come about for the following reason. It appears as if the boy Evelyn has an erect penis and two large balls a little up from where you would expect them to be. In fact, the child artist is doing his best to represent a long flap of skin that the surgeon has created with his cutting instruments, along with the hole in the patient's stomach that is exposed when said flap of skin is peeled back. At least in part, I point this out because there will be occasions enough in this exercise for dwelling on sexual matters without raising them when it would have been the last thing on the mind of a recently suffering child.

Actually, Evelyn himself in *A Little Learning*, when describing his appendectomy in words, tells us exactly what that figure standing towards the foot of the table is doing. He's strapping down the boy's legs. Following the operation, Evelyn was kept in bed for a week, so that the stitches wouldn't be broken. And it was by means of these leather straps that the boy's inactivity was ensured.

Another thing while I'm at it. Both John Howard Wilson and Alexander Waugh suggest that the figures on either side of the triumphant surgeon represent Evelyn's parents. However, in *A Little Learning*, Waugh specifically states that it was the surgeon who applied the chloroform cone to his nose, and to my mind all three figures represent a different facet of the one surgeon. In his mature writing, Waugh would occasionally split a single figure from real life into two or more characters. However, in most cases the person split into multiple roles was himself. As it happens, there is a fifth figure in the background of the appendectomy drawing. To my mind it's a second Evelyn. This Evelyn has a floppy summer hat on his head and a big sunny grin on his face and is waving a flag with one of his upraised arms. His exuberance echoes that of the surgeon, trumps it even. Yes, the surgeon may be lording it over the part of

Evelyn that's lying on the table but there is another part of Evelyn who looks on and laughs at it all. Laughs at the whole ridiculous operation from chlorocone to leg irons.

The drawing is so strong a structure that I can't help but apply it to another dazzling creation, *Decline and Fall*. How might that work exactly? Poor Paul Pennyfeather, reading for the Church, is lying on his back on the table. Lumsden of Strathdrummond is drunkenly looming above the recumbent figure, baying for blood. On either side of the moustachioed stalwart of the Bollinger Club are Mr Sniggs, the Dean of Scone College, and Mr Postlethwaite, the Domestic Bursar. They are both outraged at Pennyfeather's alleged behaviour. '*Without trousers!*' exclaims Mr Sniggs, banging a chisel into Paul's anus. 'This sort of young man does the college no good. I think we should do far better to get rid of him altogether,' says the Domestic Bursar, placing the chloroform over Paul's nose and mouth, a little too late for maximum anaesthesia. It doesn't look good for Paul Pennyfeather, the poor dim lightweight – sent down from Oxford for indecent behaviour. But what's this? The bloke in the corner of the room is grinning and waving his flag. It's got to be Grimes, who taught at Llanabba alongside Pennyfeather, Grimes the one-legged pervert! And what is Captain Grimes saying with that irrepressible smile, over and over again? 'Life-force,' Is that it? The flag sweeps to and fro, doing Grimes's talking for him: 'Life-force . . . life-force . . . life-force . . . '

Actually, there is no need to resort to such an imagined scene because Waugh himself makes use of the appendectomy scenario in *Decline and Fall*. Near the end of the novel, the governor of Egdon Heath Penal Settlement receives an order from the Home Office giving permission for Paul Pennyfeather to be transferred to a private nursing home so that his appendix can be removed. Paul insists that he had his appendix removed as a child, but that's brushed aside as nonsense. At the nursing home, there are again three figures involved in the 'operation', including the doctor who was supposed to have carried out the operation, an elderly man with a drooping red moustache who was evidently much the worse for drink. The doctor's mouser is reminiscent of the one sported by the triumphant surgeon in boy-Evelyn's drawing. The doctor signs the death certificate, while Paul sits quietly in the corner. The drunk doctor sings, 'Oh, death, where is thy sting-a-ling-a-ling?' as he signs. He is under the impression that a little girl, or a poor old chap, or someone, has died under the anaesthetic without regaining consciousness despite all his most professional efforts. In other words, the Paul Pennyfeather in the corner is the equivalent of the Evelyn figure in the background of the drawing. And if Pennyfeather isn't exactly waving a flag, then Waugh himself is, high as a kite in the knowledge of just how creative he is feeling.

Taking advantage of a lull in the traffic, I cross the road again and enter number 145 via the front gate. If anyone asks I will simply state my interest in Evelyn Waugh rather than try to pretend I'm interested in buying the property. There is a narrow passage down the right side of the house, going past the front door, and I stop after a pace or two to admire a pipe – emerging from the brick wall – that is pouring water down on to the concrete path. As I'm wondering why exactly the feature should have attracted my attention, Arthur Waugh materialises directly under the pipe. That is, a jet of water, or whatever the splashing liquid is, falls on to the crown of the white wide-rimmed hat that red-faced, grey-haired fat-bottomed Arthur is wearing. Arthur seemed like an old and decrepit figure from the time that Evelyn first became aware of his father as a physical presence, though he was only forty when he moved the family to this house.

The pipe keeps pumping out its stream of effluent. It reminds me of something I picked up from *A Little Learning*, which is that when Evelyn was a young boy he was put off requesting ice-creams when visiting Hampstead Heath by the suggestion that the ice-cream was made from something that Italians kept under their beds. Now Evelyn knew from Underhill that chamber pots were kept under beds, and assumed he was being told that the ice-cream he craved was made from urine. The day Evelyn realised that he had been misled – deliberately or not – may have been the day that Evelyn effectively began the story called 'The Man Who Liked Dickens'.

When I get to the end of Underhill's southern wall I stop walking. If

I take another step, I'll be in clear view of the windows at the back of the house. However, I calculate that I won't be in view if I take off my backpack, get down on my hands and knees and crawl along the base of the back wall. So I do that, because this is one of those times when I know that I must go all the way. Evelyn had one of those times back in the winter of 1931–2, only so much more so. He left Underhill and travelled to British Guiana. That took him a couple of weeks by boat, but he didn't stop there. He followed a tributary of the Amazon hundreds of miles inland. And there, just about as far from home – from here – as he could get, he wrote 'The Man Who Liked Dickens'. I need to read that special story again from my present perspective, so without so much as kneeling up I extract the chunky volume of *Complete Stories* from my bag.

The story starts off by introducing a Mr McMaster who has lived in Amazonas for nearly sixty years. The house that he built for himself stands in a small patch of savannah, bounded on all sides by tropical forest. Mr McMaster's house has a palm-thatch roof, breast-high walls of mud and wattle and a pure mud floor. This might not sound like Underhill, but that's what it symbolises all right.

One day Mr McMaster is told by a native that a white man is approaching through the forest, alone and sick. This is a Mr Henty – effectively Evelyn – who is the last survivor of an expedition from London. Mr McMaster leads him to a hammock in his house and gives him something nourishing and herbal to drink. Soon our Henty falls asleep. His recovery is slow. But finally, thanks to the herbs that Mr McMaster continually feeds him, he throws off the fever and is pronounced well enough to see the books. In the hut there is a heap of small bundles, tied up with rag, palm leaf and rawhide. McMaster unwraps the nearest parcel and hands Henty a calf-bound book. It is an early American edition of *Bleak House*. All the books in the hut are by Charles Dickens. Henty asks if McMaster is fond of the Victorian author. He is. They are the only books he has ever heard read out (he cannot read himself). Mr McMaster's father read the books to him when he was a child. McMaster has all Dickens's books except the ones the ants have devoured. He suggests it will take two years for Henty to read them all through from beginning to end. Henty reckons he will be long gone by then, but he is happy enough to make a start on *Bleak House*, to pay back Mr McMaster for saving his life.

So Henty reads. McMaster makes for a childishly enthusiastic and uncritical listener. At the end of the day Mr McMaster compliments Henty's reading. He comments that it's almost as if his father was alive again. Day follows day, reading follows reading, and Henty begins to wonder if he really might still be around to finish the books. Mr McMaster assures him that this will be the case. They finish *Bleak House*, anyway. When they finish *Dombey and Son*, Henty calculates that he has been gone from England for a year. In the middle of the next meaty read, *Martin Chuzzlewit*, Henty tries to withdraw his labour. But he soon finds out that for him a day without reading means a day without the food that McMaster provides. On the second day of non-reading, Mr McMaster guards himself with his shotgun as he eats. On the third day, Henty gives up his strike. Weeks pass quickly and hopelessly. They read *Nicholas Nickleby* and *Little Dorrit* and *Oliver Twist*. But now I must leave the pair to their Dickens-fest. For it's time for me to clarify exactly what's going on here.

Of course, Arthur Waugh was 'the man who liked Dickens'. As Alexander Waugh writes in *Fathers and Sons*, Arthur didn't just like Dickens, he was obsessed by him. Arthur was president of the Dickens Fellowship. He was a renowned expert who lectured on Dickens. He edited two complete editions of Dickens. For thirty years he was the managing director of the publisher who owned the Dickens copyright. And, perhaps most significant of all, he read aloud the works of Dickens night after night to a captive audience, his sons.

There can be no doubt that in 'The Man Who Liked Dickens', with Henty trapped in the house of the Dickens nutter, Evelyn was expressing both his reservations about his literary upbringing and his frustration about still being based at Underhill. The irony is that even on a trip to the other side of the world he couldn't get away from the thought of his despised home. Trapped in a hell hole called Boa Vista, writing his story in a ramshackle abode while he waited for a boat to get him back to civilisation, a boat that might never come, Evelyn was both homesick and sick with horror that Underhill was still his home.

So Mr McMaster is Arthur Waugh, with a cunning reversal going on. That is, in the jungle hut, McMaster is read to by Henty. Whereas at Underhill Arthur did the reading, thank you very much. Day after day, night after night, he did the reading.

Mr McMaster is surely also a very close relation to the Reverend Kenneth McMaster, friend and confidant of Arthur Waugh for forty years. Arthur wrote at length to Revd McMaster about the pleasure of having his bare buttocks massaged by a young female nurse. I don't think Evelyn liked his father's chums much. Another was Edmund Gosse, the man who knew every famous literary man of the day and who was a regular visitor to Underhill. In his autobiography, Evelyn recalled the day that Gosse asked him where his knees were taking him. The boy had promptly replied that his knees weren't taking him anywhere, instead *he* would be taking his knees wherever he wanted to go. Apparently, Gosse had then turned to Arthur and remarked on the confidence of youth: to both be able to envisage a journey and to foresee the attainment of the desired destination. Evelyn, in *A Little Learning*, recalled thinking that his father's friend was both silly and dismal. He didn't think much of any of decrepit old Arthur's friends: they lacked panache.

Anyway, Evelyn's intrepid Henty has both envisaged a journey and he's made it all the way to the Amazon forest, bless him. He's taken his knees to the middle of the jungle. What next for the intrepid explorer? First, as I'm so comfortable here, lying on my back now, with the thick paperback book preventing the sun from shining directly into my eyes, let's recap the position. Henty has read *Bleak House*. A cheap American edition, Evelyn makes clear. That's to say, *not* the memorial edition published by Chapman and Hall in 1920, complete with black-and-white frontispiece and forty-odd plates, a smart volume half-bound in red morocco leather. Henty has read *Dombey and Son*, *Martin Chuzzlewit*, *Nicholas Nickleby*, *Oliver Twist* and *Little Dorrit*, all in the same cheap American edition. That's to say, *not* in the best Chapman and Hall edition of them all, the Oxford India

Paper Dickens, an edition seen through the press by Arthur Waugh himself.

So we're up to speed. What next? One day Mr McMaster is in a fine mood. He imparts the news that Henty, who has been in a drugged sleep for two days, has missed the visit of a small party of Englishmen. The search party was shown a grave marked with a cross, and given Henty's distinctive watch to take away with it. Mr McMaster does not envisage the peace of their little neck of the jungle being disturbed again.

So it's back to *Little Dorrit*, that book about a selfish father and his put-upon child. Not that day, though. Mr McMaster appreciates that Henty is not feeling at all well. But in the morning they could do no better than begin on *Little Dorrit* again. There were some passages in that book which Mr McMaster could never hear without the temptation to weep.

I'm lying on my back in the back garden of Underhill, blown away by a story written about seventy-five years ago by Evelyn Waugh. It concerns the helplessness of childhood and a pulsating black maturity. Any temptation to weep with McMaster, or for Henty, is dwarfed by admiration for the author.

So where does that leave us? In a room on the second floor of the house built by Arthur Waugh, his sensitive-yet-tough second son begins to stir. The boy soon comes to realise that his father has two loves in his life: his brother and a literary phenomenon from the previous century. When I look closer, I see that the boy is waving a flag of his own back and forth, a two-way movement, endlessly repeated. Let me read its semaphore signal: 'Lacking in love . . . Lacking in love . . . Lacking in love . . . '

OXFORD

Nor Dreaming Spires a Cage

We're on a fast, comfortable train from Paddington to Oxford. It was always in my plan that the loved one sitting opposite would accompany me on this leg of the journey. Having said that, I didn't get any response from Kate when I sent her my book's opening pages by e-mail. And when I came across a printed copy of the Underhill and Lancing College chapters in her flat the other day, I realised why. On each page, every fifth line was faulty. Waving the sheaf of paper in front of her face, I said: 'So you don't think my Evelyn writing has got quite the flow of my Enid material, do you?' She had the grace to look embarrassed. I pressed home my advantage: 'You don't think I manage to reward the reader in quite the way that I have done in the past?'

Kate admitted she'd been having problems with her printer, and invited me, who surely knew my own words well enough, to read the Lancing College chapter aloud from her defective copy. So I did that, managing to cope with the flawed line fairly well. The reading reminded me that, for Evelyn, perhaps the main thing about his time at public school was the intellectual stimulus given by his two mentors: the closet homosexual calligrapher Francis Crease and the gay aesthete J. F. Roxburgh. And so, perhaps not surprisingly, for me the most striking things about the period were the signs of Waugh's precocious intellectual development. Not only did Evelyn keep a detailed and astute diary, but he set up a debating society for the fifth form, wrote a play that was staged by his peers, and edited the school magazine. However, by the end of my reading, it became clear that for Kate, the main thing about Waugh's Lancing years was the relationship between Preters and Precoshers.

'Preters' was the nickname of fellow schoolboy Hugh Molson, whose 'Preternaturally so' answer to the question: 'Are you interested in politics?' earned him his moniker. An elderly Molson, who'd gone on to be a Conservative MP for decades, appeared in the *Arena* documentary about Waugh, wearing trousers whose waistband encircled his body at nipple level. 'Precoshers' is my nickname for Evelyn because of the astonishingly knowing diary he kept at Lancing. For example, there is an entry in it where he declares – on reporting that his brother has used nearly the same phrase in reviews of a Compton MacKenzie novel in two different journals – 'I should hardly have thought he could afford to do that sort of thing yet.' Yes, the diary is full of evidence that Evelyn was raised in a literary hothouse called Underhill.

At Lancing's sixth-form debating society, Evelyn proposed the motion: 'This House believes that reincarnation of souls is the most reasonable solution to the problem of human immortality,' even though – as he made clear in his diary – he knew that it wasn't. When the debate took place, everyone who stood up from the floor spoke against the proposal, with the exception of Molson, who, according to Evelyn's diary, 'will take any view so long as it is unconventional'. In my Lancing chapter, I suggest that I would have liked to hear Preters propose the motion: 'This House believes that chest-banding of trousers is the most reasonable solution to the problem of masculine dignity,' with everyone else opposing it except Preters's trusty pal Precoshers, whom I see slowly rising to his feet and unbuttoning his blazer to reveal the highest waistband ever seen inside an English public school. Again a link with Bowie seems irresistible, and in particular a line from the *Ziggy Stardust* album that describes Ziggy's appearance on stage: '*Came on so loaded, man; well-hung and snow-white tan.*'

Anyway, for the rest of the day following the reading it was Preters this and Precoshers that, with Kate taking to the role of Preters with relish. At Kate's instigation we 'ragged the Corps' (playing at soldiers being an aspect of school life that Evelyn derided in his diary entries of 1921) by marching in a daft way through her flat. Then, when we got to the end of the lounge, Kate gave a solo rag as I sat on the sofa and watched.

'*Atten–shun,*' said Kate to herself, and pulled up her make-believe eighteen-inch trouser zip from crotch to chest. Kate made an ideal Preters – standing there, keen as mustard, fresh-faced as a public-school boy, and facetious from the top of her head to the tips of her toes.

'*Stand at . . . ease,*' said Kate, pulling her trouser zip down again and – as indicated by a flick of her wrist – letting make-believe male genitals flop out from the crotch of her trousers.

In case Kate had got the wrong idea, I explained that Evelyn and Hugh Molson did not have an affair with each other, either at school on the South Downs or when they went up to Oxford. Although in his Lancing diary Evelyn does mention his attraction to certain boys at school, he held himself back from having affairs.

After listening to this, Kate told me that in her opinion my Lancing chapter didn't cut the mustard and that I should omit it from my book. Once I'd got over the impudence of this advice, I considered whether I could indeed bear to omit the material, in particular the story of the blue-skyed day I walked across the South Downs, from Lancing College Chapel – one of the most impressive religious buildings in England – to Lychpole Farm, where Evelyn received lessons in the art of calligraphy from the mincing Francis Crease. Maybe I *could* afford to leave it out. Nothing is sacred, after all. All that matters, whether in an Evelyn Waugh novel, or in any book I might write, is style and structure.

Where are we? The train is drawing to a halt. 'This is us,' says Kate. We get off at Oxford Station, as Evelyn would have done many times himself. Umbrella up against the rain, we walk smartly east, minding the odd patch of what's left of yesterday's snow. We are in the university town precisely eighty-five years and two months after Evelyn first came up in January 1922.

'How exciting!' says Kate, squeezing my arm.

'Evelyn, the freshman, had a couple of quiet terms settling in. But by the end of the summer term, only his second, he'd struck up a close friendship with Richard Pares, a clever academic young man from Balliol.'

'Were they partners?' asks Kate.

'Mmm, probably. Harold Acton reckons the relationship was platonic. But in later years Richard Pares told a friend that Evelyn and he had been deeply in love, sharing everything, and that the relationship had been more intense than anything he'd subsequently experienced. Also, in a letter to Nancy Mitford written in the fifties, Waugh talks about paying a visit to his "first homosexual love" who by then was a professor, married with four children and, alas, succumbing to a disease that was slowly paralysing him.'

We've reached a crossroads. To the right, Cornmarket Street leads on to St Aldate's. I tell Kate that it was there, in a place called the Hypocrites' Club, in premises close to the river, that Evelyn and Richard Pares shared passionate times together. Evelyn had particularly fond memories of the place, describing it in his auto-biography as the stamping ground of half his Oxford life. However, it was also the root of the disintegration of Waugh's relationship with Pares. Evelyn increasingly sought the bliss of drunkenness, which was when he felt most at ease with himself and most intimate with others. However, Richard didn't have much of a head for alcohol.

'First and foremost, Evelyn wanted a partner who could hold his drink,' suggests Kate.

'And that's what he soon got,' I replied. Though I don't say any more for the time being.

Kate and I have turned off Broad Street, passed the Bridge of Sighs and are entering Hertford College. We pass through an arch and walk by the sign that says the college is presently open to visitors. The arch leads straight into inner-city peace and quiet. The quad is small and the cloistered atmosphere seems to take us back a hundred years from the bustle of modern Oxford. There is more sign of snow here than in the streets because the middle of the quad is a lawn and it's not the done thing to walk on the grass. Slowly we walk round the stone path of the quad, soaking up the architecture and the ambience. It's glorious here. Evelyn never admitted as much, though he did accept that Oxford as a whole was superb. To enjoy Oxford to the full was Evelyn's only aim when he went up. And in this he spectacularly succeeded. Though not straightaway.

When Evelyn came back for his second year in college, he had rooms here in the front quad of Hertford. But where exactly? I thought I'd recognise the windows from the images I've seen, but in fact I'll have to enquire at the porter's lodge. However, before we do that I want to tell Kate a story as we continue to circle the quad. 'Portrait of Young Man with Career' was published while Evelyn was at Oxford. It's written in the first person. Evelyn tells us that 'Jeremy', whom he'd known at school, and who was now intending to become President of the Oxford Union, comes into his room at half-past six. That is, during the awkward hour before hall.

'Could Evelyn's visitor have been Preters?'

'Definitely. Hugh Molson went on to be President of the Oxford Union.'

'Oh, goody, a story about Preters and Precoshers!'

'Evelyn is about to have a bath and intends to leave Jeremy to

entertain himself with a glass of sherry. However, on finding his sherry bottle empty – the implication being that Evelyn has drunk nearly a whole bottle that day – he feels he should abandon the bath and entertain his guest with conversation until it is time for them to go to their respective halls. Jeremy props his feet on the fireplace. He is wearing shoes that Evelyn thinks are detestable, the sort of dark brown suede shoes that always look wet.'

'Preters cut a sartorial figure at Lancing. And he intends to do the same at Oxford.'

'Jeremy asks Evelyn if he would introduce him to Richard Pares.'

'Ooh, exciting! – a mixture of real and fictional names.'

'But Evelyn doesn't want to introduce Jeremy to Richard, because Jeremy was apt to get a bit too familiar with new acquaintances. However, forceful Jeremy insists on setting up a meeting. Then Jeremy starts to speak about his forthcoming Union speech. Now at that point in the story, Evelyn finds his brain filling with a fiery mist. He takes hold of his room's poker and caves in Jeremy's forehead with it. He then has a quiet chat with his scout about the corpse and the empty bottle of sherry.'

Kate is laughing as we walk around the quad of Hertford College. Evelyn's beautifully judged little story is going down nicely.

'Then Evelyn's brain clears and he finds that Jeremy is still in his room, talking to him about recent speeches he's made at the Union and what other people have said about those speeches. Luckily, it is seven o'clock and time for Jeremy to go to hall. As he departs, Evelyn tries to think that one day he shall be proud of having known Jeremy. But until then . . . '

'Until then he will have to resist the temptation to crack his skull open every time they meet. That's hilarious!'

I'm glad I've got that story told. Much of today is going to be concerned with what Evelyn wrote in 1944 about his time at Oxford, when he was in a mood of nostalgia twenty-odd years after the event itself, and I can hardly wait to get stuck into that. But it's good to bear in mind Evelyn's state of mind as he recorded it in print at the time: violent mood swings and irrational impulses.

Kate asks me if Waugh wrote anything else when he was at Oxford. The answer is that he wrote several short pieces for magazines between May and September of 1923. They take up thirty-odd pages of *The Complete Stories*, about the same as his juvenilia. And if the juvenilia is mostly about incidents at public school, then the Oxford stories are mostly about college life. An exception to that is 'Antony Who Sought Things That Were Lost'. This is a chivalric tale about a pair of lovers who are locked up together in a cell. When the woman succumbs to the advances of their jailer, her lover Anthony kills her by strangulation.

'More violence.'

'It may allude to the split between Evelyn and Richard Pares. Because that spring, in Evelyn's second year, Richard had become the intimate friend of an intellectual don, "Slicker" Urquart, the Dean of Balliol.'

'Did Evelyn see the dons as being his jailers then?'

'On some level he did, as I might be able to show. The longest of the Oxford stories is called "Edward of Unique Achievement", though it's still only runs to a few pages. In this, a senior History scholar (like Waugh) kills his tutor, a Mr Curtis. Now Evelyn got on extremely badly with his History tutor, Mr Cruttwell, whose name crops up, always in a disparaging way, in much of Waugh's post-Oxford writing. In the Oxford story, Edward speaks at the Union debate (as Waugh did a few times) and then sneaks back to college and stabs Curtis, who, as was his habit, has continued to write a sentence after his visitor has entered his room to emphasise his superiority, a sentence that ends up merged into a pool of blood. Edward gets off with the murder thanks to the self-serving instincts of the other senior members of the college.'

'Evelyn did get hot under the collar when he was a student here.'

'He got hot-headed on fiery liquor, that's for sure. And when he got drunk he got noisy. Apparently, when visiting Balliol, after he'd broken up with Richard, he was in the habit of shouting out that the Dean of Balliol slept with men. Slicker had not only played a part in ending Evelyn's relationship with Richard Pares but had also closed down the Hypocrites' Club, Evelyn's preferred stamping and snogging ground.'

'Snogging?'

'I forget the reference. But someone in the Waugh literature is quoted as having seen Evelyn and a young man, probably Richard, rolling around on the furniture with their tongues down each other's throats. So, no Richard for Evelyn; No Hypocrites' Club for Evelyn. Instead he has to be content with bawling out at the top of his voice: "THE DEAN OF BALLIOL SLEEPS WITH MEN." '

'Poor mixed-up Evelyn. Evelyn Who Sought Things That Were Lost.'

'That's about right. Similarly, Evelyn was known to sing under the rooms of Cruttwell, who was Dean of Hertford College as well as his unfortunate History tutor. The song was one Evelyn had devised after a chum and he had got caught up in a fantasy that Crutwell was sexually attracted to dogs and was in the habit of consummating his passion in the privacy of his rooms here at Hertford. The song goes:

> "Cruttwell dog, Cruttwell dog, where have you been?"
> "I've been to Hertford to sleep with the Dean."
> "Cruttwell Dog, Cruttwell Dog, what did you do there?"
> "I bit off his penis and pubic hair." '

'Oh, Evelyn of Unique Achievement! – it doesn't even scan.'

I'm more concerned that I don't know where the appropriate room is located in the quadrangle. But actually I don't need to know where a dim old don lived. What I do need to know now is where exactly Evelyn lived in his second year. So we stop circling the quad and make for the porter's lodge. Politely and promptly – the porters are used to being helpful to their young charges – the ground-floor room in question is pointed out to us.

Ah, yes. Now I can link up the room's windows with the scene in the TV biopic about Waugh when Tony Bushell – a college contemporary of Evelyn's – talks the viewer through the time when there was a party going on in the rooms of another mutual friend.

The old man uses a walking stick to indicate the whereabouts of the party, and says that, when it dispersed, several individuals went out of the main entrance back to their own colleges but one straggler wandered over to this window – one of Evelyn's – and was sick. The documentary footage leads in to the equivalent scene in *Brideshead Revisited* – filmed right here – when Charles Ryder, in the middle of a serious discussion with a colleague called Collins, a watered down Richard Pares, watches expressionlessly as Sebastian wanders over to his room and elegantly pukes into it. Evelyn Waugh – or whatever you want to call yourself – welcome at last to the real Oxford! It is just so admirable that the Granada TV production went to the trouble of getting authentic locations. In itself, the overhead shot of Hertford College – only on screen for a few seconds – is priceless.

Evelyn's rooms were at the opposite end of the quad from the chapel, but apparently Evelyn had had enough of chapel from Lancing days and rarely attended. The hall was upstairs to his right, but in the second year Evelyn often ate out with friends in the evening and provided 'offal' in his own rooms for lunch. The offal, being good traditional English fodder, was washed down with lots of beer, which Evelyn and chums would consume until it was time for them to give serious thought to their evening's recreation. Tony Bushell is quoted as saying that in all the time he knew Evelyn, he never once saw him reading a book relevant to his History course.

Evelyn did read though. Charles's room – pre-Sebastian's influence – is very particularly described in the first chapter of *Brideshead*. The room's books are said to be meagre and common place. Waugh then lists Roger Fry's *Vision and Design*, a Medici Press edition of *A Shropshire Lad*, *Eminent Victorians*, some volumes of Georgian poetry, *Sinister Street* and *South Wind*. The point of the listing is pretty well lost on a reader now. I think the suggestion is that these were the books an average undergraduate of the time would have had in his possession. But the Medici Press is a very specific reference and the volumes of Georgian poetry were published by his father's firm. Surely, this gives away the fact that Evelyn – or his book's main character – was already something of a connoisseur of culture. If Charles's mind was about to be opened by Oxford aestheticism, it hadn't been anything like tight shut to begin with.

It's no longer raining. Having dried its top surface, Kate and I are sitting on the bench conveniently situated outside Evelyn's old room.

'Can you smell the gillyflowers?' I ask.

'What are gillyflowers?'

'They're mentioned repeatedly in *Brideshead*. They bloom in summer outside Charles Ryder's room, giving off a musky smell. I looked up the word, it means carnations, or pinks, or sweet williams, or any flower that gives off the scent of cloves.'

'It's too early in the year,' says Kate. 'All I can smell is Sebastian's sick.'

I tell Kate that there is a March/June structure to the first chapter in *Brideshead*, with the action switching between spring and summer. I suspect that March of Evelyn's second year was when Evelyn first met Alastair Graham, his second lover, and that the relationship was in full bloom three months later. This all feeds back into *Brideshead* in a way that fascinates me. The Prologue makes it clear that the book is written in 1944, by Charles Ryder, an army officer, a man who has reached an age of disillusion. But things were once different for him. And for Chapter One, Charles Ryder, the narrator, takes the reader back to Oxford in the early twenties. It's Eights Week at the university, which means that, unusually, there are women around. Sebastian enters Charles's room and asks what on earth is happening at his college. It's as if a circus has arrived, he declares. And, what's more, Oxford as a whole is pullulating with women.

'Is pullulating Evelyn's word?'

'Yes, it comes out of Sebastian's mouth though. The exquisite young man – dressed in dove-grey flannel suit with white crêpe de Chine shirt and a Charvet tie that belongs to Charles, goes on to say that he's come to take his friend out of danger. He's got a motor car and a basket of strawberries and a bottle of Château Peyraguey – which isn't a wine that Charles has ever tasted so he needn't pretend.'

'Is that the wine that's said to be "heaven with strawberries"?' asks Kate, who spent at least some of today's double train journey –

Westcliff to London; London to Oxford – reading my annotated copy of *Brideshead*.

'That's the one. And to help explain that reference, there's a letter from Alastair Graham to Evelyn saying that he's found the ideal way to drink – if not sauternes – burgundy. You peel a peach, place it in a finger bowl, then pour the burgundy over the exposed flesh of the fruit. The peach brings out what he calls the "happy Seraglio contentedness" that the old wine evokes. In the same letter Alastair says that when he comes to Oxford later that week, he and Evelyn might carry some bottles into a wood, or other bucolic place, and drink like Horace.'

'I like that phrase "happy Seraglio contentedness". What sort of person was Alastair?'

'Indolent, cultured, sweet-natured, profoundly sensual. In *A Little Learning*, Waugh says of his young self that he could not have fallen under an influence better designed to encourage his natural frivolity, dilettantism and dissipation. That is, young Evelyn could not have fallen under an influence better able to expose as vulgar and futile any promptings he may have felt to worldly ambition. Alastair was sent down – or ran away – from Westminster, his public school. And he only lasted a couple of years at Oxford where he did no work whatsoever.'

Kate smiles. 'I suspect that Alastair was much indulged in his heyday. What did he look like?'

'Small and good-looking with pale face and glossy brown hair, neatly side-parted. There is a picture of him at eighteen in the Selina Hastings biography of Waugh. Anyway, that day in June, with Aloysius between the *Brideshead* boys, Sebastian drove Charles out of Oxford in the direction we came in from the station, along the Botley Road. At Swindon they turned off the main road into a cart track and stopped. On a sheep-cropped knoll, under a clump of elms, they did for the strawberries and the wine, finishing off by lying on their backs smoking Turkish cigarettes. They were on their way to Brideshead Castle for what would be Charles's first glimpse of Sebastian's stunning childhood home. But the specific references to the Botley Road and Swindon are deliberate red herrings, I've decided.'

'How do you mean?'

Alastair lived with his mother in Barford House about forty miles to the *north*, not west, of Oxford. Alastair got to drive about in his mother's car, and, without question, Evelyn and Alastair visited Barford from Oxford. Obviously, there would have been a first visit, in which I strongly suspect Evelyn would have been struck by the splendid house, faced in white stucco, with pilasters on either side of the front door and a glass cupola on the roof. The house also featured stables, a fish-pond, box hedges and a stone gazebo: a big step up from the suburban setting and style of Underhill.'

'Was Barford an influence on Brideshead, do you think?'

'Brideshead, the house, and *Brideshead* the novel, take on certain attributes from Evelyn's later friendship with the Lygon family, who lived in a house called Madresfield which he didn't visit until 1931. And by the time Waugh came to write the book in 1944 he had stayed in many splendid country houses, perhaps even Castle Howard where the Granada production was set. But while Waugh was writing the early stages of the book, the set up at Barford House in Warwickshire would have fed into the portrait of Sebastian and the description of the time they spent together at Brideshead.'

'Have you been there yet?'

'I had a quick look, with an old friend from university. But I'll go again when the time is right. For now I need properly to take in Evelyn's Oxford.'

Where are we again? Sitting on a bench outside Evelyn's rooms at Hertford. We are strawberryless and entirely without Château Peyraguey, I can't help noticing. And Kate's right, it is too early in the year to smell the gillyflowers. But that's all fine and dandy because we're building up to something. Something that will be in full bloom by the end of the day if all goes to plan.

For now I need to re-focus on that morning in March when a note from Sebastian was delivered to Charles asking him to come for lunch because Aloysius wouldn't speak to Sebastian until he knew that he had been forgiven for his behaviour of the previous night. Needless to say, nothing so coarse as the word 'vomit' was mentioned. Nor was there an address on the note. But Charles had seen the conspicuous gentleman going about town with the classically named teddy bear under his arm, and he knew where the exotic one lived. So do I know where Sebastian hung out. 'Come on, no time for a cigarette, Turkish or otherwise,' I say, pulling Kate to her feet.

The Bodleian Library makes for quite an eyeful – straight ahead as we exit Hertford. We need to veer sharp left so as not to get embroiled in a lot of musty old history books, so we veer away just as sharply as Evelyn did. We walk along wide roads and narrow lanes, negotiating the yellow puddles. Now and again I refer to a city-centre map on which every college building is clearly marked in a purple colour that complements the warm yellow of the actual stone. Thanks to it, I navigate a route that means we always seem to have a college wall of Cotswold stone alongside us. We pass All Souls on our left, Oriel and Corpus Christi on our right, and now have a view of the grandest of all the colleges: Christ Church. The splendour of Christ Church partly explains why Waugh always referred to his own college in disparaging terms. Though that was typical of Evelyn, always looking to what he hadn't got rather than counting his own considerable blessings.

Harold Acton had rooms at Christ Church. In fact, as Waugh states in *Brideshead* about Sebastian, he lived in rooms painted bright yellow high in Meadow Buildings. Kate and I are looking up at the building now. It is *the* most fantastic location. The three-storeyed terrace is castellated, with balconies. On the parapet of one balcony are five glasses left over from a party. Two of the glasses look as if they once contained red wine but, in the time that has elapsed since the party, rainwater has turned the liquid rosé. What a view there must be from that balcony! Christ Church meadows, a huge loop of grassland cut off by the River Cherwell, are at your personal disposal. You could be partying in your room, look out over the meadows and suddenly have a hankering to be on your own. You might make your excuses to your guests, walk downstairs, then loop the waterside loop and be back twenty minutes later, just as another bottle of Bordeaux was being opened. And your glass would be glugged full of ruby-red wine

again. And you would chink it against Harold's glass and drink deeply of the shared privilege.

Acton came up to Oxford in October of 1922 and had an immediate impact on the university. He'd been raised in an exquisite home called La Pietra near Florence. He'd had his poems published while at Eton and was already a friend of the Sitwells. He soon attracted people like Evelyn, who did drawings for the magazine that Acton edited called *The Broom*. Evelyn was impressed by Acton's intellect, his panache. Just as Acton was seduced by the faun-like Waugh. Acton would partake of offal in Evelyn's rooms at Hertford, and in the process fall in love with some handsome, rugged, silent lad he'd find there. Evelyn would accept invites to Harold's more rarefied parties, enjoying the idiosyncratic Victoriana his rooms were full of. Apparently, Acton would stand on the balcony of his room and recite parts of T. S. Eliot's *The Waste Land* across the meadows. I think the use of the megaphone came about through a party in London that Acton took Evelyn too. On that occasion, Edith Sitwell wore a mask and recited her poems through a megaphone.

We sit on a bench that looks directly on to Meadow Buildings. Not for the first time today I remove from my pack a paperback copy of *Brideshead Revisited*, and I find the extract from *The Waste Land* that Evelyn quotes in Chapter One, via a megaphone held to the lips of lisping, gay, Anthony Blanche:

> 'I, Tiresias, have foresuffered all
> Enacted on this same d-divan or b-bed,
> I who have sat by Thebes below the wall
> And walked among the l-l-lowest of the dead . . . '

'He recites that at the end of a lunch party, doesn't he?'

'Yes. Charles, followed by other undergraduates, turns up in Sebastian's rooms by invitation. Anthony is the last to arrive.'

'But why isn't it Anthony Blanche's rooms if *he's* really Harold Acton?'

'First, I should say that Anthony Blanche's more outrageous mannerisms, as opposed to his aestheticism, are based on another person Evelyn knew of when at Oxford: Brian Howard. But, more importantly, Evelyn was killing two birds with one stone. Alastair Graham actually had rooms at Brasenose. But that's another middling college, so Evelyn couldn't have Sebastian live there.'

'Certainly not!'

'No, Sebastian had to live high in Meadow Buildings. But as it was Harold Acton who actually did that, and as he, after Alastair, was the biggest influence on Evelyn while he was at Oxford, Waugh made sure he turned up at the party – in the form of Anthony Blanche, to do his r-r-recitation.'

My lispy stutter doesn't sound convincing to my own ears, and nor can I bat enormous eyes the way the Anthony Blanche character does in the Granada serial.

'I love his lines when he first comes into the room,' says Kate. She takes the book from me and finds the page.

' "My dear," ' says Kate, who *can* bat huge eyes, and whose voice has all the rich cadences necessary to put across such fruity speech. ' "I couldn't get away before. I was lunching with my p-p-preposterous tutor. He thought it was very odd my leaving when I did. I told him I had to change for F-f-ooter." '

I'm reminded of the lines right at the start of the first chapter of *Brideshead*, where Evelyn writes nostalgically of Oxford. How does it go? I regain possession of the book: ' . . . bells rang out high and clear over her gables and cupolas . . . soft vapours of a thousand years of learning . . . It was this cloistral hush which gave our laughter its resonance, and carried it still, joyously, over the intervening clamour . . . '

'Where are our plovers eggs?' asks Kate in her own voice.

The party in Sebastian's rooms that March day in 1923 began with everyone helping themselves from a basket of plovers' eggs. Eggs from birds that laid especially early for Sebastian's mummy, according to the host.

However, I don't think Kate is really complaining that there are no plovers' eggs to start, or lobster Newburg to follow, because we stopped off at Pret A Manger earlier and from a bag I now extract the most succulent-looking vegetarian sandwiches. Black olive-studded wholemeal bread stuffed with avocado, beetroot, lamb's lettuce, humus, pumpkin seeds, puréed chestnut. I chomp though my sandwich and have opened our packet of parsnip crisps before I feel the urge to communicate again with my lunch companion. With the help of the back of the crisp packet I'm able to tell Kate that these crisps were made for Pret at Tyrells Court, a family-run farm in Hertfordshire. 'The crunchiest parsnips are prepared by hand by Mummy, who slices small batches straight into hot oil.'

'My dear,' says Kate, in Anthony Blanche mode, 'you have eaten more than half the p-packet before I've had so much as a g-g-grain of salt.'

When we've eaten our fill I tell Kate what I know about the extract from *The Waste Land* that Evelyn plants towards the end of the lunch scene in the first chapter of *Brideshead*. T. S. Eliot was a fashionable and influential poet in the early twenties. And Waugh was briefly fascinated both by the depths and difficulties of the poetry. *The Waste*

Land juxtaposes scenes from the mundane modern world with classical allusions. The lines quoted by Waugh are from the third part of the five-part poem. A typist has returned to her untidy little suburban home at the end of the working day. She's visited by an estate agent's clerk, a self-assured young man, and they dine together. She is bored and tired but he forces his attentions on her . . .

'I take it T. S. puts it a bit more poetically.'

'She lets him have his way with her.' Though Kate's quite right, the poet puts it a lot more obliquely. 'It's at that point in the poem that Tiresias announces that he's foresuffered whatever sordid event has taken place on the divan or bed – "I who have sat by Thebes below the wall and walked among the lowest of the dead." '

'What does that mean, exactly?'

I shrug: 'Just take it as classical allusion, can't you?'

Kate ponders this, and says: 'I suppose it's T. S. Eliot – and Harold Acton and Evelyn Waugh – rejecting the limitations of grim early-twentieth-century existence.'

'A rejection of the commuters disembarking at London Bridge and flowing into the City towards the Bank of England and the Stock Exchange, an image that comes up in the first part of the poem. Not hard to reject if, like Harold Acton, you have been raised in a palace on the fringes of Renaissance Florence and, in your golden prime, are living in the best rooms that Oxford has to offer.'

'And whatever Evelyn's got planned for himself after he goes down from Oxford, I don't suppose getting a clerk's job at an estate agent's is very high on his list of might-dos.'

'Let's be clear. Evelyn has no intention of getting a job in the motor trade. He will not be found in a cheap brown suit and horrid wet-look suede shoes pacing up and down the forecourt of a garage in Wolverhampton.'

'Neither will our Evelyn be spending his Friday nights seducing some common little typist.'

'You won't find him pumping her on a divan that by day boasts piles of stockings and camisoles.'

'Oh don't say p-p-pumping, darling,' says Kate in her best Anthony

Blanche manner. 'It's more than my delicate sensibility can s-stomach so soon after such a HUGE helping of c-c-crisps.'

We take turns to sip from a brightly decorated bottle that Pret has labelled '*Flower Fantastic*'. Basically it's still water, made with orange blossom and a hint of rhubarb. But it hits the spot as far as we're concerned: 'Château Prêt à Guey,' I clumsily pronounce. When finally I screw the top on the vitamin-drained bottle I say: 'Now come on, we must go to the Botanical Gardens!'

'Why?'

'To see the ivy, of course. At least that's what Sebastian says to Charles after the long initiation lunch in *Brideshead* When Charles says that he's never been to the Botanical Gardens, Sebastian is scathing: what a lot his new friend has to learn.'

'Can Aloysius come?' asks Kate.

'Of course Aloy-sius can come.'

'He's only coming if you pronounce his name properly.'

'Aloy-sius.' No, that's not right.

'Alo-y-sius.'

'Aloy-sius. Damn, why does it come out like that?'

'Say it slowly. Al-o-y-sius.'

Eventually I do get the classical hang of the teddy's name and then we're all happy. Kate, Aloysius and I walk arm in arm under the walls of Merton for a short distance, then pass through an arch which is a side entrance to the Botanicals. The first thing I notice about the wall-bound gardens is that there are no flowers. No flowers in a garden? Well, only a few. It's too early in the year, and they don't go in for daffodils here. Which reminds me that on that morning of March in 1923, along with the invitation to lunch, Charles finds his rooms at Hertford full of yellow daffodils. The real flowers put the print of *Sunflowers* that Charles has hanging on the wall in the shade. It's a detail in the book that doesn't work for me. Van Gogh was a great original, a true sun-worshipper, and would surely have passed any test set of him by Harold Acton, Evelyn Waugh or Alastair Graham.

Anyway, no flowers on this March morning. Which is maybe why Sebastian was taking Charles to see ivy – in lieu of there being nothing more colourful to look at. Though there's at least one academic article in the *Evelyn Waugh Newsletter* interpreting the ivy – and the arch we've walked through – metaphorically. That's to say, Charles, in walking through the arch was taken by Sebastian into a world of paganism that ultimately led to a world of Roman Catholicism. Crikey, what have Kate and I let ourselves in for?

Actually, there is something growing in the narrow flowerbeds that we're now passing, a forest of labels. Each two-foot-long metal pole displays the Latin name of a plant.

'Alli-um acu-min-atum,' I stumble aloud.

'Let Aloysius read the names.'

'Go on, then.'

'Euphorbia stygiana . . . euphorbia sikkimensis . . . eryngium variiforlium.'

'What mysterious names,' I say. 'I bet the euphorbias will turn the whole place yellow come May or June.'

'Aloysius says that euphorbia sikkimensis is just another name for gillyflowers and that they smell of sick all the year round.'

We wander about the peaceful, calming flowerbeds for a while, enjoying our stroll round exquisitely proportioned, flowerless beds, when Kate asks me a question: 'If Sebastian was so keen on the Botanical Gardens, I suppose Alastair must have been too.'

'Well, he liked nature. He liked it for itself and as a place of escape from conventional social life. In her biography of Waugh, Selina Hastings quotes from a letter from Alastair to Evelyn that was written at the time. Alastair goes on about how he thinks of all the beautiful things that he's seen or heard or thought growing like bright flowers or musky herbs in a garden where he can enjoy their presence, a garden where he can sit in peace and banish the harsh realities of life.'

When we exit the Botanical Gardens, it seems like a natural thing to follow the riverside path. This is the loop of the river that takes us round the front of Meadow Buildings. I point out Christ Church in the distance.

'So these are the Meadows,' says Kate. 'Let's stop a minute, and see if we can hear Harold Acton or Anthony Blanche on the megaphone.'

I help her out by quoting the bit I've ended up knowing from the end of *The Waste Land*'s third part. It mostly involves the word 'burning' and nonsense about the Lord plucking me out.

I don't think Kate's too impressed. She wants to know more about the relationship between Evelyn and Alastair instead. I tell my partner that in their correspondence they exhibit a puerile attitude towards sex. The original letters from Alastair were subsequently bound by Evelyn and given a Latin tag. They are still in the Waugh family, I believe, because, in *Fathers and Sons*, Alexander Waugh quotes from a letter that was written in April 1924, Evelyn's third year at Oxford, when Alastair was staying for a week with the son of a canon at Wells Cathedral. I'm not sure if the original letter is in the form of a list of points, but that's how I remember Alexander Waugh putting it across. Nor can I recall his actual words, but I can let Kate hear the gist of each point.

'One. The Dean of Wells has "kinderlust" and seduces children in what he calls a "pudenda" hidden within the Cathedral library.

'Two. The authorities at Downside School keep a collection of female birds and animals at their sexual disposal.

'Three. Alastair's mother performs sexual rites on her pet dog and would be aroused if she saw Alastair's picture (enclosed with the letter) of a dog with a sticky-out bottom.

'Four. The Dean's wife, having discovered her husband's paedophilic tendency, is now lying with her own bitch.'

Kate interrupts: 'Those clever boys at Oxford really have it in for deans 'n' dogs, don't they?'

I treat that question as rhetorical: 'Five. Alastair thinks it would be interesting to dress as a dog and sit in the Cathedral to see what would transpire.'

Kate snorts disparagingly.

'Six. Alastair saw a horse masturbating in a field. Then, on the way to buy an envelope for Evelyn's letter, he saw four dogs copulating on the Cathedral green.'

After a pause, Kate asks me what I make of such material. Well, it reminds me of communications I had with special male friends from the age of about seventeen to twenty-four. That period – post-adolescence, perhaps, but pre-adulthood for me – was a time of sexual obsession, because I had not yet found, or at least proven, my sexual identity. Certainly, I had little experience of girls or women, and I don't think Evelyn did. The young man feels closer to other young men, because they have similar values and desires. This strange world of sexuality can be explored together. Not necessarily in a sexual relationship – I didn't have a sexual relationship with my close male friends. But one way to explore sex is to joke about it. I recall doing that with various pals. And it's obviously what Evelyn and Alastair did together, judging by their ribald correspondence. Though my conclusion is that they did much more than make smutty jokes.

As we walk along the muddy riverbank, past the ducks and a rowing boat, another writer comes to mind. I tell Kate that Charles Dodgson had rooms in Christ Church, and under the *nom de plume* of Lewis Carroll he published the Alice books while he was in residence as a mathematics don.

'Did he have rooms in Meadow Buildings?'

'No, he was in first-floor rooms in a corner of the main quad. I mention him because he became important to Waugh. Richard Pares was very keen on the works of Lewis Carroll and it was he who made Evelyn take the Alice books seriously. Waugh never forgot Lewis Carroll or Alice. Chapter One of his travel book set in Ethiopia, *Remote People*, ends with a sentence that states that Waugh's *Alice in Wonderland* fortnight had begun, meaning his attendance at the prolonged celebrations to mark the coronation of Haile Selassie had kicked off. And the second chapter starts by again mentioning *Alice in Wonderland*, where rabbits carry watches in their waistcoat pockets, the monarch paces the croquet lawn beside the chief executioner and litigation ends in a flutter of playing cards. The mood and imagery of this is what Waugh feels he needs to convey the crazy enchantment of his Ethiopian adventure.'

'Evelyn in Wonderland.'

'Waugh quotes Alice again at the beginning of *Vile Bodies*. The two quotes are both from *Through the Looking Glass*. The first, where Alice claims that in her country you'd generally get to somewhere else if you ran very fast for a long time, as she and the Queen had been doing. The Queen retorts that it sounded like Alice must come from a very slow sort of country. The second quote being where Alice says that if she wasn't real, she wouldn't be able to cry. Her companion, Tweedledum this time, pipes up in a tone of great contempt with, "I hope you don't think those are real tears." '

Kate seems to have taken this in, because she says: 'Well, in my country you'd generally get to somewhere else if you walked for a very long time, as we've been doing.'

'I hope you don't think these are real miles,' I reply, as we continue to put one foot in front of the other along the Christ Church loop. I tell Kate that I know Waugh kept a long-term interest in Lewis Carroll because in 1939 he reviewed for the *Spectator* an edition of *The Complete Works of Lewis Carroll*. In the two-page review he gives the editor of the volume a good dressing-down for including material Charles Dodgson originally published under his own name. Waugh takes umbrage because Dodgson was so scrupulous about using the Lewis Carroll name for a certain kind of imaginative work and for that alone. Waugh feels that it would have pained the fastidious don to have completely different kinds of his work juxtaposed. In the review, Waugh goes on to show his comprehensive knowledge of Lewis Carroll's oeuvre, though not in a showy way. He hardly mentions the Alice books and states that *Sylvie and Bruno* – marred as it is by a sentimentality that is entirely absent from the Alice books – is the creation that best allows an understanding of how Dodgson came to be motivated to produce great imaginative literature as Lewis Carroll. Waugh's own theory is that Dodgson, being a devout Christian, but finding himself plagued by doubts, tried to escape from the rational speculation that was doing his head in. He made his escape by entering a child's world of daydream, peopling his con- sciousness with fantastic creatures whose job, fundamentally, was to distract Dodgson from the possibility that there was no God.

'No God?' says Kate. 'Oh, don't say that, Mr Godson, or whatever your name is. Say anything but that.'

We've looped around Christ Church and are now at the bottom of St Aldate's. The Hypocrites' Club used to be here but the building has long been demolished. However, if we go over to the other side of Folly Bridge I'm hoping we might find something even more important to our shared cultural heritage.

It's a boat-hire place, deserted, boating being out of season. That's to say, in front of us are the boats, bobbing up and down in their mooring lane. But there is not a single person other than Kate and myself down here by the riverside on this blustery March day. I tell my companion about the golden afternoon of 4 July 1862. Charles Dodgson had been given permission from the Dean of Christ Church and his wife to take their daughters out on the river for the day.

'Not another dean?'

'I think deans must have been more common in the past than they are now. Anyway, Dodgson – and another adult male, invited along to help with the rowing – walked with the girls from Christ Church down along St Aldate's and clambered into a rowing boat here along-side Folly Bridge. The sun was shining, and though it's several miles upstream, the plan was to row to Godstow where they would have afternoon tea in the picturesque countryside there.

Kate and I set off in that direction, walking smartly so that we might actually get to Godstow by early evening. Bearing the 1862 scenario in mind, I ask Kate to jump ahead to that golden afternoon during Eights Week in 1923. Sebastian and Charles drive in their borrowed motor car out of Oxford along the Botley Road, stopping for Château Peyraguey and strawberries under some elm trees near Swindon. I tell her: 'Eventually, Charles and Sebastian make it to Brideshead by mid-afternoon. Sebastian takes Charles to a room at the top of the house to meet Nanny Hawkins. On the way back out, Charles expresses his interest in everything he sees and requests that he might see more, but basically the house is shut up while the family is enjoying the dancing season in London and the only other thing Charles gets to visit properly is the chapel.'

'What about Aloysius?

'Alo is there throughout that afternoon, carried everywhere by

Sebastian. In fact he's there throughout that golden summer. In the Granada production of *Brideshead Revisited* there is some fine footage of Charles standing at the back end of a boat, punting on this river, while Sebastian and Aloysius are lying on their backs alongside the hamper in the front of the boat. Limp-wristed, Sebastian lets the fingers of a hand dangle nonchalantly in the smooth, river water. Aloysius, lying back with a bib on, looks ready to do some serious damage to the picnic when given half a chance.'

Kate and I cross bridges as the towpath requires, making steady progress towards our destination.

'The voice-over at that point in the adaptation is taken from Chapter Two of *Brideshead* the book. The Charles Ryder narrator (an army captain in the Second World War, remember) states that he'd had a lonely childhood, a time dominated by the premature dignity and authority imposed by the school system. But that summer term he was blissfully happy with Sebastian. He tells the listening viewer that towards the end of term he did a lot of cramming of neglected history texts in an effort to pass his preliminary exams, but all he learned in that manner was soon forgotten. However, the more ancient lesson he learned that summer would never be forgotten.'

'And what would that be?'

I put a hand on Kate's shoulder as I say, hopefully with a light touch: 'That to know and to love one other human being is the root of all wisdom.'

We walk on, admiring our surroundings. The river is high and fast-flowing. Of course there has been record amounts of rainfall over the last month or so. No way would I like to be rowing against that current. Soon I'm talking again.

'In the TV *Brideshead*, Charles steers the boat to shore and he and Sebastian are then glimpsed drinking champagne from wide-rimmed glasses. Sebastian is lying down, his back leaning against a tree, his face shaded by a straw boater. Charles is lying on his stomach supporting himself on his elbows, his jumper tied around his neck. They're talking and laughing: their bodies shake as they enjoy some joke together. Aloysius sits there slightly to one side, inscrutable as the Buddha. Or maybe simply enjoying a nap after stuffing himself.'

'I'd like to ask Aloysius a question,' says Kate.

'Go ahead.'

'I want to know if he's homosexual.'

'Well if you ask him like that, pronouncing it "ho" as in hop, the answer will be a very certain no. Whereas If you make it a nice soft "ho" as in home, then the answer might be a shy yes.'

'And what does Aloysius get up to with his home-bear lovers?'

'Well, he's got a very delicate front tail, so certain types of horseplay are off the agenda.'

'What about his back bottom?'

'He's got a very delicate back bottom, so that's a no-go area altogether.'

'No matter how handsome his bear partner?'

'No matter how hot his bear buddie.'

'What does that leave?' Kate wants to know.

'Well, it leaves a whole world of sensual adventure, as you well appreciate.' Oh, but something is troubling me. I feel I must give Kate an exact quote from *Brideshead*. So we stop on the muddy old towpath and I take the rucksack from my back and flick through the Penguin until I have the single long sentence I'm thinking of. And I read it aloud in all its nostalgia:

'Now, that summer term with Sebastian, it seemed as though I was being given a brief spell of what I had never known, a happy childhood, and though its toys were silk shirts and liqueurs and its naughtiness high in the catalogue of grave sins, there was some-thing of nursery freshness about us that fell little short of the joy of innocence.'

Kate sighs. I'm glad she feels affected by the text. But then I realise it's not that. What she's sighing about is that the towpath in front of us is under water.

I don't want to stop now. But it looks as if we might have to. The river has broken its banks and there is a two-metre stretch of water between us and a continuation of the path. I can jump that distance, but I wonder if Kate can.

'I'll give it a go,' she tells me.

She gives it a go. And gets one wet foot for her troubles. I take the pack off my back and ask her to catch it. 'Watch, it's fairly heavy.'

'What have you got in there?'

'Books.' I chuck her the bag, which she catches safely, and then I jump across. It's one of the things I do best is jumping. Especially in my dreams, where, once airborne, I seem to be able to stay aloft indefinitely.

Before putting the pack back on, I search for a volume I've already referred to a couple of times this afternoon. It's my own childhood copy of the two Alice books, bound in a single volume. As we walk on, I say to Kate: 'Waugh was twenty when he experienced his golden summer, and he wrote about it when he was forty-one. Charles Dodgson was thirty in July 1862, and at Alice Liddel's insistence he put pen to paper very soon after. When *Alice in Wonderland* was published in 1865, it was preceded by a Lewis Carroll poem. The first verse reads as follows:

> 'All in the golden afternoon
> Full leisurely we glide;
> For both our oars, with little skill,
> By little arms are plied,
> While little hands make vain pretence
> Our wanderings to guide.'

'Sounds like Aloysius was on board.'

'That might be right. Because in the final verse his name comes up.'

'Really?'

'Well, it's there phonetically as "Alice". Isn't that a legitimate way of pronouncing the bear's name?'

'I don't think Aloysius would answer to "Alice". Too common.'

'Maybe you're right,' and I read:

'Aloysius! A childish story take,
　　And with a gentle hand
Lay it where Childhood's dreams are twined
　　In memory's mystic band,
Like pilgrim's wither'd wreath of flowers
　　Pluck'd in a far-off land.'

I take a good look around as we walk on. There are houses to our right, but the path has gone very quiet. We haven't met anyone since crossing the last public road. It feels like we've got the place to ourselves. To our left is countryside, but before that the wide fast-flowing river. Fast-flowing? The branch of a tree fairly zips past me. It's quite disconcerting. Anyway, I should get back to the story I'm trying to put together.

'A few years pass in Charles Dodgson's life. As Lewis Carroll, he writes *Through the Looking Glass*. The book is inspired by that same 1862 July afternoon. Because, as Dodgson well knew, for him there would never be another afternoon like it. This time the book is prefaced by another poem, distinctly more melancholy than its precursor.'

Oh, but look at this. We are faced with another stretch of flooded towpath. I get *Alice* out again as Kate assesses the new leap that's required of her.

'You only get to hear this on the far side.'

'I know that. But you go first this time.'

I hand Kate my backpack and take a running jump and my left foot lands squarely in a depth of several inches of rushing water. But it doesn't rest there for more than an instant, and when I touch ground again I'm on dry towpath.

Kate next. She seems relaxed about the prospect. Or maybe not. Is this displacement activity on her part? She's opening my pack.

'I want to see exactly what you've got in here.'

I watch as she takes out each book and places it in a growing pile at her feet. *Brideshead*. *The Waste Land*. The Selina Hastings biography of Waugh. My travelling paperback copy of Martin Stannard's biography. Paula Byrne's more recently published *Mad World*. Alexander

Waugh's *Fathers and Sons*, which is in the same heavyweight division as the Hastings. And the slim volume by John Howard Wilson, signed for me by the professor himself.

Kate asks me how I've been using the biographies. I tell her that Martin Stannard's book is the one that goes into sufficient, consistent, reliable detail. To begin with, I was using it in conjunction with the official biography written by Christopher Sykes. But the Sykes book skips over some things and is reticent about others, so I've stopped referring to it automatically and haven't brought it with me today. The Hastings book is where I go if I need another slant on Evelyn's relationships with individuals or for more detail on the social milieu in which he lived. *Fathers and Sons* opens a great many family closets. And I check with Wilson to make sure Stannard hasn't underplayed certain aspects of Waugh's personality.

'What about *Mad World*? I like the subtitle. *Evelyn Waugh and the Secrets of Brideshead.*'

'That's there to remind me that – for the post-Oxford scenes in *Brideshead* – a major inspiration behind Sebastian Flyte is Hugh Lygon, just as the rest of the Flyte family are based on the Lygons of Madresfield. She pushes her analysis by suggesting that Evelyn had a sexual relationship with Hugh while they were both active members of the Hypocrites' Club at Oxford. However, she doesn't even come close to convincing me that the early relationship between Charles and Sebastian is anything other than unadulterated Evelyn and Alastair.'

I'm not sure if Kate is listening; she's peering at the photograph on the back of *Mad World*. In due course, she pronounces: 'Hugh Lygon looks more like my idea of Bertie Wooster than Sebastian Flyte.'

'I will check that out soonest, Jeeves.'

Kate tells me she thinks she should throw the volumes to me individually. I do not think she should do that. The paperbacks would flutter open and might drop short. The heavy books all have dust-jackets and could easily slip from her throwing hand. But she's now got hold of the Alexander Waugh volume and her arm is swinging backwards and forwards.

'Please don't, Kate!'

As I say this I get a vision of an empty boat floating past us upside down in midstream. In its wake come floating past in disarray Charles Dodgson and Alice . . . Evelyn and Alastair . . . Charles Ryder and Sebastian Flyte . . .

Kate's thought of something as well and is now standing looking at the book: 'If you had *Fathers and Sons* in your bag all day, why didn't you quote directly from it when you were going on about Alastair's letter to Evelyn about deans 'n' dogs.'

I explain that as far as various books are concerned, I am trying to get into the habit of paraphrasing, because I cannot assume I'll be given permission to quote from them.

Kate has no interest in such literary niceties. All of a sudden, *Fathers and Sons* is safely in my hands, though. Swiftly followed by the Selina Hastings brick. Followed in due course by the bag, as repacked with all the lighter books. Well done that skilful thrower!

Obviously Kate herself is going to get both feet wet this time. I advise her not to be too ambitious with her leaps – she doesn't want to fall and get wet all over. As I say this I see the empty boat again, only this time it's Kate and me that I see floating helplessly down the river . . . But no, Kate is safely over the stream. Soaked to both knees, but safely across, And she wants her reward. As do I:

> 'A tale begun in other days,
>   When summer suns were glowing –
> A simple chime, that served to time
>   The rhythm of our rowing –
> Whose echoes live in memory yet,
>   Though envious years would say "forget".'

'Sebastian and Charles broke up shortly after they left Oxford, didn't they?' says Kate, as we walk on, footsteps squelching.

'Before that, even. Neither of them stays at Oxford to the end of their course. They share a second year together, but they're nothing like as carefree as during that first spring and summer. Under pressure to conform, imposed mostly by his devoutly Catholic mother,

Sebastian falls to pieces. And by the second summer of their intimacy, Charles has had enough of it. Sebastian has been sent down from Oxford for the following autumn term, for conspicuous drunkenness. And Charles doesn't come back for a third year at all. Instead he goes to art school in Paris. And from that division of the ways, it's inevitable that they drift further apart.

'Was it the same for Evelyn and Alastair?'

'Alastair played an important role in Evelyn's life for a few years after Oxford, as we'll see. In the midterm, things ended up similarly, with Alastair and Sebastian both settling in the Middle East, Alastair as a dipsy diplomat and Sebastian as a drunken sot unofficially attached to a Catholic mission. The reader of *Brideshead Revisited* never quite knows what will happen to Sebastian in the end. In other words, he's still alive in WWII when Charles Ryder is narrating the book, twenty years after their time together at Oxford. But there is a letter that Evelyn wrote in 1960 or so, saying that he had not seen Alastair – whom he describes as his one-time inseparable companion – for thirty years.

As we turn a bend in the river, we realise we've come as far as we can today. The river has turned into a lake. Wading and swimming would be the only way to carry on. But wading and swimming the remaining mile to Godstow is not a realistic option.

'Well, in my country,' says Kate, her good humour undaunted, 'you'd generally get to somewhere else if you walked very fast for a long time, as we've been doing.'

I take the volume containing both *Alice* books from her hand and flick to the poem that's printed as a postscript to *Through the Looking Glass*. I'd hoped to read this to Kate on the riverbank at Godstow. But here might do just as well:

> 'Long has paled that sunny sky:
> Echoes fade and memories die:
> Autumn frosts have slain July.
>
> Still he haunts me, phantomwise.
> Alastair moving under skies

Never seen by waking eyes . . .

In a Wonderland he lies
Dreaming as the days go by,
Dreaming as the summers die.'

I'd set out today hoping to get exactly as far as this poem, but not realising it would feel so right when I did.

Yet again I reach for my pack. For what I expect to be the last time, I put back *Alice* and take out *Brideshead*. Soon I have the line from Chapter One that I've never given much thought to but which has crept up on me today: 'Oxford – submerged now and obliterated, irrecoverable as Lyonnesse, so quickly have the waters come flooding in . . . ' But that's just an unexpected bonus. I tell Kate the main thing, which is that after their first day together at Brideshead Castle, Charles and Sebastian drive back towards Oxford, planning to stop at Godstow.

'The Godstow connected with Alice? The Godstow that we won't get to today?'

'Yes. Sebastian's suggestion is that they eat at the Trout Inn. It's a pub that still exists and where we would have eaten tonight.'

'Oh.'

'Sebastian's plan is to leave their borrowed motor car at the Trout and to walk back into Oxford along the river. That is, to walk the route that Charles Dodgson rowed back that golden day in 1862, entertaining Alice and her sisters with outlandish tales and teasing conversation. "Wouldn't that be best?" Sebastian asks Charles. The twenty-year-old Charles Ryder of 1923 doesn't reply. Or at least his reply isn't recorded in *Brideshead Revisited*.'

'That's a pity.'

'I think we can assume that Charles would have been in agreement with his friend's plan for the evening. Because what the reader is then told is that the whole golden day during Eights Week has been remembered with tears by that same Charles Ryder, a middle-aged captain of infantry.'

Kate is silent for a minute. Then she says: 'I hope you don't suppose those were real tears?'

'I do, actually. Just as I think this is real floodwater that we're going to have to negotiate again on the way back.'

'We'll hold hands and paddle across the stream together. You and me, Dodgson and Alice, Evelyn and Alastair, Charles and Sebastian. Anyone else?'

'Selina Hastings and Martin Stannard, John Howard Wilson and Alexander Waugh, Paula Byrne and Hugh Lygon, the Dean of Balliol and Aloysius . . . '

'That's about the lot, surely.'

So I take hold of Kate's hand (and Alice's and Alastair's and Aloysius's . . .) with the intention of us all fording the flood as one.

POST-OXFORD

The Agony of Ernest Vaughan

1

Kate and I are bowling along in her mum's car. Gina lives in Witney, ten miles west of Oxford, and as our lunchtime destination for today is a village pub only five miles north of the university town, there was no need for an early start. The Abingdon Arms, Beckley, was a regular haunt of Evelyn and Alastair while they were at Oxford and for several years thereafter.

We had a strange start to the day. Kate's mum works in a shop called Teddy Bears of Witney and on display in the shop is Aloysius. That is, the actual bear, now a hundred years old, which appeared with Anthony Andrews and Jeremy Irons in the early scenes of Granada Television's *Brideshead Revisited*. The shop's owner has the original Aloysius sitting behind glass with early American editions of the novel and publicity shots from the Granada series. He told us that there is a new film to be made of the book, without Aloysius. It will be a feature-length film, with the emphasis on the Charles Ryder and Julia Flyte relationship. I do not have high hopes for this new production. After all they are planning to get rid of Sebastian and Aloysius and nine hours of transmission time. It's so difficult to make something really special. It's so easy to tear down some rare and precious thing.

Last night we prepared ourselves for this morning's pilgrimage to see Aloysius by watching the first episode of the classic Granada serial. Kate, her mother and I sat in a row in her mother's bedroom watching the VCR. Kate and I watched the programme more or less exclusively with an eye for Aloysius. So that, for instance, when he was spotted leaving the barber's in Oxford – Sebastian carrying him under his arm – we watched and listened closely as the barber told Charles that Lord Sebastian Flyte had just been in to buy a hairbrush for his teddy bear. The brush had to have stiff bristles and an ivory back so that the bear's name – Aloysius – could be engraved on it. The brush would be used to spank Aloysius when he was naughty, reported the old barber, seemingly charmed by such undergraduate antics. Kate and I were still discussing the implications of the spanking threat – sexual and otherwise – when Aloysius's name came up again. This time he was mentioned in Sebastian's initial note of apology to Charles. The 'Aloysius won't speak to me until he sees I am forgiven' line. Kate's theory was that Aloysius would use the hairbrush on Sebastian's backside to punish him for being sick outside Charles's room. 'Not *outside* Charles's room,' I corrected her. 'Sebastian was sick *into* it.'

'Oh, would you two be quiet,' said Gina, who told us she wanted to watch the programme properly.

'P-properly, darling?' said Kate, who has a tendency to revert to back-chatting teenager while in her mother's house: 'what do you mean by p-p-properly?'

Teddy Bears of Witney has produced a limited-edition full-size facsimile of the bear. Gina owns Aloysious number 2412, a valuable bear in itself, but she has allowed her Alo to take the air with us today. Kate's mother too was invited to come along (it would have been reminiscent of the days when Evelyn, Alastair and his mother went on jaunts together in her car) but she declined the offer. Maybe she knows what Aloysius is like as a driver. It's not that he doesn't *want* to change gear. It's just that with both hands on the wheel, which is a perfect size for a well-proportioned bear, his feet remain a good yard clear of the clutch. So Alo's style of driving is to delegate all the foot-pedal business to his co-driver. He sits on Kate's lap, steering and tooting. Why tooting? Because Evelyn was just as keen on *The Wind in the Willows* as *Alice in Wonderland*. For 'Toad of Toad Hall' read 'Aloysius of Brideshead Castle'.

Beckley doesn't seem to be sign-posted. But I can see where it is from the road map, and I make sure Kate and Alo don't miss the turn off. Beckley turns out to be an unspoilt Cotswold village. The Abingdon Arms looks as inviting as any building I've ever seen! We get out of the car and I plonk Aloysius in the boot. Kate protests, but to no avail. 'This is Evelyn post-Oxford we're tracking now,' I tell her. 'There can be no looking back.' Actually, there will be quite a lot of looking back, but not to the nursery freshness that Aloysius represents.

With a pint in front of me, with that first malty mouthful of midday beer swallowed, I make a start at bringing Kate up to date. 'OK, first I have to locate us. I mean I have to get Evelyn established here in Beckley. According to his diary, he left London on 27 July 1924.'

'What had he been doing since the end of his last Oxford term?'

'Making a film called *The Scarlet Woman* with Oxford chums. Partly at Underhill and on Hampstead Heath. A ludicrous piece of work about the Dean of Balliol's attempt both to sexually seduce and to convert to Catholicism the heir to the British throne.'

'The Dean of Balliol doesn't just sleep with any class of man – he aspires to sleep with the heir to the British throne?'

'Evelyn plays the Dean with relish. The bits I've seen are quite funny, I have to say. Anyway, another thing Evelyn does after leaving Oxford is to start a novel called *The Temple at Thatch*. But more about that later.'

I sip again from my pint. 'Actually, the first thing I should say about Evelyn's next three years is that he wrote a detailed diary, as at Lancing, whereas there was no Oxford diary. This means it's going to be a lot harder to give you a clear overview.'

'Do try,' says Kate. 'We don't want to get bogged down in the minutiae of Evelyn's life. After all, we've got our own lives to live.'

With those wise words duly noted, I take the plunge: 'Evelyn got to the Abingdon Arms in the late evening, having walked all the way from Oxford Station with his bag. He found Alastair in the caravan.'

'What caravan?'

'Post-Oxford, they stayed in a caravan in the garden of this pub. No doubt to save on the cost of lodgings. They'd been regular customers during their time at university and had become chummy with the

landlady. So now that they needed accommodation that was no problem – they were popular, sociable lads.'

'OK,' says Kate, who, as one half of the designated driver, sips from her lime and soda.

'They spent a quiet evening in the pub. But the next day was one of the most wretched of Evelyn's life according to this diary entry. It rained all night. The caravan leaked. Alastair was too ill to get up in the morning. Evelyn was reduced to reading in the local church to pass time. However, when he got back to the caravan at about eleven, Alastair was dressed. In the rain they walked into Oxford where they'd promised lunch to Richard Plunket Greene.' I look up from my self-stapled copy of The Twenties Diary, the pages of which were sourced from a falling-apart seventies' paperback of *The Diaries of Evelyn Waugh*. 'From now on Richard and his family become important, so you might do well to remember that name.'

'Richard Plunk-Plunk-Plunket Greene.'

'Evelyn, Alastair and Richard ate expensively at the George.'

'Where's that?

'It used to be on George Street – which is on the route into the centre of Oxford from the train station – but it's been demolished since Evelyn's day. No great loss, perhaps. Evelyn seems to have gone there a lot, but is disparaging about the quality and cost of the food.'

'Thank goodness this place hasn't been demolished.'

We don't have the inn to ourselves, but we do have a quiet corner at a table beside a window. We're sitting on chairs with high backs like thrones. We feel like royalty. But let's catch up on Evelyn, Alastair and Richard at the George.

'With lunch they had about four vodkas each. They then went down to Richard's rooms in what had been the old Hypocrites' Club and drank whisky until dinner. After dinner – again in the George – Evelyn ordered some bottles of champagne, paid for with a post-dated cheque, and they became "utterly" drunk. They then went back to Richard's rooms and drank more. Evelyn and Alastair quarrelled, so that Evelyn ended up sleeping the night on a sofa at Richard's place. The next day Evelyn hired a bike and got back here to Alastair and the caravan. In the evening they were invited to dinner with a local squire who gave them plenty to drink. Next day there was a village party here in Beckley to which Alastair and Evelyn were invited. They joined in with gusto, dancing several times with the landlady and drinking plenty of her beer. The whole village sat and ate and danced and drank and sang until three in the morning. Next day Evelyn had his viva.'

'His viva?'

'The oral part of his History finals. Presenting himself at nine-thirty, he was told to come back in an hour, so he left the building, was given a large whisky by his kindly wine merchant, and bought a little mourning ring dated 1800 for Alastair. Later, Evelyn found the viva a pure formality . . .'

'He was superbly prepared for it, I must say.'

' . . . and telegraphed his parents to inform them of his certain third-class degree, before returning here to Beckley.'

'What does that mean?'

'It means he knew he'd done really badly in the written exams and that the oral examination had not presented an opportunity to redress the balance. Next day he went into Oxford again. Lunched heavily at the George. Drank with Richard Plunket Greene. Drank at the Union.

Rode back here to Beckley where Alastair and he drank champagne. It was a very drunken night at the Abingdon Arms, apparently.' I look up from the diary. 'Are you beginning to get the picture?'

'He's drinking an awful lot. Was it a stressful time for him?'

'Yes, but it became more so in September. Alastair had signed up for an architecture course in London. As it turned out, he didn't attend a single lecture. Instead he booked himself a passage to Kenya. He'd decided he needed a break from his mother, and his sister had told him he could spend the winter with her. In the week before Alastair went off, he converted to Catholicism, something he'd long been interested in.'

'And Evelyn?'

'Evelyn was upset by Alastair's leaving. But he was devastated about no longer being at Oxford. He knew he had to do *something*, so he signed up for an art course at Heatherley's in Central London. Every day he travelled into town from Underhill and concentrated on drawing the life models. But he wasn't as talented in this direction as everyone had led him to suppose. He didn't enjoy the discipline of it and he didn't make new friends. He was hankering for a return to Oxford. And in November he did go back for a party where he was the main guest. He loved it. From then on, most weekends he'd be back at Oxford living it up. Here are the grisly details of one trip . . .'

For this I have to refer closely to the diary itself, though I paraphrase so as to keep some distance from Evelyn's doings: 'After a quiet afternoon at the cinema, Evelyn had a dinner party to go to. He arrived at that "quite blind" after a great number of cocktails at the George with his cousin Claud. When the dinner broke up, three of the guests went off on a pub crawl ending up at the Hypocrites' where another blind was going on. That was Monday and he was only warming up. Next day, Evelyn drank all morning in pubs and invited some old cronies to lunch at the New Reform Club. There he argued with the president and was expelled from the club. Alfred Duggan and he then drank double brandies until Evelyn could not walk. Alfred carried Evelyn to Worcester College where Evelyn fell out of a window and then lapsed into unconsciousness punctuated with bouts of "well-directed" vomiting. He dined four times at various places and went to a drunken party at Worcester in the rooms of someone he didn't know.'

'Do you think he was missing Alastair?'

'The binge drinking could have been a way of flushing Alastair out of his system. Because, about a week later, there is a diary entry where Evelyn wonders aloud if he is falling in love with Olivia Plunket Greene.'

'Richard's sister?'

'Mmm.'

'What was she like?'

'She liked a drink. She was intense yet she was the complete party-going hedonist as well. Maybe because of this contradiction she was prone to melancholy. Not unlike Evelyn. Evelyn also knew her other brother from Oxford, the giant David Plunket Greene. Evelyn got to know and very much like their mother Gwen, or Lady Plunket as he called her. So he began to spend a lot of time at their family home in Hanover Terrace, by Regent's Park.'

'A new direction for Evelyn,' says Kate, hopefully.

'Well, not quite. That January, things were complicated by the fact that Alastair was back from Africa, and Evelyn, fed up with the art course and with being in debt, had applied for teaching jobs. He was offered and accepted a position at Arnold House in Denbighshire. That was the most significant development, because out of that experience would come the comic masterpiece *Decline and Fall*. But not for a couple of years. At the time, the most significant development was Olivia Plunket Greene, whom he yearned for all the while he was stuck in ghastly Welsh exile with no chance to think about anything but teaching duties. Come the Easter holidays, Evelyn was full of the sorrows of unrequited love. Because when he saw Olivia again, though they shared a friendship, socialising together every day and talking together late into the night, she did not offer Evelyn anything physical. It exasperated Evelyn that he couldn't cure himself of being in love with this person. But, showing a trace of maturity, he acknowledged in his diary that it must be trying for her as well. What really annoyed him was that Olivia was flirtatious with other men, particularly Tony Bushell, one of Evelyn's friends from Oxford, who was at the start of a promising acting career. After a holiday with the Plunket Greene family on Lundy Island, Evelyn took himself off to Barford for a few days drinking with Alastair.'

'What did Olivia look like?'

As well as The Twenties section of *The Diaries*, I've got *A Little Learning* at the table with me. Most of the illustrations in the book are of Evelyn's artwork. But there is a full-page photo taken of the Lundy Island group. Evelyn is sitting in front of the Plunket Greenes. I point out Olivia, who is shown in profile. ' "A tiny mouth and big goo-goo eyes", according to Harold Acton.'

'She's got a very period look about her. I should think that bob would suit the shape of her face. But you can't really tell from a profile shot alone.'

'She looks like butter wouldn't melt in her mouth. When all the time she's subject to the usual human cravings.'

'But she doesn't fancy Evelyn. I wonder why.'

'One of her brothers was six-foot-nine, remember. To her Evelyn probably seemed like the shortest man in England.'

'The shortest man in her upper-class world.'

'Look at him in his high-necked jumper. He mentions buying a jumper like that in the *Diaries*. He says the style is very popular in Oxford as it allows young men to cover up love bites they've received from other young men. Evelyn notes in his diary that the style makes him look precisely ten years old.'

'He looks cute,' says Kate, smiling at the photograph; 'the shortest, youngest man in England.'

'Looks cute; feels miserable. But the truth is he's young. He's got friends, and really good friends at that. True, he does not have the lover he wants, but he's got time on his side – he's still maturing. Pity for Evelyn that he couldn't see that.'

'Who can see that when they're twenty-one?' asks Kate. 'Youth is taken for granted. It's experiences and a sense of fulfilment that's top of everyone's wish-list at that age.'

Our lunch arrives. I'm more interested in carrying on with my pint but I have to admit that Kate's meal in particular looks delicious: 'What is it?'

'It's goat's cheese – which I love – with shallots and walnuts encased in crumbly pastry. Oh, it's delicious. Try a mouthful.'

It is gorgeous.

'No wonder Alastair and Evelyn used to come here.'

'I doubt if it's the same chef, eighty years on.'

'No, it won't be the same chef, but this place won't have changed that much. It's got a great fabric – the building and the village – why should it change?' asks Kate, enjoying her food. 'So update me with Alastair.'

'His sister reported back to their mother that he was interested in *absolutely nothing* in Africa.'

Kate smiles. 'He probably went on to his sister about the wonderful English cooking you could get at the Abingdon Arms.'

'When he got back to England, with Evelyn about to go off teaching, Alastair got a job at the Shakespeare Head Press in Stratford. So he was around for get-togethers in Oxford and at Barford and here in Beckley. But by May, Evelyn was back at Arnold House in deepest Wales. By this time he'd finished *The Temple at Thatch* and had sent the exercise book it was written in to Harold Acton, who was still at Oxford. The story was about someone who'd inherited nothing but a classical folly in the grounds of a once-rich estate, and in the folly he practised black magic.'

'Doesn't sound like an Evelyn theme.'

'No. But there is one story he published while at Oxford, called 'Unacademic Exercise', which does have a black-magic theme. An older man takes three undergraduates out to a heath. The youngest is required to strip naked, draw a circle round himself, take a potion and drink some human blood. He is beginning to go wild in the moonlight when one of his young companions summons up the willpower to knock him out of the circle and break the spell. Another Oxford story that embraces an irrational cast of mind.'

'So you think *The Temple at Thatch* would have been dark?'

'There is a diary entry written just after Alastair had gone off to Africa saying that Evelyn had read again and with vast delight Drummond of Hawthornden's *A Cypress Grove*. Evelyn goes on to say that he's writing more of *The Temple at Thatch,* which he is considering calling *The Fabulous Paladins* after a passage from *A Cypress Grove*.'

'What sort of book is that?'

'It's a treatise on death written early in the seventeenth century by a religious Scot. It goes from despair to hope. Hang on, I've made a note in the diary of the "fabulous paladins" passage, which is from early on in the essay. Here it is. Ready for a blast from the past?'

'Mmm.'

' "Death is the sad estranger of acquaintance, the eternal divorcer of marriage, the ravisher of children from their parents, the stealer of parents from their children, the interrer of fame, the sole cause of forgetfulness, by which the living talk of those gone away as of so many shadows, or fabulous Paladins." '

'It must have caught Evelyn's attention because Alastair had just gone off to Africa.'

'*A Cypress Grove* was published in a very nice edition in 1919 by the Shakespeare Head Press, the very organisation that Alastair went to work for when he came back from Africa. So there can be little question that both Evelyn and Alastair were into books and into a dark and mystical view of life.'

'You're not saying that *The Temple at Thatch* would have been all dark, are you?'

'Actually, no. Another influence on it would have been the dandified prose of Ronald Firbank. The exquisite book of his that was published in 1923, and which Evelyn would no doubt have read in his second Oxford year, was *The Flower Beneath the Foot*. It's full of aestheticism and innuendo: a modern equivalent of Firbank would be Kenneth Williams, or any arrestingly camp stand-up comic. Anyway, whatever came out of Evelyn's mixing-pot of a mind, Harold Acton didn't think *The Temple at Thatch* was any good. Too much "nid-nodding over port", he told Evelyn in a letter when returning the book. "Sub-Firbank and not worthy of Evelyn's talents" is what Acton said in his memoirs. Evelyn must have agreed, because he threw it in the school boiler. And so we'll never know how good or bad it was.'

'It must all have got him down a bit.'

'Evelyn was depressed all right. His brother Alec had given him some hope that Scott Moncrieff, the Proust translator, would employ him as a secretary. Evelyn was looking forward to moving to the Mediterranean to take up this post, though how he thought his language skills would be up to the job, God only knows. Also, he couldn't type and he'd never been abroad! Anyway, it turned out that Scott Moncrieff could not afford to employ a secretary, so that was that. Specifically, that was Evelyn at the end of his tether, as he says in his diary. He'd given his notice at the school and was pretty sure that even if he withdrew it the headmaster wouldn't have him back.'

'So what did he do?' asks Kate, still eating happily.

'He says nothing about it in his diary. But forty years later in *A Little Learning* he admits that he attempted suicide. He went down to the beach, took off all his clothes and left them in a pile under a note he'd written in Greek, and then he swam out to sea with the intention of not coming back.'

'What did the note say?'

'It was a quote about the sea washing away all our sins.'

'Sins or troubles?'

'Mmm. Good point. Let's look it up . . .

'It's "ills". And the quote is from Euripedes. Anyway, before poor Evelyn has got to the point of no return, he gets stung by jellyfish. This brings him to his senses and he swims back to shore. There is no towel to dry himself, but I dare say he manages that with his clothes. Then he tears up the note and walks the steep – sorry, "sharp" – hill that leads to the rest of his life.'

I tell Kate that Evelyn's autobiography ends with the aborted suicide attempt at the age of twenty-two – there are no further volumes because most of what happened to him thereafter was covered by his fiction. But the great thing is that so much of what I've been saying to Kate in the last hour was itself transformed into a little known piece of fiction by Evelyn. A story I must tell Kate about. But in order to do justice to 'The Balance' we must move to a pub in Oxford.

'Can't we stay here?' she asks. Kate needs to be convinced that we have to move from this lovely spot. Maybe she's right, we shouldn't rush off just yet. So I tell her a few things about 'The Balance' that are appropriate to say in Beckley. 'First, Evelyn got the idea for the story in May 1925 while teaching in Wales. The story was put to one side when Evelyn became excited about the prospect of the secretary's job in Italy, and it remained on one side while he was depressed in the aftermath of the Italian job falling through. However, on returning to civilisation after the end of term, he finished the story at Barford House in the room that Alastair's mother had kitted out for him to work in. The diary is worth looking at in detail for the next few days.'

'Do you want another drink?'

I do want another drink. But in a few minutes it really will be time to move on. So I persuade Kate to make do with diary now, drink later.

'On Wednesday, 26 August, Evelyn takes a bus into Stratford to lunch with Alastair. When Alastair goes back to his printing in the afternoon, Evelyn goes to see a performance of *Two Gentleman of Verona*, which he describes as a silly play. In the evening, back at Barford (proto-Brideshead, remember), Evelyn and Alastair dine together in high-necked jumpers and together they do "much that could not have been done if Mrs Graham had been there".'

'Oh, love bites! I thought Evelyn had given up that sort of thing.'

'Saturday, 29 August. The intention is for Alastair to drive Evelyn to Oxford from where he will get a train to London. They lunch in Banbury on bread and cheese and then go to Beckley where everyone at the Abingdon Arms is so sweet that Evelyn decides to stay the night.'

'*We* should do that! That woman who brought us lunch is so sweet that we should spend the whole day and then the night here.'

'Note that Alastair didn't stay the night here. He may have had a dinner engagement back at Barford as it was Evelyn's intention to be back at Underhill by Saturday night. Anyway, on Sunday, 30 August, Evelyn feels it is pleasant to wake up in Beckley. He sits in the inn porch reading newspapers until noon when two former cronies come down for their morning drink. At lunchtime Alastair arrives from Barford and they eat roast beef and celery with those cronies. One of those Beckley bods, without saying anything to Evelyn, pays for his food and lodgings, which clearly delights and moves Evelyn when he finds out about it. Alastair and he drive to Tring and they have dinner at Aylesbury. During dinner, Alastair reads Evelyn's story which he has had typed up at great expense.'

'And?'

'And nothing. Evelyn is much too modest to say that Alastair pissed himself laughing at "The Balance". Which he surely must have done.'

'Is it funny then?'

'You'll soon see. But let me finish this. Monday, 31 August, Evelyn writes in his diary that he has forgotten to say that throughout these journeyings he has been carrying a kitten with him for Olivia, with whose family he is about to spend a week.'

'A lovely kitten? Does he say anything more about it?'

'Just that the next day he spends two hours feeding Olivia's cat.'

'It goes from being a kitten to a cat in one day flat?'

'It does. And it reminds me that we've got a pet of our own to see to.'

'Oh, you mean the bear,' says Kate, suddenly ready to go. So we make our way out of the pub and we open the boot of Kate's mum's car. Neither of us supposes that Aloysius will be too happy at having been locked away in the dark with various Waugh biographies for two solid hours when he could have been lying in a punt with Sebastian or having some other such Oxford treat. I for one am braced for the mother of all tantrums.

'EVELYN WAUGH SLEEPS WITH PUSSY,' announces Aloysius.

Prompted by Kate, the bear corrects himself: 'EVELYN WAUGH *ASPIRES* TO SLEEPING WITH PUSSY.'

It turns out that Aloysius must have heard every word we exchanged in the pub and doesn't feel left out at all! What's more he's driving again and there's nothing he likes more. *Parp, parp.* Let him make the most of it, because in only a few minutes we'll be at a Park and Ride, and that's as near as Aloysius will be getting to the dreaming spires of Oxford today.

2

We're sitting in a bar in the centre of Oxford called the Crown. The reason why we're in these licensed premises will become apparent to Kate soon enough. The Crown is a few yards down a lane off Cornmarket Street, the city centre extension of St Aldate's, so it's not far from Christ Church. However, it doesn't look as if there are many students on a 'blind' this weekday afternoon. This generation of students is nothing like as decadent as the one in Evelyn's heyday. Not that the lack of an old-fashioned student atmosphere is going to prevent us from thoroughly enjoying what I've got lined up for ourselves. I sip from what is only my second pint of the day as Kate follows suit from her half.

We've sat down at one of the few tables with natural light falling on to it. The tabletop is dry, so it really is the ideal place for us to consider *Georgian Short Stories*. This is an American edition of the anthology published in 1927, a year after the UK edition, which cost me a fiver plus the same again in postage from the States. It contains sixteen stories, and because of Waugh's position in the alphabet he gets the ultimate slot – last and longest story in the book. Chapman and Hall originally published the work, the stories being chosen by Alec Waugh. But the fact that Evelyn's father and brother were closely involved in the production is nowhere apparent, at least not in the American edition.

A nice detail is that each author's portrait is included as a full-page black-and-white photograph near the start of his or her story. In the bottom-right corner of Evelyn's portrait, it says 'For Terence from Evelyn', so the photograph dates from the time of his friendship with Terence Greenidge, an Oxford pal. Although the story is subtitled 'A Yarn of the Good Old Days of Broad Trousers and High-Necked Jumpers', the portrait of Evelyn shows him wearing shirt and tie, woollen jersey and tweed jacket. He looks *precisely* ten years old.

'Tell me about this marvellous story, then,' says Kate,

challengingly. She briefly holds open the book at the beginning of Evelyn's contribution, then allows the pages to flick over, several at a time.

'It's peculiar to start with. The action settles down at an art school. But the reader has to take it in as if it were a film. What I mean is, the bits that are in italic are supposed to be the responses of members of the cinema audience watching the film (the main narrative, set at the art school). And the lines in capital letters are supposed to be the film's captions. All the rest of the dialogue – at the art school and elsewhere – is what the intelligent film watcher is supposed to deduce from what they are seeing.'

'I'm not sure I follow.'

'Yes, it's a pretentious set-up. Written under the influence of T. S. Eliot and the rise of Modernism, you have to remember. Once you know the story well enough, most of the pseudo-cinematic side of things just falls away. I'll tell you the story straight, shall I?'

'Yes, please.'

'Adam Doure is a student at a London art school that obviously represents Heatherley's, the place where Evelyn studied art for three months. He's in the middle of some lacklustre life-drawing when he's called to the phone. It's Imogen Quest, who tells Adam that she can't meet him that night. They arrange a lunchtime rendezvous instead. Imogen orders expensive food and then doesn't eat. She tells Adam that her mother is against their relationship continuing and has arranged for her to be sent off to Thatch.'

'Thatch as in *The Temple at Thatch*?'

'I suppose so. Adam accompanies Imogen to Euston to see her off. That's the first part of the story, throughout which Adam behaves like a lovesick puppy.'

'I take it Imogen is based on Olivia.'

'Yes. Though the indicators are subtle. First, her inconsistent and maddening – though, of course, irresistible – behaviour. Second, the references to Imogen's brother and her mother, Lady R, which bring to mind Olivia's brothers and Lady Plunket. Third, Adam's home is said to be at Hanover Gate from where he can hear the animals in Regent's Park Zoo. A map of London shows that Hanover Gate is next to Hanover Terrace where the Plunket Greenes lived when Evelyn first knew them. Evelyn may have slept there the odd time after one of his long talks into the night with Olivia. Heart-to-heart chats which may have been punctuated by baboon howls. But perhaps the niftiest parallel is where, while standing on the station platform waiting for the train that will separate them for ever, Imogen looks at a weekly publication and draws Adam's attention to a striking picture of someone called Sybil.'

'How does that connect with Olivia?'

'Apparently, she was fascinated by magazines like *Vogue*, as well as by traditional religious imagery of madonnas. Anyway, Imogen goes off in her train. And Adam, upset about having lost the object of his unrequited love, and depressed about his prospects in life generally, decides he will kill himself with a bottle of pills. But first he must write his suicide note.'

'Was this story written before or after Evelyn's suicide attempt?'

'Waugh's diary shows that he began the story at the school in Wales in May 1925. The suicide attempt was at the beginning of July. The story was finished at the Grahams' house in Barford in August. So it's difficult to know for sure whether Evelyn's suicide attempt or Adam's came first. But if the main chapter, with its cinema structure, was written as a whole shortly after his initial inspiration, a time when Waugh reports in the diary that he's been writing furiously, then the fictional suicide came first. Which means that when Evelyn swam off, leaving the note in Greek, he was leaving a longer suicide note in modern English prose. In the middle of this extended suicide note, Adam's suicide note was written in Latin. It was placed in an envelope with Imogen's name on it.'

I direct Kate's attention to the page.

'It's one of those lines that are put over in capital letters. In other words, Evelyn would have us believe that the people in the cinema watching the film are given the words of the note as an on-screen caption.'

Kate takes up the book and reads aloud: ' "AVE IMPERATRIX

IMMORTALIS MORITURUS TE SALUTO." Do you know what it means?'

'I looked it up with one of those translator functions you can get on the Internet. According to that it means: "HAIL, IMMORTAL RULER, HE THAT IS ABOUT TO DIE SALUTES YOU." '

Kate smiles: 'I bet that's what Aloysius will say when we next open the boot of the car.'

'Maybe he'll give us a better translation.'

'He'll give us the original Latin. He's a classical bear, don't forget. But back to the story. Did Adam top himself?'

'Well, Adam is not going to top himself in London, is he? He's going to end it all in Oxford. But first he's going to have one last blind. So when he gets off the train at Oxford he goes round all his old haunts in a taxi trying to get a chum to spend a last evening with him. However, no one is available. Only as a last resort does he call on Ernest Vaughan. This is where the fun starts. Do you want another drink?'

'I'd better not. I'm driving if you remember.'

'I better had. Evelyn's Adam is on a blind and he needs company.'

When I get back to our table I tell Kate that if Adam Doure is one facet of Evelyn – which he clearly is – then Ernest Vaughan is a much more vigorous chip off the original block. He's described as being a short, sturdy young man with fierce little eyes and a well-formed forehead. Evelyn to a T. His rooms stand in the front quadrangle of one of the uglier and less renowned colleges.

'I suppose he means Hertford but I can't think of it as anything other than a privileged and special place.'

'Nor me. Ernest's rooms are described as a pillar of cloud by day and a pillar of fire by night.'

Kate reads aloud: ' "Inscriptions and drawings, ranging from almost inspired caricatures to meaningless or obscene scrawlings, attest to Ernest's various stages of drunkenness." '

I draw attention to another line. Ernest has written across his bedroom door in red chalk: 'Who is this Bach? I have not so much as heard of the man. E. V.'

Kate, her nose in the book, tells me: 'And above a drawing of

Lord Basingstoke, Ernest has written, "UT EXULTAT IN COITU
ELEPHAS, SIC RICARDUS." '

She lowers the book and leans her face towards mine. 'I suppose
you've looked that up on your Internet thingie.'

'Of course, I have. It translates something like: "IN ORDER TO
LET ONESELF GO IN THE CASE OF HAVING SEX WITH AN
ELEPHANT, THIS IS WHAT ONE MUST DO, RICHARD." '

'I prefer that to Adam's Latin tag.'

'I prefer it to both Adam's sad Latin tag and Evelyn's insipid Greek
one.'

'Tell me,' says Kate, leaning forward again, smiling, 'is Ernest by
any chance going to join Adam on his BLIND?'

'Affirmative,' I say, glancing at my glass. 'And it's only by exerting
all my willpower that I'm going to remain behind as narrator.'

'It's only fair that if I'm the designated driver, you're the designated
narrator.'

'OK. Well first Ernest pours out the whisky. Just to break the ice
between them, you know. Waugh tells us they have not been close
friends in the past. Half an hour later they leave Ernest's college,
having to put up with the muttered disapproval of undergraduates
who are queuing for Hall and who hate Ernest and anyone who
associates with him. Homophobia, I think. An hour later our pair of
college undesirables are just finishing dinner at the Crown, both
showing marked signs of intoxication.'

'The Crown – great! I feel we're part and parcel of the blind just by
being here.'

'Me too.' I have the book in front of me now, so that neither Kate
nor I miss out any of the fun. 'Evelyn describes the place as being
pathetically frescoed with views of Oxford. At a table near that of our
heroes who are drinking double whiskies, three young men wearing
gowns order coffee and cream cakes and discuss the Union elections.
Ernest insists on sending a bottle of gin over to their table. The offer
is gracelessly rejected.'

'I wonder if that's another dig at Preters,' says Kate.

'At a public house in "the slums" Ernest gets embroiled in a heated exchange about birth control with a beggar whom he has just defeated at "darts".' I look up from the book to add: 'God, there is so much anger and arrogance in that single sentence. But I'll just point out, in case my pronunciation hasn't done the trick, that Evelyn puts double quotes around the word "darts" to distance himself from such a beyond-the-pale pursuit.'

'Yes, but it's a joke as well.'

'The whole thing is certainly intended to be funny. Ernest is then beset by two panders.'

'What are panders?'

'Pimps, I think . . . To whom Ernest loudly maintains the abnormality of his tastes.'

'Ernest is gay?'

'Well, he maintains his tastes are abnormal to the pimps, but what conclusion can one draw from that? Meanwhile, Adam tries to give the bottle of gin to a man, the man's wife interposes and the bottle falls to the ground and smashes.

'Our sociable pair hire a taxi but are too drunk to be allowed into any colleges. They do manage to get into the grounds of Balliol, where Adam is recognised and hauled from the quad into a party. Suddenly Adam hears his name being called from outside. It's Ernest, and Adam feels he must introduce "this marvellous man" to Henry Quest. The introduction does not go well. When Henry's second name is announced a bell rings in Ernest's disorientated mind. "QUEST? ANY RELATION TO ADAM'S WOMAN?" Henry takes exception to Imogen's being described in this way. Things look like turning nasty. Ernest saves the situation by announcing that he is going to be sick. He makes his way unmolested and with perfect dignity to the quad.'

'It's like that bit you were reading me from the diary in the Abingdon Arms. The day that Evelyn ended up being carried by his chum into Worcester College and falling out of the window.'

'It is like that. Evelyn doesn't say whether Ernest's projectile vomitings are well directed, but I think we can assume they were. Anyway, next stop is a Liberal Association dance at the Town Hall.

Which is back on to the main road here, almost opposite. A band is playing, Liberals are dancing and Ernest is going around with a radiant smile on his face offering plum cake to couples sitting at tables. An MC in evening dress asks Adam to take Ernest away. Outside the Town Hall, Ernest climbs into the first car he sees – a decrepit Ford – and starts the engine. Adam and a policeman try and stop him but to no avail. Halfway down St Aldate's the car mounts the kerb and runs into a shop window. There is movement in the crowd that converges, to make way for something that is being carried out.'

'Oh dear, I hope Ernest is all right.'

'Ernest is more than all right. He's a star! I can't believe that most of the commentaries I've seen on this story place emphasis on the modernist trappings of the story and the Evelyn / Adam side of things, without even mentioning Ernest. Ernest represents a vital side of Evelyn's character.'

'Of course he does!'

'More about him anon. For now, let's go with Adam to the end of the story and the crux of *The Balance*. Just half an hour later, Adam is alone in his hotel bedroom.'

'Hotel?'

'I think Evelyn mentions in his diary staying in a hotel in Beaumont Street. There's an old-established one there now opposite the Ashmolean Museum. Maybe it was there. Anyway, Adam drinks the poison and lies down to die. But in the middle of the night he wakes with the coldness of death about his heart. He stumbles to the window with the drumming of blood in his head. He tries to keep down his sickness but can't. He vomits uncontrollably into the yard below.'

'So that's Evelyn, Ernest and Adam all having gone through the projectile-vomiting experience,' says Kate.

'He goes for a walk along the river.'

'Along our Alice-and-Alastair-and-Aloysius route?'

'I think so. Actually, I'm glad you bring that up. Note what a difference there is between this story, written about Oxford in the immediate aftermath of Evelyn's undergraduate life, and the Charles and Sebastian stuff from *Brideshead*, which was written twenty years down the line. It's tempting to write off the latter as the product of looking through rose-tinted specs. But I think 'The Balance' isn't really about the time at Oxford at all. It's Evelyn in exile, immediately post-Oxford. The Adam character is Evelyn recognising the unhealthy obsession he's got with Olivia. And the Adam/Ernest binge is in the style of the binges Evelyn had when he revisited Oxford in the autumn after going down. Oxford was a great time for Evelyn, and in due course he would preserve that period for posterity. In the meantime he would express his anguish about having had the place taken away from him . . . Where was I?'

'Adam has gone out for a walk along the river.'

'Right. He stops on a bridge and looks at his reflection in the water. His reflection asks what's been going on. And Adam's reply, which is not that clearly expressed I have to say, talks about the balance between reason and appetite. Reason remains constant, so that's not really part of the equation at all. It's a matter of what you have an appetite for, life or death. The reflection sums up: "That is the balance then – and in the end circumstances decides." Adam agrees with this bleak summation.'

'Is that it?'

'Not quite. There is a final scene set at Thatch, which is evidently a country house close to Oxford. Imogen and some male friends from Oxford are having lunch. In his absence, Adam is being talked about disparagingly. Ernest's name comes up and he is talked about even more disparagingly. Imogen asks if he is the short, dirty man with masses of hair. This description is confirmed. "Always drunk," someone elaborates. Perversely, Imogen says she finds him attractive and would like to meet him properly. This is shouted down as an impossible idea. She asks first one man and then another if they will introduce her, but no one will. "Really, he is *too* awful," says one man. In that case, Imogen will get Adam to introduce her to him. And with that the story ends.'

'How strange.'

'Yes, I hadn't really thought about it before today. It's as if Evelyn isn't giving up on Olivia. If Olivia is sick of the lovelorn side of his personality, maybe she will go for the fiery, drunken side of his nature.'

'Oh, but she won't.'

'No I don't think she ever did. But I recall something that Selina Hastings states in her biography. She goes into the Olivia–Evelyn relationship in more depth than any other commentator and is particularly strong on describing and analysing Olivia's personality. Hastings doesn't date this anecdote, but she tells of how there came a time when Evelyn was becoming increasingly frustrated with Olivia's behaviour. She would get off with all sorts of men but never him, much to Evelyn's fury. So Olivia laid it on the line for him: she didn't and could never fancy him. Evelyn was smoking at the time – perhaps it was one of their late-night drinking-talking-smoking sessions – and he took her arm and pressed the lit cigarette against the flesh of her wrist. Although this no doubt greatly pained her at the time, it actually put Evelyn up in Olivia's estimation. First, because she was getting more into religious mysticism and the idea that physical sacrifice might be the way to personal salvation. But also because she knew that in hurting her in this way he was expressing the depth of his own suffering. "Feel my pain," was what Evelyn's cigarette said. Just as "Feel my pain," was what Evelyn's Adam and Ernest said in a different language.'

Kate looks thoughtful.

'But that reminds me. When Adam wakes up and finds he's still alive, he muses about a time from his childhood when he was cruel to his cat. The cat's name was Oz-y-man-dias.'

'Goodness! – I wonder how Aloysius is doing at the Park and Ride.'

'Forget him for a moment.'

'Poor Alo-all-alone.'

'On days when Adam was left alone, he would find Ozymandias and take him to the day nursery. He would then chase him from one hiding place to another until the cat was terrified. The boy Adam would then change tack and try to win back Ozymandias's affection by talking to him nicely, until, sure enough, the cat was purring and reconciled to the peculiar boy. But one day, after Ozymandias had been rounded up, he short-circuited the whole process by leaping on top of a high cupboard. To get the cat down, Evelyn – sorry, Adam – placed a chair on a table and stretched up. However, the chair wasn't resting on all four legs; it toppled over and down the boy went to the floor via the table. In the few seconds, after landing on the floor and before his nurse arrived from downstairs, the boy felt at a distance from his damaged body.

'Now Evelyn spends three pages describing what is clearly an Underhill memory. And by the start of the memory he's only one page into what he calls the "Conclusion". In this section, film captions have been dropped and the writing is more conventional. So it seems likely that this is where the writing takes up again in August, post-suicide attempt. That means, as I said before, that the section concerning Adam at art school, Imogen's rejection of Adam, Adam going on a blind with Ernest and Adam taking the poison was all written before Evelyn's suicide attempt.

Kate considers: 'So a month or two later, he's gone back to the story, more or less going straight into the Ozymandias recollection, because the kitten he's obtained for Olivia has triggered the memory?'

'It's tempting to think that. And it's tempting to analyse Evelyn's position before and after his own suicide attempt using his own reason /appetite motif.'

Kate leans forward: 'Are you going to do that for me, Precoshers?'

'I'm going to try. So here goes. At Arnold House, a public school of lower quality than Lancing, Evelyn is in a job he has no appetite for, and a trusted friend has told him his writing is crap. What does reason say?'

'Reason says he should kill himself.'

'Well, Preters, that is ridiculous. Evelyn hasn't really *tried* to find his position in life yet. But, to be fair to his analysis, as the main section of 'The Balance' suggests, the thing that is really getting him down is the rejection from Olivia. It's that that has sapped his appetite for life. Agreed?'

'Women are vermin. Don't you think so, Preco?'

'Let's leave that to one side for the time being. A couple of months later, after Evelyn's seen the back of the Welsh school and he finds himself installed at Barford House with his high-necked-jumpered boy-friend, things don't seem so bad after all. Especially since, thanks to Richard Plunket Greene, he's just been offered another job as a school-master at the same school Richard works in. This time the job is in Aston Clinton, which is just ten miles east of Oxford. The job might be just as tedious as the last one, but at least Evelyn will get to party regularly in Oxford, Barford and London. What does reason say?'

'Reason says, "Rejoice." '

'Reason even says, "Buy a kitten for Olvia and finish off that promising story." '

We've finished our drinks.

'Did Evelyn have a favourite pub in Aston Clinton by any chance?' asks Kate.

'Funny you should ask that,' I reply. 'A place called the Bell, which I've Googled. It's still there.'

And we rise from the table as one.

When we get to the car, I can't help wondering what Aloysius's contribution to the afternoon's entertainment will turn out to be. As the boot rises, I glimpse a pile of well-pawed books in a dark corner as the bear lets rip: 'WHO IS THIS OZYMANDIAS? I HAVE NOT SO MUCH AS HEARD OF THE CAT.'

3

It takes us a while to find the Bell, because straggling Aston Clinton has no centre and the Bell, its most prominent landmark, has recently changed its name to the Duck Inn.

We're glad to have persisted though, because what was the Bell is an astonishing place. It's an enormous old coaching inn, with so many public rooms on the ground floor that some are locked this midweek evening. But there are plenty of lounges open and the room we choose to sit in is wood-panelled. It's a superb room on account of the hardwood alone that surrounds us, though the furniture is substantial as well.

I go to the bar and order our drinks. And as I do so, it comes to me what I've been feeling today: nostalgia for those times when as a very young man I would go out with friends for an afternoon or evening in the pub. I would drink as quickly as everyone else and be in the bubble all session long. I would never notice what was happening at other tables: I was concentrating – to the exclusion of all else – on our banter: the joy of being out on the razz. For me every pub was an opportunity to get a few heads together and to enjoy what came out of the mix. Obviously Evelyn felt the same. I think many introspective young men feel and have felt the same way. It's a situation where they can relax and make the most of themselves. Jokes, logical analysis, innuendo, complete bollocks: all fuelled by the uninhibiting and stimulating effect of alcohol on brain cells.

I sit down at the table and smile at Kate. Because, while I may be thinking fondly of a former way of life, I wouldn't swap it for what I've got today. Besides, what have we had today if not a constant flow of good humour, literary analysis, double entendres: all fuelled by the odd beer? But there must be more to it than that: I've never felt so . . .

'So what went down here?' asks Kate, breaking into my reverie.

'Aston Clinton School was across the way, an ugly building in the middle of a lovely park, according to Evelyn. The food served at school wasn't good, so he was in here a lot. And of course he and Richard would come to the Bell every night just to get away from their workplace and to chill out over a beer or two.'

'He was good friends with Richard?'

'Yes, but Richard was engaged to marry Elizabeth Russell, so it was often the three of them together. It's clear they got on well as a three-some. Richard had a car, so Evelyn was to some extent dependent on him for trips to Oxford. But then Alistair and his cousin Claud would visit Aston Clinton from Barford. Unquestionably, Evelyn had a better time here than in Wales. He was in Aston Clinton for three times as long: for the eighteen months from September 1925 to March 1927.'

'Did the relationship with Olivia peter out?'

'Well, there are diary entries concerning her. Let me look them up; I've highlighted the vivid ones . . .

'On 25 November 1925, Olivia has a look round the school at Aston Clinton then Evelyn and she go off to a party in Oxford. Olivia "as usual" behaves like a whore, being embraced on a bed by various people . . .

'On Christmas Day 1925, Evelyn is in London. He describes Olivia as being "literally" crazy about the Charleston. Evelyn reports that at a party she had to find an empty room to do what Evelyn refers to as her ridiculous dance, after which she relapsed into drunken melancholy . . .

'On 15 March 1926, Evelyn writes of travelling to London from Aston Clinton just to see Olivia and very much regretting doing so. He finds her "packing bottles" in her bedroom, which is "littered with stockings and newspaper". He notes that she seems "fatter and larger generally" and is "unable to talk of much except herself and that in an impersonal and incoherent way". Evelyn sits down on her bed for some time "trying to talk to her with my heart sinking and sinking".'

'Oh, dear. That sounds bad.'

'Yes, but at least Evelyn is showing sympathy for another human being. He then hardly mentions her for a year. And when they do meet for a lunch with her mother in London, Evelyn finds Olivia can talk of nothing but black men.'

'Black men?'

'In the twenties, jazz was *the* cultural sensation. There weren't that many black people in London, but those who were in town found themselves very much in demand.'

'Not much has changed then.'

'There are plenty of blacks in London now. It's no longer a fashion thing, though a certain amount of stereotyping still goes on. Anyway, as you guessed, the relationship between Evelyn and Olivia peters out.'

'What happens to her later in life?'

'Like her mother – like Alastair – she converts to Roman Catholicism. I think she came to terms with her own nature by forgoing her nymphomania. Giving up something she really wanted – sex with black men, actors and pretty well any male as long as it wasn't Evelyn – took her closer to God. I suppose it's a self-esteem thing.'

'A bit like Julia Flyte in *Brideshead*?'

'A lot like that – Julia giving up Charles, the thing she wants most of all, in order to be reconciled to God. Having said that, Julia comes out of her Catholic commitment a stronger person, whereas I'm not sure Olivia does. She ends up unmarried, living with her mother in a cottage on the Longleat estate.'

Kate sighs. 'Better get back to Evelyn himself then. Any more romances on the horizon?'

'With the demise of his friendship with Olivia, the person he feels closest to reverts to being Alastair. However, he must have felt at a loose end following Christmas 1925, because he went to Paris with a gay acquaintance. Evelyn's first ever trip abroad, as it happens. The diary describes the meals they ate, a bit of cultural tourism and then there is a lurid account of a trip to a male brothel. Evelyn's travelling companion was really into his boy, while Evelyn was on the point of paying for a tableau he'd set up whereby a large negro was to penetrate the boy who'd been making up to Evelyn – admiring his check trousers and using that as an excuse to squeeze his legs. In the end, Evelyn decides he can't afford the three-hundred-franc transaction and goes back to the hotel.'

'That's all a bit sordid. And contradictory.'

'Come to think of it, the same contradiction comes out in his behaviour the next Christmas. By then Alastair has left the Shakespeare Head Press and has begun a career in the diplomatic service. He's posted to Athens and Evelyn visits him for New Year. In his diary Evelyn expresses distaste for the set-up in the flat that Alastair shares with a colleague, complaining there are always "Dago youths" about the place, Greeks that will sleep with "the English colony" for twenty-five drachmas a night.'

'That's *Brideshead* again, isn't it? Sebastian and the German in Morocco.'

'Yes, the man Kurtz that sponges off Sebastian. It's also Evelyn very slowly coming to the conclusion that he's not really into sex with men after all.'

'What else happened at Aston Clinton?'

'It was a quiet time. Maybe the only period in his life when, if looked at in summary, you would not conclude that Waugh was going to be a creative writer. I get the impression that he was gradually coming to terms with normal life. For a start, he was trying to live within his means.'

'Fancy.'

'When Richard left the school at the beginning of 1926 – to take up a music post at Lancing, of all places – he bought a motorcycle for Evelyn so that he wouldn't feel stranded at Aston Clinton.'

'What good friends Evelyn had! They really cared for him.'

'Yes, they did. Mind you, he nearly came a cropper on the bike, what with drink-driving and so on. Also, the bike that Richard gave him kept breaking down. Three times on a single trip to Barford! So he needed to buy himself a more reliable model. He began to get on a bit better with the boys in his charge (they respected his motorbike) and he mentions a couple of them quite fondly in his diary. Just as he took *Alice in Wonderland* with him when he went to Wales, so he had *The Wind in the Willows* with him at Aston Clinton. He used to read it aloud to his favourite pupils.'

'What about his own writing?'

'In the whole time he was at Aston Clinton, from September 1925 to February 1927, he wrote next to nothing. But an interest in creativity just about manages to tick over. The diary tells us that in the autumn of 1925 he sends "The Balance" to a couple of publishers. But the story gets rejected and it's not until the spring of 1926 that brother Alec comes to the rescue with the offer to place it in *Georgian Short Stories*. Then, that summer, Alastair, while still at the Shakespeare Head Press, asks Evelyn if he will give him something to print. So Evelyn spends four days writing up a twenty-five-page essay on the Pre-Raphaelite Brotherhood, which Alastair proudly prints for him.'

'Any good?'

'It's never been reprinted so I'll have to wait until I'm in a good reference library and have a chance to read it. Full of misprints, apparently. Though whether those would have been Alastair's care-lessness, or Evelyn's lack of interest, I'm not sure. On publication in

October 1926, 'The Balance' was favourably noticed by a few people. In February 1927, one editor commissioned a story from Evelyn for a book entitled *The New Decameron*. Evelyn had just recorded this fact in his diary when something rather upsetting happened.'

'Tell me.'

'Well, Evelyn had been drinking here in the Bell with Richard's replacement, whom Evelyn was trying to get out of the tedious habit of talking seriously to him about education. When they got back to the school, Evelyn became involved in what he thought of as a light-hearted discussion with the new matron. That's not what she thought, however. And after she reported to the headmaster what Evelyn had said to her by way of evening banter, Evelyn was sacked on the spot. So, rather to his surprise, he found himself living back at Underhill until he could fix himself up with a new job. The setback in his school-teaching career gave him a chance to write the story he'd been asked for. Apparently, it took him just two days to write 'The Tutor's Tale: A House of Gentlefolk'.

'Have you read it?'

'I'm still waiting for my AbeBooks copy of *The New Decameron* to arrive from the States. But the story is reprinted in *Complete Stories*, so, yes, I've read it. And it is very revealing. Revealing in a completely different way from his diary of the time. Guess who the first-person protagonist is?'

'I can't.'

'Yes, you can. Look deep into the pint glass of Adam Doure, and you'll see the answer!'

'Ernest Vaughan?'

'Yes. But he's on his best behaviour. He's been sent down in disgrace from Oxford and he's applied to be tutor to a duke's son. He gets to Vanburgh where the Duke of Vanburgh's house, called Stayle, is located. Ernest meets the elderly duke and his two sisters. They're all nuts, but according to them it's the grandson that's not all there. Although he's eighteen, he's only had two terms of schooling. They've decided it would be in the boy's best interests to go abroad with a tutor for a while. Ernest is not too keen on looking after a mad student for any length of time, but when he gets to meet the boy – deplorably dressed and socially ill-at-ease though he is – Ernest takes a shine to him.

'So Ernest takes the boy, George Theodore Verney, back to London with him. George is keen to experience London life in all its glamorous variety, but before he can do so he must be bought some decent clothes. Ernest takes him to his own tailor and in the process his own credit is extended in order to allow him to buy a couple of new suits for himself. To Ernest's pleasure, George shows good taste in clothes. He also gets on well with everybody Ernest introduces him to. After just four days of the social round it's obvious that the boy has been held back by his immediate family and early environment. In fact, he has the potential to be a thoroughly charming and accomplished young man. Ernest's plan is to take George to Athens via Brindisi, but before they can go anywhere a letter arrives from George's grandfather, the duke. There has been a change of heart at Stayle. George is to be escorted back to his guardian by his solicitor as it is felt that the boy is not ready to see the world after all. George isn't too disappointed. He had a feeling life with Ernest had been too good to be true and consoles himself with the thought that in three years he will be twenty-one at which point he will inherit money from his mother and be free to do as he wishes . . . And that's it.'

'Not really an Ernest Vaughan story at all,' says Kate, looking a little disappointed.

'Well, although the story states that Ernest has just come down from Oxford, you get the feeling that he's been with Evelyn throughout every one of the eighteen months at Aston Clinton. Ernest plans to take George to Athens via Brindisi in a story written just a couple of months after Evelyn, on his first trip abroad other than to France, came back to England from Athens via Brindisi. What a strange transformation! It's almost as if the trip to Greece to see Alastair didn't happen on some level. And, just as significantly, George is not being allowed to develop as he could. His family are holding him back. Perhaps in the same way that Evelyn feels his middle-class heritage holds him back from really getting on with the aristocracy he's been introduced to at Oxford, the peer group for which nature so clearly intended him.'

'You think both the main characters are alter egos of Evelyn?'

'Yes, and just as Adam Doure, Evelyn's alter ego, introduces the reader to Ernest Vaughan in "The Balance", so Ernest Vaughan, Evelyn's altar ego, introduces us to George Theodore Verney in "The Tutor's Tale". In fact, Evelyn, sacked by the school at Aston Clinton (just as Ernest is suddenly taken off the Stayle job), may feel he has been dragged back to Underhill, where he has had to make the most of things by writing the story. A story that is – subtly, but distinctly – autobiographical. Which is what gives it such intensity. The reader feels that something is at stake. And the thing that is at stake is Evelyn's position in the world.'

I may to be going on a bit. I suppose it's the drink talking. Oh, well, as long as Kate is happy to listen, I'll carry on.

'This autobiographical frustration comes out most strongly in the scenes involving the buying of clothes. In his diary, Evelyn mentions buying clothes on several occasions in 1925 and 1926. He's pleased with the pair of check trousers he wears in Paris, just as in the story Ernest is pleased to see that George "has a well-bred leaning towards checks". In October 1926, Evelyn mentions going to his tailor's and trying on a suit they are making for him that will cost him fifteen guineas. It is well made, he acknowledges, but he admits to a little disappointment in the article. It makes him look distressingly dapper. However, a month later when he wears his new suit for the first time, he no longer feels the worst dressed person in the room. So that's something.'

'But does he still feel distressingly dapper?' asks Kate. 'In his new suit he wants to feel like a pillar of fire.'

'Of course he does. Evelyn wants to be able to stand there in his new suit in the staff quarters of Aston Clinton School and show off. In February 1927, he's half-cut after an evening at the Bell, and to impress his fellow teachers, who are all as dull as ditchwater, he announces: "IN ORDER TO LET ONESELF GO IN THE CASE

OF HAVING SEX WITH AN ELEPHANT, THIS IS WHAT ONE MUST DO, MATRON." '

'But matron takes this the wrong way,' says Kate. 'There and then she reports to the headmaster that she's never been so insulted in her life.'

' "Let's get this clear," ' I say, taking on the role of the headmaster. ' "Dapper Waugh, the dimmest of schoolteachers, called you an elephant, matron?" '

' "Standing there, bold as brass in his new check suit, he said that it was a toss up as to whether he'd prefer to make love to me or an elephant, headmaster . . . It was then, when he saw that I'd taken umbrage, that he tried to hand me a bottle of gin." '

' "Refused, of course?" '

' "I was in my nightgown, headmaster!" '

' "I see. Well, we'll send him down for indecent behaviour." '

' "He's already been sent down from Oxford for indecent behaviour any number of times. But what we *can* do is to dismiss him from his dismal teaching career and send him back to his unfortunate parents." '

I sip from my pint before going on with this story we seem to be putting together without much difficulty.

'So Evelyn, back in his old room at Underhill . . . '

'Looks at himself in the mirror . . . '

'He sees a pillar of dapper.'

'Dapper is as dapper does.'

We're in danger of dappering out. But never mind, I think the picture that emerges is clear enough, so I spit it out: 'Evelyn is twenty-four years of age and back living under his parents' roof for the foreseeable future. He's without a job, without a lover. One short story has been published courtesy of his dapper brother and even dapperer father. Another has been written out in longhand on the dressing-room table but has petered out into an obsession with quality tailoring and inside-leg measurements. To cheer himself up, he reads aloud from *The Wind in the Willows*.'

For this I have to get my copy of the book out of my coat pocket. But that is the work of an instant. Soon I'm reciting:

'The clever men at Oxford
   Know all that there is to be knowed.
But they none of them know one half as much
   As *dapper* Mr Toad.'

I scan the remaining verses and see that there is one more I can make use of:

'The queen and her ladies-in-waiting
   Sat at the window and sewed
She cried, "Look! Who's that handsome man?"
   They answered, "Dapper Toad." '

'Do you know, the longer I consider Dapper,' says Kate, 'the shorter the poor man seems to get.'

'I see what you mean. His backside is literally scraping against the floor of the night nursery at Underhill; literally brushing the pavement when he goes out for a stroll. Those suit trousers clearly will not last. His bottom will be hanging out of them before he gets as far as Golders Green Tube Station!'

'It would be useful if he could drive around on a motorbike rather than having to walk everywhere,' reckons Kate. 'But Dapper is too short. The most he could expect would be to sit on the lap of someone with regular-sized legs and maybe steer a bit.'

Oh, Lord, now we've gone too far. I think we both feel that we've been sitting in this pub too long. Now we'll have to face the music. Arm in arm we exit the pub and cross the road to the car park. The boot of the car looms ominously.

But before we get there, Kate breaks away from me. I keep trudging towards the vehicle until she calls my attention to the little dance she's doing. Her arms are held straight down by her side as she bobs about, her legs flicking up from the knees to both right and left.

'My Charleston, darling. You try. Doo-doo, doo-doo, doo-do-do-do-do-do'

I stand rooted to the tarmac.

Kate pouts her lips, bats her eyelids, flicks busy fingers on the ends of flexed wrists, and generally looks the part that I imagine Olivia oh-so-briefly played in her own life.

I give the Charleston a go, but without much conviction.

'Think Flapper, not dapper, Preco.'

'I can't. Alo's put the evil eye on me. Besides, I think I know what he's going to say when we open the boot. And you're not going to like it.'

'What?' asks Kate, her timeless little dance falling in on itself. I wonder if she is now finding the cool night air as sobering as I do. Then I remember that Kate's not been drinking. Well, in my opinion, one and a half pints consumed in eight hours is not drinking. But then nor have *I* been drinking. Four pints consumed in the eight hours of today spent in licensed premises is not what Evelyn Waugh or Adam Doure or Ernest Vaughan or I would call drinking.

I open the boot and, sure enough, Aloysius, sitting on Selina Hastings, with John Howard Wilson and Martin Stannard as arm rests and Alexander Waugh as backstop, announces soberly and sanely: 'Thursday, 7 April 1927. I have met such a nice girl called Evelyn Gardner.'

SHE-EVELYN

The Making of an Englishman

1

So far, today has been all about getting from Westcliff-on-Sea, Essex, to the M25 in Kate's car, then grimly hanging on in there among the lorries and the white vans as we've proceeded in a clockwise direction from the M25's easterly edge to a south westerly point on the monster. We're safely on the M3 now, and pointing in the direction of our Dorset destination. A chance for Kate to relax a bit behind the wheel, and for me to get her up to speed re Evelyn.

'In the same April 1927 diary entry that Waugh mentions meeting Evelyn Gardner for the first time, he writes that he's in some doubt as to whether to work for the *Daily Express* or write a biography that the publisher Duckworth was interested in. In fact, he chose to go to the newspaper and it wasn't until he was sacked after six weeks as a non-performing journalist that he turned to the book project.'

The road is relatively clear ahead. Kate is able to spare enough attention to ask: 'How did the invitation to write a biography come about? Last I knew, Evelyn was the obscure writer of a couple of odd little stories.'

'Tony Powell, an acquaintance from Oxford and not yet famous, liked the Pre-Raphaelite essay of Evelyn's that Alastair had printed privately, and managed to secure the interest of his publisher employer. On learning this, Waugh suggested he write a biography of Rossetti, as the centenary of the senior Pre-Raphaelite's birth was coming up in the next year. Gerald Duckworth thought this was a jolly fine idea. So on 1 July, Waugh began writing the book at

Underhill. Three weeks later he noted in his diary that he had finished twelve thousand words "without much real difficulty".'

'Without much real difficulty?'

'Basically, he just copied out the beginning of a biography written twenty years before by H. C. Marillier. At first I thought it was a joke. But I came to the conclusion it was Evelyn being lazy. Chapter Three of *Rossetti* is about nineteen thousand words and takes up forty-eight pages of the two-hundred-and-twenty-page printed book. As much as thrity-five per cent of the chapter consists of direct quotation.'

'What impressive stats!'

'There are eleven people quoted. Ruskin alone writes almost ten per cent of the chapter – quotes from his letters to Rossetti. And Ford Madox Brown writes another ten percent – quotes from his diary.'

'What do all the quotes imply?'

'They mean that at this stage Evelyn didn't see himself as a writer. Rather, he saw himself as a historian (which he missed the opportunity of being when an undergraduate), a craftsman (piecing together a book rather than writing it) and, potentially at least, a painter. He goes into Rossetti's techniques in some detail. Indeed, Evelyn seemed to find the writing side of things both hard work and tedious.'

'I wonder what motivated him to take it on.'

'I suspect he noticed when doing his Pre-Raphaelite essay that there were striking similarities between himself and Rossetti. Their faces were alike; same build and height; same theatrical and literary father combined with emotionally supportive mother. Rossetti ended up living a life full of romance, poverty and art. Evelyn might have felt he was trying out such a lifestyle, once removed.'

Kate goes into the outside lane long enough to sweep past a heavily loaded lorry.

'The book was written at a series of Evelyn's old haunts. After getting the ball rolling at Underhill, he moved to the Abingdon Arms from where he would take a bus to the Oxford Union every day. He favoured its library at least partly because Rossetti had himself been commissioned to produce frescoes for that building, and I'm supposing Waugh enjoyed working in the same place his subject had once laboured. But after a chapter or two Evelyn got restless. He continued the book at Barford. But when Alastair was in residence, he couldn't concentrate and returned to Underhill. He couldn't concentrate there either, with his father driving him to distraction. He did seem to need familiar surroundings though, even writing at Aston Clinton for a spell. Anyway, he was finding the writing process a struggle, only occasionally getting into his literary stride.

'How does the book end?' asks Kate, hurrying me along.

'It ends with a chapter called "What is Wrong with Rossetti?" The main point Waugh makes is in regard to the moral position of the artist. In this respect he finds Rossetti suspect. Specifically, what Rossetti lacked was what Waugh calls the "essential rectitude that underlies the serenity of all really great art". Waugh reckoned that all Rossetti's brooding about magic and suicide was mediocre. Apparently, Waugh wrote after the last line of the manuscript: "The End. Thank God." I can't help doubting that essential rectitude was operating in his mind when he wrote that.'

Kate looks thoughtful. Then tells me: '*Please*, don't include a chapter on *Rossetti* in your own book. Just mention it in passing.'

'I've already written a twenty-pager!'

'Junk it. You've got to keep cutting to the chase.'

'Do I? OK, here goes. The most intriguing thing in *Rossetti* is a statement that Waugh makes near the beginning of the book. He criticises the 1920s' trends in biography of over-dramatising the life of the subject and of seeing his or her life through the standards of the biographer's own life and times. Specifically he writes: "We have discovered a jollier way of honouring our dead. The corpse has become the marionette. With bells on its fingers and wires on its toes, it is jigged about to a period dance of our own piping." Waugh was clearly of the opinion that he'd avoided such a subjective approach in his biography of Rossetti. Could the criticism be made of the book I'm writing?'

Kate nods. 'It makes me think about the image of dapper Evelyn, dancing with flapper Olivia at the end of your Post-Oxford chapter.'

I wouldn't have it any other way. But nor do I want to dwell on the image. Soon I fill our minds with the alternative image of Evelyn lying on his back in the middle of an appendectomy operation cum autopsy: 'Martin Stannard is standing over the sunken-eyed Waugh, brandishing a pair of scissors and a long knife in such a way that it's obvious he means business. I know it's Stannard because I recognise the distinguished moustaches from his author portrait on the jacket of his Waugh biog.'

'He looks competent.'

'He looks more than competent: expert diagnosis can be taken for granted and surgical incisions will be the order of the day. Having said that, following some deft preliminary work, he goes straight for Evelyn's sex.'

'Poor dead Evelyn.'

'Evelyn speaks accusingly up from the slab: "I see you have discovered a jollier way of honouring your dead. The corpse has become the marionette, jigged about to a period dance of the biographer's piping." '

'Flap, dead Evelyn, flap!'

'In addition to Stannard on knives, there would appear to be Selina Hastings on chlorocone and John Howard Wilson on leg irons. But I realise it's not them that Evelyn is chiding. It's the bloke in the corner waving a flag of his own design. Me, as it happens.'

'So what do you do? Keep waving your home-made flag, or pipe down in respect for the dead?'

'I like to think that the answer to that is happily bubbling away inside the question.'

2

So here we are in another lovely old pub, this one thatched. But it hasn't been easy to get here and it will take a while for the strain of today's travel to leave our systems. All that driving to get to Wimborne. All that walking from our B&B only to get here and find the Barley Mow stone-cold shut at 4.30 p.m. on a bleak afternoon in November.

Walking back to Wimborne, ultimately in the dark, along un-pavemented, steep-sided lanes, was harrowing. I need to swallow a bit more Badger Ale before I can forget about that experience. There was no problem with the second trip here, by car. Except that one of us is going to have to go easy on the Badger so that we can drive back to the B&B at closing time. That'll be Kate, who is sipping from a half-pint. There is no way I could be expected to come to the Barley Mow of all pubs and stay sober.

In return for the privilege of drinking tonight, I must tell a good story. It's no more than Kate deserves. After all, that part of the day when she's not been coping with traffic as a long-distance Renault driver, she's been trying to avoid being run over as a pedestrian caught in the glare of oncoming headlights. Yes, I owe her some quality time. Here we go then.

'In the middle of writing *Rossetti*, while staying at Underhill at the beginning of September 1927, distracted by noise by day and unable to sleep at night, Waugh noted in his diary that he had begun a comic novel.'

There! – At last! – We're off and running.

'Apparently he had ten thousand words, to a reading of which he treated Anthony Powell that autumn. By the time Waugh gave a reading to Dudley Carew, his faithful old Lancing chum, there were fifty pages in the manuscript. In *A Fragment of Friendship*, Dudley recalls the reading, with Evelyn back to how Dudley remembered him at school: pugnacious and laughing at his own jokes, revelling in a piece of work he knew was special. Waugh must still have had doubts, however. Because he also wrote to Harold Acton enclosing the beginning of the novel and asking his friend's advice as to whether he should carry on with it. Ultimately, *Decline and Fall*'s dedication is to Acton, so it's clear what his advice must have been: 'On, Evelyn, on.' I suppose we must be grateful that he didn't rubbish the book the way he did *The Temple at Thatch*.'

This Badger Ale is beginning to hit the spot. The words are coming in a relaxed flow now: 'An encouraging contribution was also made by Henry Lamb. He knew that this Dorset pub, miles from London or

Oxford, would be a place where Evelyn could live quietly and cheaply while getting on with his book. But there was more to it than that. Lamb, a painter in his mid-forties and a bit of a Bohemian, was having an affair with Pansy Pakenham, twenty years his junior, who shared rooms in London with Waugh's fiancée, Evelyn Gardner. Lamb was living on his own in Poole, waiting for a divorce from his first wife. So the idea was that Pansy and She-Evelyn move into lodgings in Wimborne, five miles inland from Poole, with He-Evelyn a further two miles north, here in the Barley Mow. A thoroughly respectable arrangement then, with no illicit mixing of the sexes. And that was how things stood from January 1928 until late spring, with Pansy and the two Evelyns all working on novels.'

'If Waugh was based in this pub, why aren't we? That would have saved us almost getting run over.'

'The Barley Mow doesn't do accommodation these days. It's cheering that the place is still going at all, nearly eighty years on, selling real ale and good country grub. Mind you, most of Evelyn's bolt-holes seem to have survived the test of time, either by luck or

sound judgement. After all, a thatched pub like this, a drovers' inn from the sixteenth century, was built to last.'

'Tell me more about Henry and the girls.'

'Henry Lamb was a friend and supporter of Stanley Spencer, so that establishes him in my good books. I suppose the set-up would have been for Evelyn to write during the day and then hook up with Henry and the women in the evening. Though it's possible that socialising had to wait until the weekends.'

'What would the sleeping arrangements have been?'

'You tell me. If Pansy occasionally stayed over at Henry's house, would He-Evelyn have joined She-Evelyn at the lodgings?'

'I don't suppose that would have been acceptable to a landlady of those times.'

'Another possibility is that She-Evelyn might have sneaked into He-Evelyn's room here.'

'That wouldn't have been easy either. There wouldn't have been en-suite bathrooms then, so I don't think She-Evelyn would have been able to stay over without the owners of the pub knowing. Besides, He-Evelyn's room would have been furnished with a single bed, suitable for a commercial traveller.'

'We don't know if there was any variation on their normal sleeping arrangements,' I conclude. 'That is the fact of the matter.'

'So what kind of book was Waugh writing this time?' asks Kate. And as she utters these words of invitation, I know exactly how a dog feels when it's let off the leash.

'Let me quote the first lines:

Neither her Gaudiness the Mistress of the Robes or her Dreaminess the Queen were feeling quite themselves. In the Palace all was speculation. Would they be able to attend the *Fêtes* in honour of King Jotifa and Queen Thleeanouhee of the Land of Dates? – Court opinion seemed largely divided.'

'Is that how *Decline and Fall* begins, then?'

'Actually, no. That's the beginning of *The Flower Beneath the Foot* by Ronald Firbank. Waugh's first novel begins:

Mr Sniggs, the Junior Dean, and Mr Postlethwaite, the Domestic Bursar, sat alone in Mr Sniggs's room overlooking the garden quad at Scone College. From the rooms of Sir Alastair Digby-Vaine-Trumpington, two staircases away, came a confused roaring and breaking of glass.'

'So the books have ornate names and parties in common?'

'Waugh's novel is a sort of autobiography, rendered in the prose style of Firbank. *Decline and Fall* starts off with Paul Pennyfeather getting sent down from Oxford for indecent behaviour. Oh, that Bollinger Club! Oh, those dons! He then finds himself teaching at Llanabba Castle, an obscure public school in Wales – just as, after Oxford, Waugh spent a desperate six months at Arnold House in Denbighshire. While working as schoolmaster, Waugh felt like a fish out of water, and he communicates his anguish through Pennyfeather in scene after scene of farce that is made hilarious by the panache of Waugh's Firbankian style. Or, rather – in the joy of being engaged to Evelyn Gardner, in the comfortable surroundings of the Barley Mow – he retrospectively transforms his anguish into something altogether uplifting. With the paederast Grimes providing much of the sauce.'

Kate smiles at my summary. It's a cheering sight and incites me to push on.

'Paul Pennyfeather is saved from servitude at Llanabba Castle by Margot Beste-Chetwynde, the glamorous mother of a pupil. Pennyfeather then finds himself in an aristocratic environment – country houses, Mayfair and Bright Young Things – and is about to marry Margot when he finds himself arrested for dealing in prostitution, a crime of which he is entirely innocent. Pennyfeather gets on fairly well in prison, meeting again the characters he knew at Llanabba, but when Margot marries the Home Secretary, Pennyfeather suddenly finds himself released from jail and back reading Theology at his old college in Oxford. Decline and Fall? Decline, Rise, Fall and Back To Square One would be more like the thing.'

I get to my feet. Summarising the whole book in a couple of flowing paragraphs has been thirsty work. Making sure my head doesn't come too close to the old beams in the ceiling, I walk over to the bar for another instalment of Badger. But soon I'm back talking to my partner.

'The character Margot Beste-Chetwynde is a key figure in the novel, and decidedly autobiographical ingredients have gone into the making of her. While at Hertford, every time Evelyn walked down New College Lane, he would read the names of two New College undergraduates that lived in a particular block flanking the road: 'Best' and 'Chetwynde'. The character would have been named long before Evelyn got to the Barley Mow. Otherwise, she might have been called after words that Evelyn would have noticed every time he approached the bar: 'Best' and 'Badger'.

'Shame. Margot Beste-Badger has a certain ring to it.'

'It's pronounced "Beast-Cheating" by Rik Mayall in his audio recording of the novel.'

'Margot Beast-Cheating! Neat.'

'Pennyfeather first meets Margot at the school's farcical sports day, not long after young Lord Tangent has been shot in the foot by a starting pistol fired by a master who was the worse for drink. She rolls up in an enormous limousine of dove-grey and silver which seems to be related to the Phantom Rolls Royce that a society lady once turned up in to see Evelyn and Richard Plunket Greene at Aston Clinton School.'

'I like the way Evelyn always writes about the things he knows.'

'Margot is accompanied to the sports day by a smartly dressed black man, Mr Sebastian Cholmondley, whom she calls "Chokey". Margot is patronising about his love of culture. But then Chokey asks for it, with his overstated enthusiasm for all things English: "Why I'd give all the jazz in the world for just one little stone from one of your cathedrals," he fawns.'

Kate smiles.

'At one point Chokey proudly tells Dr Fagan, headmaster of the school and owner of Llanabba Castle, that he's read *Hamlet, Macbeth* and *King Lear*, and asks the head if he's ever read these plays. The reply is as dry as Evelyn can make it: "Yes," said the Doctor; "as a matter of fact, I have."'

'So where does the racist undercurrent come from?'

'Well, in July of 1927, not long after Evelyn had started *Rossetti*, his diary records that he received a despairing call from Olivia Plunket Greene. Rudolph Dunbar – a black guy – was on his way from Manchester for the day. What was Olivia in despair about? Waugh doesn't say, he just states that after luncheon he went to Knightsbridge to help out Olivia with Rudolph, that he secured a couple of people to make up a party, but that the continual playing of a noisy gramophone had made his head ache. By this time, Waugh had already made several comments in his diary about Olivia's obsession with black men. Sexual jealousy would seem to account for Waugh's digs at Chokey's expense in *Decline and Fall*. One character at the sports day says that it's hardly something to talk about before the ladies, but that black people have *uncontrollable passions*. And in making the point he uses the unfortunate term "niggers".'

Kate tuts.

'The minor character goes on to say that you can see "them" in Shaftesbury Avenue, any night of the week, the women "just hanging on to 'em". After the sports day, when Paul Pennyfeather realises he's rather taken with Margot, he asks Grimes what he thinks is the relationship between Mrs Beste-Chetwynde and "that nigger".'

Kate tuts again.

'You must bear in mind that another of Ronald Firbank's books was called *Prancing Nigger*, so it was an acceptable term of the day. Anyway, Grimes replies that he doesn't suppose the lady trots round with the black dude for the uplift of his conversation, and diagnoses a simple case of good old sex.'

'Evelyn laying bare his own sexual frustration with Olivia?'

'Well, not quite. I'd say that He-Evelyn, in the happy position of being engaged to Evelyn Gardner, in the soothing surroundings of the Barley Mow, retrospectively transforms his sexual angst into something much more life-enhancing. With man-of-the-world Grimes providing the zip and the zest.'

A waitress takes our order for food. Though I'm not that interested because I'm still getting on so well with the banquet of words.

'Once Paul has moved to King's Thursday, Margot's ultra-modernised ex-country house, and an engagement is mooted, then it's Evelyn Gardner who seems to fill the character's lizard-skin boots. Like She-Evelyn, Margot has to sleep on her man's proposal of marriage before she can accept it. In Margot's case she sleeps with Paul – in Paul's bed – just in case it's only a romantic idea of his that he's in love with her. Happily there is no mistake and the next day their engagement is announced.'

'Sleeping arrangements again.'

'It would seem likely that Waugh and Evelyn Gardner got engaged prior to sleeping with each other. But in the months living in close proximity in Dorset, notwithstanding what you said earlier, surely the idea of He-Evelyn smuggling She-Evelyn into his room at the Barley Mow for the night – just to make sure they were sexually suited – was at least thought about by both parties.'

I can't help dwelling on this point. Indeed, I lean towards Kate and ask her a perfectly straightforward question: 'How about slipping upstairs with me tonight, darling, for a bit of "how's your father"?'

Kate looks offended. 'That's just the Todger talking, Evelyn.'

'Badger, Evelyn, darling. It's delicious *Badger* Ale I'm knocking back as if there was no tomorrow.'

Which reminds me. I tell Kate that Grimes, because he's been especially nice to young Percy Clutterbuck, gets offered employment by the boy's father. The job is as taster of the ales that his family brewery makes and sells, 'God's own job' as Grimes puts it. His elation fades when he comes to the conclusion that the job offer must be a joke. But, reassured by Pennyfeather on that score, Grimes perks up again and declares that he's going to take the job even though he's gone and got himself engaged to the charmless and unattractive Flossy, daughter of the headmaster. God's own job comes to nothing, of course. Except as a piece of comic writing.

Kate seems more interested in Margot than Grimes. I tell her that beautiful Margot, for plot reasons, has to be the mother of one of the boys at the school, and in her thirties. This is handy for Waugh as it keeps his creation at arm's length from the real women in his life. The last chapter in the King's Thursday section is called 'A Hitch in the Wedding Preparations'. Paul has asked an old college friend, Potts, to be best man, but Potts is in Geneva (just as Alastair will be in Athens when it comes to Evelyn's own wedding). Although the Evelyns marriage has to be a hole-and-corner affair, kept secret from She-Evelyn's mother, Paul and Margot's wedding is to be a big society do. However, not everybody agrees about Margot Beste-Chetwynde's high-society credentials. Lady Circumference for one would like to boycott the marriage.

'Would Waugh be thinking of She-Evelyn's mother at that point?'

'Lady Burghclere? Perhaps not. Selina Hastings writes that in *Decline and Fall* there are two characters who are dead-ringers for real people. Grimes being the Dick Young who worked alongside Waugh at Arnold House, and Lady Circumference being Alastair Graham's mother, not Lady Burghclere. Mrs Graham does feature in many entries in Waugh's diary from 1925–8, and is portrayed there as an unpredictable, indomitable old bat (of whom Evelyn is obviously very fond). Mrs Graham is Alastair's *mother*, of course, whereas in *Decline and Fall*, Lady Circumference is the aunt of Alastair Digby-Vaine-Trumpington. Though, satisfyingly enough, in the absence of Potts in Geneva, this Alastair takes over the role of being Paul's best man. So there are tantalising links between the marriage due to take place in Waugh's book, and the one due to take place in his life.'

Kate asks me about the marriage of Paul and Margot in *Decline and Fall*. I tell her that ten days before the wedding, Paul moves into rooms at the Ritz. Why the Ritz? Perhaps because Ronald Firbank has a joke about the Ritz that runs through *The Flower Beneath the Foot*. Perhaps also because that's where Evelyn proposed to She-Evelyn in December 1927. Meanwhile, Margot's villa in Corfu is being made ready for the honeymoon. Why Corfu? Certainly because on the way back from visiting Alastair in Athens in January 1927, as noted in his diary, Waugh stayed for two hours on the island, long enough to be won over by the place. If he was ever rich enough to buy a villa for himself, this is where it would be located . . . God, I'm seeing connections everywhere. Partly, this is due to the Badger I'm necking; it seems to refresh parts that other beers cannot reach. I continue.

'The hitch in the wedding comes when some of the girls that Margot is shipping out to Rio get stuck in Marseilles. She asks if innocent Pennyfeather will go out to France and "sort out the paperwork". In Marseilles, Pennyfeather dines at Basso's, a bottle of Meursault washing down his bouillabaisse. In June of 1927, Evelyn joined his family during their annual French holiday, and spent an evening in Marseilles with brother Alec. Then it was caviare that was eaten at Basso's, though washed down with Meursault sure enough. Later in the evening, Paul finds himself in the red-light district, specifically on Rue Ventomargy, where Alec and Evelyn ended their evening together. In other words fact and fiction constantly collide all through this witty riot of a book.'

'What about the wedding itself?' asks Kate.

'At ten o'clock on his wedding morning, Paul Pennyfeather is back at the Ritz. By two o'clock, Paul, best man Alastair and Peter Beste-Chetwynde, Margot's fifteen-year-old son from her first marriage, have finished lunch. One of Margot's limousines is waiting outside to transport them to the church. Paul asks Peter to have one more drink with him as they still have heaps of time to spare. Young Peter feels that it would be a mistake if he did have another drink. So Paul and Alastair alone refill their glasses with brandy. Alastair notes how strange it is that the Boller blind he had in his rooms in Oxford has led to all this. Paul turns the liqueur round in his glass, inhales its rich bouquet and proposes a toast: "To Fortune, a much-maligned lady!" At which point the police enter and arrest him for trafficking in white slaves.'

Kate smiles from the cheekbones. She can sense what an irresistible moment that toast is. So let's stay with it. I must take the opportunity of fleshing out the scene.

'Evelyn Waugh is sitting right here at this table in the Barley Mow in early April of 1928. He is the author of the about-to-be-published

Rossetti of which he has an advance copy on the table before him, alongside a pint of Badger, his third of the evening. Cover, wrapper and illustrations are all excellent. The book is open at the dedication page: "To Evelyn Gardner". He's spotted a few misprints that had escaped him during proofreading but they are purely literal and not worth an errata slip. The presentation copies will be going out soon and he has taken the trouble to ask Anthony Powell at Duckworth's to try and make sure that Lady Burghclere gets the "with kind regards" card and *not* one of the seven "with love" cards to 1) She-Evelyn . . ., 2) Olivia . . ., 3) Alastair . . ., 4) Harold . . ., 5) Henry and Pansy . . ., 6) Alec . . ., 7) Mr and Mrs Waugh.'

'Do you know that these people got the books with inscriptions? Or are you making that up?' asks Kate, cheekbones waning.

'Don't be so anti-intuitive. Go with the flow! Suddenly Evelyn gets to his feet and raises his pint glass, which he clinks against the equally raised glass of his alter ego, Adam Doure. Evelyn is aware that his new book, the one being written, is merely an expansion of "The Balance", in the sense that it is still circumstances that dictate the fate of the protagonist. But circumstances have taken a distinct turn for the better for Evelyn himself now that he has got a *lover* and a *career*. Evelyn goes on to clink glasses with Ernest Vaughan, George Theodore Verney and Paul Pennyfeather ("clinkity clink-clink-clink"). "TO FORTUNE," the happy laughing group say as one, "A MUCH-MALIGNED LADY!"'

After Kate and I have finished toasting ourselves, I do a spot of rearranging of our table. I've now got seven copies of *Decline and Fall*, of which six are Penguins, in a pile on the tabletop before us. I lead Kate through them. Three are variations of the early design, a white horizontal band between two orange bands at the top and bottom of the book. In 1937, the penguin that appears on the cover is distinctly flabby, but in the 1940 edition the bird is a slimmed-down and stylised version. There is surprisingly little difference in design between the 1940 edition and the 1953 edition. It's not until the mid-seventies that Penguin got the design absolutely right, which is when my other three Penguin editions of *Decline and Fall* were printed.

'Lush,' reckons Kate.

The cover shows a languid young man, head surrounded by blue sky, stepping out of a building that could be an Oxford college, a public school, a country house or a pub. The back of the book has a concise summary of the novel, and it's to the first page that one turns for biographical details about the author. Why have I got three near-identical copies from 1973, 1974 and 1976? Well, the 1974 copy is the one I bought and read in my teens, to the accompaniment of Bowie's *Young Americans*. The 1976 copy is a pristine copy bought off the web for a few pounds, which I have been displaying in various parts of my home since buying it a month ago. The 1973 copy I came across in a charity shop in Oxford, and at 50p I just couldn't walk away from it. I'm glad I didn't because I found a carbon copy of an exam paper, neatly folded, tucked into the middle of the book. It's a document that takes me back to something I left behind some time ago: a narrowly academic approach to books. However, it's not without interest, and I want to read to Kate how the text is prefaced:

> *Decline and Fall*. This novel would seem to belong to the tradition of novels in which an innocent is swept up by events and shown many sides of life before the happy ending.

'Is the ending happy?'

'The whole book is steeped in a perverse kind of happiness. But the ending, in my opinion, is not happy.'

Kate takes the exam paper from me. In a stern voice she asks me: 'Question one. How relevant is the title to the novel?'

I reply as lightly as I can: 'Originally the book's working title was *Picaresque or the Making of an Englishman*. By April 1928 Waugh was leaning towards *Untoward Incidents*. The first title can't make up its mind, the second has no structure. *Decline and Fall* is the right kind of title because it hints at the book's shape.'

'You haven't answered the question, just shown off a bit,' says Kate, refusing to give me a pass mark. 'Question two. Show how in the first two and a half pages Waugh uses the dons and their language:

a) to establish that this is a comic, satirical novel;

b) to present victimisation in a light-hearted way, without arousing our normal sympathies or indignation.'

'Well, as a matter of fact, this reader *was* indignant when Lumsden of Strathdrummond swayed in front of Paul Pennyfeather and announced, *"Here's an awful man wearing the Badger tie."* What I mean is, I fully agreed with Strathdrummond's desire to rip off Paul's tie and trousers and dump him in the fountain.'

Kate does not seem impressed: 'That's an even less acceptable answer. It's all very well demonstrating that you understand what irony is. But to start using it in an exam without an explicit invitation from the examiner is a big no-no. Marks deducted for insolence!' Kate leans towards me and whispers: '*You're in danger of failing your Oxford Entrance exam.*'

'We can't have that: Next question!'

'Give another example of a potentially shocking or unpleasant incident that is handled lightly, and show how this is done.'

'Little Lord Tangent is shot in the foot. Then his foot goes septic. Then he dies.'

But that's enough of the exam paper. Which I know I've failed having bottled out of writing long well-argued sentences. The fact is, it makes me feel uncomfortable thinking about such a sublime novel in an academic context.

Striking out on my own, I venture: 'Near the beginning of Part II, Waugh explicitly states Paul Pennyfeather's role in the novel. He is a shadow. He is the shadow of the real Paul Pennyfeather, the real Paul Pennyfeather being a shadow of Evelyn Waugh. And this works: both as entertainment and autobiography. Whereas Evelyn's first book, *Rossetti*, full of shades of Waugh as it is, simply does not come to life in the same way.'

I sip from my drink. Our meals arrive. Before starting to eat, Kate returns to the exam paper despite my distaste for it. 'Question four. Give three examples of attitudes or ideas satirised in the prison sequences in Part III, and indicate through which characters this is done.'

Ah, yes, the prison sequences, I can't resist answering a question about that. Any reservations I have about an exam context no longer signify. 'These are much more products of Waugh's imagination than are the public-school scenes, which are based on his actual experience as a teacher. Nevertheless, it's still useful to explore the prison sequences from an autobiographical perspective. First, in the chapter "Stone Walls Do Not a Prison Make", Paul is locked up in Blackstone Prison. He meets again Philbrick and Prendergast, who were part of Llanabba Castle's flawed school regime. However, Paul's first four weeks are spent in solitary confinement, which he experiences as among the happiest weeks of his life. He doesn't have to worry about meals or clothes, nor about having to make any decisions about anything. He is a free man.'

I eat a mouthful of juicy pie, then get back to pondering the book aloud.

'I wonder if Waugh was thinking about himself at the Barley Mow when he wrote this section. Of course, he was not entirely free when he was here, because he had his novel to write. But then Paul Penny-feather too has to work. He has mailbags to make out of a heap of sacking. Not that Paul minds this, because he finds that with minimal exertion he can finish his allotted task before supper. So let's envisage a particular day when Paul has made his quota of mailbags, and Evelyn has written his allotted number of pages. What has he written in his dense longhand on lined sheets of foolscap? It's the day that Waugh has been mocking the optimistic socialist principles of the prison regime. The governor has allowed a dangerous inmate to work with carpentry tools (Waugh was on a carpentry course himself just before getting engaged to Evelyn Gardner), insisting that the man's problems stemmed from his not having enough attention paid to his latent creativity. The inmate wastes no time in showing his appreciation of being treated so considerately by sawing off the prison chaplain's head. Poor Mr Prendergast. Paul hears about this unfortunate event in chapel under cover of the hymn "O God, our help in ages past".'

It seems right that Kate does not wish to interrupt what is developing into quite a satisfactory answer to her question. Or is it simply that she's concentrating on her pheasant *bourguignon* to the exclusion of her exam marking? Anyway, I carry on.

'Soon after, in the chapter "Nor Iron Bars a Cage", Paul is transferred to Egdon Heath Penal Settlement. Egdon Heath is Thomas Hardy's fictional name for the wild area of heathland that lies between Bournemouth and Dorchester. Waugh was living in this pub on the northern edge of exactly that area, though there's not much sign of bleak marshland now. And even in Waugh's time, the heath would have been long drained and turned over to crops. Still, the past lives on in the present. Wessex is something that Evelyn had been brought up with at Underhill, inheriting a good working knowledge of Hardy's fictional world from his father.'

Actually, this pie is rather good.

Which reminds me: 'At Egdon, Paul finds delicacies popping up in his meals (caviare one day, oysters another). Could someone have been sending Evelyn delicacies from London to brighten up the simple country fayre provided by the Barley Mow? And when the Egdon schoolmaster comes round with a book for Paul from the prison library, it's not the book on elementary grammar written in 1872 that he was offered at Blackstone Prison, but the latest offering from Virginia Woolf, brand new and bearing the label of a Piccadilly bookseller.'

'Foyles?'

'Well, that's Soho, but you've got the right idea. So, again, where does this motif come from? I wouldn't be surprised if it was Harold Acton sending Evelyn metropolitan treats in anticipation of receiving the dedication of *Decline and Fall* and to encourage its author to keep going to the end of it. But as Evelyn's diary for this period was either not kept up, or, more likely, retrospectively destroyed, that can only be the wildest of speculations.'

'This prison bird is a bit tough,' remarks Kate.

'The venison in my poacher's pie simply melts in the mouth. Try it.'

'Ooh, that is nice. I'll swap you a bit more if you don't mind. Let me try a bit of rabbit as well.'

119

While Kate is chewing contentedly, I get on with the job of entertaining her. 'Grimes is also incarcerated in Egdon Heath. Whereas
Paul thrives in his cage, Grimes just languishes in captivity like the
lark. As Grimes points out, Paul may like reading and thinking, but
Grimes likes a drink and a bit of fun and chatting now and then to
his pals. Of course, while part of Waugh too enjoyed reading and
thinking, another part of him would most definitely be languishing
like the lark, confined to the Barley Mow for weeks on end. So when
Grimes makes a dash for freedom on a foggy day, making off on one
of the jailer's horses, I can't help imagining Waugh doing much
the same thing, rushing off to Wimborne to call on She-Evelyn and
Pansy.'

'Oh, I don't think so. That road is terrible.'

'There wouldn't have been anything like as much traffic back then.
And in the light of a spring evening it would have made a great walk.'

Soon Kate is getting the picture. She tells me she can imagine She-
Evelyn opening the door of her Wimborne lodgings to the man she is
engaged to, and her face lighting up: ' "Hello, Evelyn. What are you
doing here? Have you been languishing like the lark?" '

I have little difficulty answering on He-Evelyn's behalf: ' "Yes, you
see I like a drink, and a bit of fun, and chatting now and then to
my pals." '

Kate: ' "Oh darling, you're well out of that Barley Mole-hole. That
place is just too languish-making!" '

I tell Kate that Grimes's flight to freedom doesn't end so well as the
one that we've imagined for his creator. The hounds follow Grimes's
scent as far as Egdon Mire. A shepherd finds his hat on the surface at
the most treacherous part. It seems that Grimes has died a horrible
death. But Evelyn can't bear the thought of that. Besides, wasn't
Grimes of the immortals? He would pop up again elsewhere, no
doubt about it.

We eat and drink for a bit in silence. I feel the need to go back
to that image of Evelyn having done a good day's work here and
suddenly feeling like spending the evening with the girls. He decides
he's been cooped up inside these four walls for long enough. So he

exits the pub through the front door and turns left on to Long Lane. There are green fields to his right, a row of mature trees to his left, and larks all around him. Actually, it was not larks that we passed earlier, at the beginning of our walk, when it was still light. The dark faces of the flighty twitterers suggested goldfinches, but I needed to wait until the light caught one in such a way that I could make out its red face and the gold bar on its wing. Goldfinches sure enough.

We walked along the long straight country road thinking about just one goldfinch. The bird carried by Michael Henchard, ex-Mayor of Casterbridge, in the gutsy Thomas Hardy novel. He was walking with the caged bird at a rate of sixteen miles a day from a little place inland and west of here to Casterbridge, Hardy's codename for Dorchester. I pointed out to Kate that Henchard's route wouldn't have crossed our path, but it would have run parallel to it, just a few miles to the west. Henchard had the goldfinch in a little wire cage covered with a sheet of newspaper. Bought out of wages earned from manual labour in the fields, it was to be a wedding present for his stepdaughter, a last attempt to gain her forgiveness for his past sins. What happened again? Kate had to remind me. Henchard's stepdaughter was too stunned to respond positively to his unexpected appearance at her door. Henchard was too proud to give her a second chance. In the blink of an eye he was walking away. Kate couldn't remember what happened to the caged bird. I wasn't sure either. But I was able to tell Kate in the gathering gloom that Henchard walked on to his doom. Then I remembered that, in his agony and shame, he ditched the goldfinch. And his daughter found it a few weeks later, starved to death, just a few feathers and featherlike bones to bury. I wasn't able to tell Kate about that part of the story during our walk to Wimborne. We were walking in single file by then, getting anxious about the passing traffic. So I fill her in now. Once she's back in the loop, I push on with my analysis.

'A year after *Decline and Fall* came out, Waugh wrote about Thomas Hardy in the *Spectator*. (The same year as he wrote approvingly about Ronald Firbank in *Life and Letters*.) He wasn't happy about what he called the bogus tragedy in *Tess of the D'Urbevilles*. But he did say something positive about the Wessex novels as a whole. Waugh admired the structural magnificence of the plots. He thought highly of the solidity and continuity of the life that the books revealed.'

'So do I.'

'I think Hardy was the kind of artist that had solved the problem that Waugh had identified in *Rossetti*. The real world was there in Hardy's work all right, a "necessary relation of forms" as Roger Fry would say. But this necessary relation of objects, places, people and institutions was lit up by the passionate vision of an individual man. As for essential rectitude – if glorious little Thomas Hardy didn't have that, then nobody did.'

'The Wizard of Wessex!' says Kate.

'Though it was the wizardly Ronald Firbank that Waugh himself claimed was the first *modern* writer to solve the aesthetic problem of representation in fiction. Waugh wrote that Firbank's novels were almost totally devoid of any attribution of cause to effect. The compositions were instead built up of a balanced alternation of the wildest extravagances and the most austere economy, with conversational nuances. Which is certainly how one could describe *Decline and Fall*.'

Enough literary theorising. Let's get back to He-Evelyn walking to Wimborne in the spring of 1928. Where exactly was the lodging house that Pansy and She-Evelyn occupied? I have no idea. So let's assume it was in the central square, close to where we're staying tonight at the Albion Inn. I inform Kate that Evelyn is knocking on the door and is eagerly expecting to see that door opening and a particular female face looking pleased to see him.

Kate responds in kind: ' "Hello, Evelyn. What are you doing here? Have you been languishing like the finch?" '

I try and look doleful as I say: ' "I bring you my last will and testament." '

'Let's hear it then,' says Kate, brightly.

' "That Evelyn Gardner be not told of my death, or made to grieve on behalf of me . . . " '

' "Oh Evelyn, you're all languished up." '

' " . . . And that I be not buried in consecrated ground. And that no sexton be asked to toll the bell. And that nobody is wished to see my dead body. And that no mourners walk behind me at my funeral. And that no flowers be planted on my grave. And that no man remember me. To this I put my name . . . MICHAEL HENCHARD!" '

I describe to Kate how I imagine Evelyn being led through the hall and into the girls' sitting room. He's asked how his day's work has gone. Pansy and She-Evelyn may be writing novels as well, but no one is allowed to forget the only novel that really matters to He-Evelyn. Waugh assures them that his day's writing has gone very well indeed. He reports that in his latest chapter, Paul Pennyfeather has received a prison visit from Margot. Of course, Margot was far from comfortable in the surroundings of Egdon Heath Penal Settlement, not with a prison warder *standing within earshot of their conversation.* She-Evelyn smiles at the veiled reference to their landlady who is sitting in a corner of the lounge, knitting. The woman looks up and tells the young people not to mind her, but to carry on talking about their nice books.

'Evelyn relates how Paul Pennyfeather asks Margot how business is doing. In reply, Margot asks Paul not to be horrid to her. But Paul isn't being horrid, he just wants to know. Anyway, after updating him on the sex trade, Margot goes on to hint that Alastair is getting sweet on her. Then she blurts out that she's going to marry Maltravers, something she's just realised there and then.'

'Is that the old bore of a politician who was at the party at Margot's country house?' asks Kate. Just as She-Evelyn might have done.

'That's right, at King's Thursday. And when Maltravers gets made Home Secretary he'll be able to OK the arrangement to get Paul Pennyfeather out of jail. But Margot has difficulty explaining her decision about this to Paul. After all he is doing chokey for her, and she has promised she'll be there waiting for him when he gets out. The prison warder breaks into their conversation at this juncture to say that if they should want to kiss goodbye – not being man and wife, it wasn't usual – he wouldn't mind stretching the point for once. As Evelyn finishes his summary of the scene he's written that day, he stares with mock malevolence at the benevolently smiling landlady knitting in the corner of the pokey sitting-room. This prompts Pansy and She-Evelyn to laugh out loud.'

I see the scene almost as clearly as I see Kate and myself sitting here at this table. Clearer, in fact. So I go on, trusting that Kate is seeing the historical/fictional scene as well: 'At that point (Evelyn tells the girls in the lodging-house), Margot rushes from the prison visiting room without looking back. Paul is returned to his cell where he finds his supper waiting for him. It's a pie from which protrude the feet of two pigeons. There is even a table-napkin wrapped around the pie. But Paul has very little appetite to bring to his meal, for he is greatly pained at how little he is pained by the events of the visit.'

The waitress asks us how our meal was. 'Delicious,' I tell her, though Kate does mention the toughness of her bird. 'It might have been the way it was shot,' says the waitress. Shot? Penguins aren't shot for the table. A perspective I will pass on to Kate when the waitress is out of earshot. Instead, by the time the waitress has gone, I say: 'Come to think of it, Evelyn can only write with such style and detachment about the demise of Paul's love affair with Margot because he is so sure about his own relationship with She-Evelyn. That relationship nourishes He-Evelyn deep inside. It's that well-nourished self that keeps bobbing up throughout the novel to toast "Fortune, that much-maligned lady".'

When paying for the meal, I try to explain my interest in the Barley Mow to the waitress. She has never heard of *Decline and Fall* or Evelyn Waugh. I cite that on *Desert Island Discs* recently *Decline and Fall* was chosen by David Mitchell, star of Channel 4's *Peep Show* and all the wittiest Radio 4 quiz programmes, to be marooned on the island with him alongside a few records, the Bible and the works of Shakespeare. She looks at me blankly. I shut up.

Kate carries on chatting to the waitress, and it turns out that she has known the building for thirty-odd years. She tells us that where we're sitting is indeed the original part of the establishment. And that if anyone was lodging back when we mentioned, it would have been in a room right above us. She adds that the pub is thought to be haunted, and goes on to describe three occasions when she and the landlord have been sitting at a table at the end of the evening when one door or another has mysteriously opened. I'm studiously polite in the face of this. At least Kate now knows how Margot must have felt when in the visiting room at Egdon Heath Penal Settlement, having to listen to the stuff that the warden was spouting, however well meant.

The exchange with the waitress has dispelled the Wimborne fantasy and brought me well and truly back to Evelyn's base at the Barley Mow. This prompts thoughts about Paul Pennyfeather's eventual return to his Oxford base via a false death certificate and a new identity. I try and interest Kate in this: 'At the beginning of *Decline and Fall*, Pennyfeather is at Oxford reading for the church. Specifically, he is on his way to his rooms and will smoke a pipe before going to bed. The next day, after he has been so unjustly expelled from the college, the chaplain asks Pennyfeather if he will return his copy of Dean Stanley's *Eastern Church*. The significance of this detail only comes to light in the epilogue. In that concluding section, having returned to his theological studies at his old college, in his third year of uneventful residence at Scone (a phrase Waugh repeats from the Prelude), Pennyfeather is visited by Margot's son. Peter is now up at Oxford, and has had the Bollinger Club blind in his rooms that night. At the end of a long chat – drunken and repetitive on Peter's part, cold and unresponsive on Paul's – the host sees his visitor out and settles down again at his table with Dean Stanley's *Eastern Church*. Pennyfeather reads that the ascetic Ebionites used to turn towards Jerusalem when they prayed. Pennyfeather makes a note of it while thinking that it had been quite right to suppress them.'

'What is Waugh getting at?'

'It seems that Paul Pennyfeather has turned into an ultra-orthodox Christian, disapproving of anything that deviates from the most conservative of rule books. It's no longer circumstances that dictate Pennyfeather's life – he's not going through all that again – God's word will do for him from there on in.'

Kate looks thoughtful. Finally she asks: 'What did Evelyn do when he'd finished the book?'

'Well one thing he did was to travel the seven miles to Poole so that Henry Lamb could paint his portrait. The painting is lost, but a black-and-white photograph of it is on the back of the dust-wrapper of Volume One of Martin Stannard's Waugh biography. Have a look.'

I take the book out of my bag and hand it to Kate with the back cover uppermost. 'That is one weird portrait,' says Kate. 'Evelyn is sitting there looking pin-headed and mean-spirited and *humourless*.'

I look too. A pipe is poised in front of his mouth and he is making entries in a notebook with a pencil. Surely this is a defeated Paul Pennyfeather at the end of *Decline and Fall*, not an effervescent Evelyn Waugh.

'Perhaps it is another of Evelyn's jokes,' I suggest. 'Evelyn asks Henry if the picture is finished. Henry replies that he's given Evelyn exactly what he asked for – Paul Pennyfeather made flesh through the medium of paint.'

However, I'm not happy with this summing up. So I add a few words more: 'But Paul Pennyfeather has already been made flesh through the medium of literature. There is a scene in the last chapter that is echoed in the very last lines of the book. At a lecture, Paul learns that in the second century AD there was a bishop in Bithynia who denied the divinity of Christ, the immortality of the soul, the existence of good, the legality of marriage and the validity of the Sacrament of Extreme Unction. Pennyfeather reckons that the Church had been absolutely spot on to condemn him.'

As my eye flicks to the portrait featuring the big serious eyes and the sneering mouth I can't help snorting my amusement. Henry, Pansy, She-Evelyn and now me, all laughing aloud at his antics. I try and bring Kate in on the joke, which is all too easy. All she has to do is imagine the four of them having an evening here together, as they surely did many times in that magical spring of 1928:

Kate: ' "Oh, Pansy, make him stop. If he doesn't stop I'm going to make a puddle in the middle of this Barley piddle-hole." '

Evelyn has finished his comic novel but he just can't stop celebrating his happiness and his achievement. At least that's what I'm trying to convey when I say to Kate: ' "Do you see that man behind the bar? The so-called 'landlord' here? Well, in the three months that I've been quietly living on the premises, minding my own business, he has consistently referred to me in public in the most insulting terms. He has called me a Moabite, an abomination of Moab, a wash-pot, an unclean thing, an uncircumcised Moabite, an idolater and a whore of Babylon." '

Kate: ' "Stop it, Evelyn. Just because he won't serve you yet another pint of Todger for the very good reason that you've had one-over-the-eight already." '

'Actually,' I say, coming back to my normal voice, 'that Moabite stuff is a quote from Evelyn's book. A warder at the prison reports to the governor that a convict has called him these names. On consideration, the governor reckons that the most significant thing is that the stream of insults was delivered while the prisoner was holding on to a piece of wood from a broken stool. The governor's conclusion is that the foul-mouthed prisoner should be given a set of carpentry tools to work with. Perhaps a set of tools like the set that Evelyn had to give up because Lady Burghclere wasn't happy about the prospect of her high-born daughter marrying a tradesman who could only be expected to bring in the measly sum of £4 a week.'

Kate: ' "And so you've been writing a comic novel that will earn you a fortune and enable you to take my well-bred hand in marriage!" '

Suddenly I'm bang into the spirit of things again. What else would account for my next fiercely whispered words? ' *"DO YOU SEE THAT MAN STANDING BEHIND THE BAR? HE IS A MOWBITE, AN ABOMINATION OF MOW, A WASH-POT, AN UNCLEAN THING, AN UNCIRCUMCISED MOWBITE, AN IDOLATOR AND A PIDDLE-PUDDLING WHORE OF BABYLON."* '

'If you're telling me that his chef doesn't know how to cook pheasant, darling, I couldn't agree more.'

I'm lying awake in our bed at the Albion Inn. Of course, I'm lying awake – how could anyone sleep with the inn sign creaking just outside their bedroom window, blowing back and forth in the wind. Actually, Kate *is* managing to sleep, no doubt knackered from her day's driving and her evening's Evelyning.

This place is not really geared up for B&B. At the Barley Mow, the inn sign is a good thirty yards from the window, so that even if it squeaked I dare say anyone sleeping in the old part of the building would be able to sleep on undisturbed. I must recommend that they go back to offering budget accommodation to literary types.

I try and imagine He-Evelyn and She-Evelyn making love together in lodgings in Wimborne on nights when Pansy was in Poole with Henry. But that doesn't work out very convincingly. On the other hand, I have little difficulty imagining Evelyn suddenly taking a hankering for another pint of Badger Ale. So he dresses himself, goes down the stairs of the lodging-house and walks all the way to the Barley Mow. There, he lets himself in with his precious key, switches on the light in the lounge bar and – with practised ease – pulls himself a pint. He's official beer taster for the local brewery, the job that Grimes held briefly in *Decline and Fall*. Evelyn takes his duties very seriously. Basically, he considers himself on call twenty-four hours a day.

As he tastes the Badger (God's own brew) he thinks of his bride-to-be lying serenely in the bed in Wimborne, waiting for him and him alone. As he sups the Badger (God's own nocturnal nectar) he thinks of the novel that's fast taking shape by day, just waiting for him to resume where he left off from it in the morning. Having finished his pint, Evelyn considers returning to the lips and hips of his loved one. But Evelyn can't face walking back to Wimborne at four o'clock in the morning. No way, José! So it's upstairs for five hours of kip before rising with the larks in the morning. He was simply gagging to get back to *Picaresque*. Gagging meaning the opposite of languishing. He was simply gagging to get back to *The Making of an Englishman*.

4

It's taken us a day to get from the Barley Mow to Canonbury Square in Islington. It took the Evelyns three months to get here, but their journey was more eventful. The Selina Hastings biography is the most informative about this period in Waugh's life, so it's the book that's open between Kate and me on the bench we're sitting on.

I tell Kate that in May of 1928, Pansy, Henry and the Evelyns came back to London from Dorset. The girls took up residence in lodgings in Montagu Place, north of Hyde Park, not too far from Evelyn, who was still calling Underhill his home, and not too far from Henry in Maida Vale. But the Evelyns soon got impatient with this arrangement and they speedily organised a wedding for June.

Actually, I can't help wondering about this. Waugh made five line drawings for *Decline and Fall*, which he described on the title page as an illustrated novelette. One is of the sports day at Llanabba, one is of Paul in the red-light district of Marseilles, two feature Grimes, but the one I've studied closest was used as a frontispiece in the first edition. It's a drawing of Margot and Paul's wedding. Well, not of the wedding itself, because that didn't take place. But a drawing of the church and all the people gathered in the vicinity in readiness for the marriage ceremony. Above the church there is a hot-air balloon from where some people have a bird's eye view. And an aeroplane's slipstream has written the word 'Margot' in the sky above St Margaret's. St Margaret's is in Parliament Square (not that Waugh tells the reader this: he just expects him or her to know that) and it's where Winston Churchill got married. The church has been accurately drawn. Why has Waugh chosen this scene? Well, the logical conclusion of his own engagement to Evelyn Gardner would be preying on his mind, and having sat drawing such an upbeat scene, for however long it took, perhaps a plan for his own wedding suddenly gelled. Of course, St Margaret's could not be booked at the drop of a hat. But St Paul's in Portman Square could.

I tell Kate: 'Only Harold Acton, Robert Byron (another Oxford chum), brother Alec and Pansy were invited to the church ceremony. The same afternoon, the Evelyns caught a train to Oxford and a taxi to Beckley.'

'Beckley?'

'Well, why shouldn't they honeymoon at the Abingdon Arms where He-Evelyn had already spent happy times with Alastair?'

'Maybe for exactly that reason.'

'He-Evelyn told his parents about the wedding, and they were pleased for the couple. They told Lady Burghclere and she was "inexpressibly pained". After a month or so of less than comfortable living at Underhill, the flat at Canonbury Square was found for them by friends. It came unfurnished, but there were plenty of junk shops around where they could buy cheap furniture which He-Evelyn, with his carpentry skills, enjoyed repairing and decorating.'

Kate looks happy for the young couple. So here they took rooms in the splendid three-storey terrace that runs close behind this bench. The newlyweds moved into number 17a in August of 1928. There are still bells for flats a, b and c. It's unclear which floors relate to which bells, but, according to the literature, the Evelyns occupied five rooms on the first floor. In front of the terrace are the neatly-laid-out gardens of the square itself. We're enjoying the exotic trees and the colourful flowers of this tranquil spot, just a stone's throw from busy Highbury Corner, and I believe the Evelyns would have been pleased with their first home together. There is a chirpy letter from Evelyn to Harold Acton telling him that a number 19 bus from the corner of Theobald's Road, opposite the school where Waugh learned carpentry, would get his friend to the Evelyns' new place in about ten minutes. Waugh describes their residence as in a 'dilapidated Regency square'.

'Well, there's nothing dilapidated about it now,' says Kate. 'This is prime real estate.'

'I don't have Stannard with me today, but that's the book that includes a photograph of the Evelyns' dining room, which I've pored over with a magnifying glass. The table is set for a meal for two (three different wine glasses stand to the right of each place-mat: Waugh has had enough of Badger Ale to last him a lifetime). A candelabra – perhaps a wedding present – dominates the dining-table. On the wall are a sketch of He-Evelyn and a painting of She-Evelyn, both by their friend Henry Lamb. Also on the wall is a photograph of the two Evelyns sitting on a couch, reflections of their distinctly similar heads appearing in the mirror behind them. That's six images of one or other of the Evelyns altogether.'

'A very self-referential decor.'

'Harold Acton – once of Meadow Buildings, Christ Church – duly visited the pair, though I doubt if the number 19 bus was his preferred mode of transport, and found them happily working away at their home in what he described as a sparkling nursery atmosphere. A pair of fauns, according to him; a couple of prize pigeons, according to another Oxford friend, Peter Quennell, who had upset the Evelyns with a lukewarm review of *Rossetti*.'

'The reference to pigeons makes me think of that pie in *Decline and Fall*.'

'I hadn't made that connection. It reminds me that Pansy had written in her diary shortly before her friend's wedding that although the relationship with He-Evelyn was making She-Evelyn happier than she'd seen her before, Pansy doubted the strength of the bond on She-Evelyn's part.'

'I can't get that pie out of my head now. With the two pairs of legs sticking out from the pastry.'

'In October She-Evelyn fell ill with chickenpox. After two weeks of lying ill in bed at Canonbury Square, she began to recover. Her sister Alathea, who was married to Geoffrey Fry, inheritor of the Fry's chocolate fortune, invited them to stay at their country home on the Wiltshire Downs.'

'So the pair of fauns enjoyed a free holiday in the country, the sparkling nursery freshness was back in their lives.'

'In November the Evelyns gave a cocktail party. The invites were backed with a map showing the route from Buckingham Palace to 17a Canonbury Square. And why not? The daughter of Lady Burgh-clere was a well-connected young lady. Waugh was now rubbing shoulders with Nancy Mitford, and her sister Diana, who had married Bryan Guinness, heir to a brewing fortune. Beautiful, RICH, clever people.'

'Brightest of BRIGHT young creatures!'

'But at the end of the evening, according to Hastings, Geoffrey Fry was heard to murmur: "And when they buried her, the little town had never seen a merrier funeral." '

'So he wasn't convinced that this marriage was right for She-Evelyn either.'

'In December, Waugh landed commissions from several publications, his byline being in demand following some great reviews of *Decline and Fall*. He also plugged away with the research for a book on John Wesley, which was proving as laborious a chore as *Rossetti* had been. They spent Christmas with Pansy and Henry Lamb, who had also married that summer, at their new home near Salisbury.

However, She-Evelyn was soon ill again with a bad sore throat that needed operating on in January.'

'The poor lamb. And I don't mean Pansy.'

'Actually, I must stop. I don't want to get into 1929, the year Evelyn Waugh's world was turned upside down. I want to linger in the autumn of 1928 when *Decline and Fall* came out. Arnold Bennett gave it a glowing review in the *Evening Standard*. He wrote that *Decline and Fall* was an uncompromising and brilliant satire. So the Evelyns invited him round to their flat for lunch.'

'Pigeon pie for three.'

'Cyril Connolly gave the book a glowing review in the *New Statesman*. He wrote that the book displayed a love of life, and consequently a real understanding of it. He emphasised that it was a funny book, and the only one that, professionally, he had read twice. So the Evelyns invited *him* round for lunch later in the week.'

'Pigeon pie all round.'

Connolly later recalled that meal, which lasted all day. He wrote: 'It was a very small spick-and-span little bandbox of a house, and his wife was like a very, very pretty little china doll, and the two of them were this fantastic thing of the happily married young couple whom success has just touched with its wand.'

I stand up, turn around and look across at the Georgian terrace. The blinds are pulled down over the first-floor windows at number 17. But I can see in there all right. A scene with one, two, three, four, five, six, seven, eight Evelyns in all. No sign of Arnold Bennett or Cyril Connolly. Well, actually, there is a sign of their recent visits. He-Evelyn is firing some figures at She-Evelyn.

' "Friday, 12 October. Sales of *Decline and Fall* for the week of 157, making a total of 1093." '

Kate: ' "Cheers!" '

' "Friday, 19 October. Sales of *Decline and Fall* for the week of 827." '

' "Bottoms up, darling." '

' "Friday, 23 November. Sales of *Decline and Fall* for the fortnight of 398. The second edition has been put to bed!" '

' "Oh, what a good idea. Let's us go too. You can touch me with your magic wand." '

' "First a toast. Try this in your dessert wine glass – it's delicious if you sip it while nibbling strawberries." '

' "Nipples like strawberries? Sounds lush, darling." '

' "To Fortune, a much-maligned lady!" '

' "To Fortune, a *much*-maligned lady . . . " ' pouts Kate in She-Evelyn's clothing. Then she adds more thoughtfully: ' "I wonder how Pansy's book is doing. Didn't Chapman and Hall publish it the month following yours?" '

' "Dearest, there is only one book in town, a delicious concoction from yours truly. A great lump of a thing called *The Old Expedient* is just sitting there in bookshops, taking up space that should by rights be given to extra copies of *Decline and Fall*." '

' "Oh how can you say that, *Faux*-Evelyn? Besides, didn't you design the wrapper?" '

' "Too true. And to do that I had to read the ruddy book. It's about a castle on an island off the coast of Ireland, clearly Pakenham Hall. Pansy tries to have her cake and eat it by having the plain, short girl in the family – a representative of the masses – inherit everything. But true also, alas, is the expression that you can't polish a turd. Not that easily." '

' "Oh, don't speak like that, dearest. Henry and Pansy have been marvellous to us. They're our best friends." '

' "Of course they are." '

' "While we're clearing the air, you haven't asked me for months now how my own novel is going." '

' "Haven't I? Well, you are going to have to forgive me for that little omission, O Evelyn-of-the-weaker-sex." '

' "I'm not sure that I can." '

'In case it makes you feel any better, this is what Chapman and Hall himself thought of *Decline and Fall* . . . '

'Arthur?'

'Old Arthur wrote a bit of doggerel in a copy that he presented to a friend and with some effort I've committed it to memory:

'The sons decline, the sons decline and fall.
The fathers stand at gaze, deploring all.
Say are the daughters better? you who know;
I doubt it, but I like to think it so.'

5

A couple of days later, back at Kate's Westcliff-on-Sea flat, I get on with writing up our visit to Dorset. Kate pursues a line of enquiry of her own in the bedroom. By mid-evening we come together to swap notes.

'I've made a lovely discovery.'

I open a bottle of wine, all ears.

'Following in the footsteps of Waugh has made me remember something similar I once did concerning Graham Greene.'

'Oh, yes.'

'For my birthday, a few women friends and I went to Cuba. We were reading *Our Man in Havana* on the way over, and – rather to our surprise – we were enjoying it.'

'I read that once upon a time. Greene was one of those Penguin authors that were unavoidable during my adolescence.'

'I read the novel when I was a teenager too. Probably a copy of Gina's that was lying about the house. I have to say though, that I was pleased when Virago came along with their all-female publishing programme. The books of Margaret Atwood, Angela Carter and so on quickly replaced those of Waugh, Greene and Co. on my all-time-favourites list.'

'I couldn't relate to those Virago titles when they came out.'

'You don't say.'

'I like to think I would get on better with that kind of thing nowadays.'

'Well, I'll lend you Fay Weldon's *Life and Loves of a She-Devil*. But back to *Our Man in Havana*. My friend Annette realised that for our one-night stay in Havana we would be in the hotel that crops up in the book. She and I went up to the fifth floor, found room 501 as mentioned in the text, and had quite a giggle imagining who was in there and what they were up to. Annette and I didn't get as far into the literary-pilgrimage thing as you and I have done at the Barley Mow. I was thinking that when I picked up my copy of *Our Man in Havana* this afternoon and began to read the relevant section.'

As Kate flicks through her Penguin, she tells me: 'Wormold – a vacuum-cleaner salesman – is the book's protagonist. He is given the key to room 501 of the Seville-Biltmore Hotel . . . The room belongs to Hawthorne, a British spy, and when Wormold enters it he finds on the table some spy stuff, including a copy of Lamb's *Tales from Shakespeare* which Hawthorne explains he uses both to compose and decode messages . . . Anyway, on the way to room 501, Wormold finds himself in the company of a Dr Hasselbacher. And when making their way through the bar of the Seville-Biltmore Hotel, an exchange takes place between Hasselbacher, who is drunk, and someone whom they meet in the bar.'

Sipping wine allows me to follow this easily enough.

'Hasselbacher tells the man – who is from Miami and in the real-estate business, with a wife and two kids – that he is only a figment of Hasselbacher's rather pedestrian imagination. Hasselbacher goes on to say . . .' And at this point Kate zeroes-in on a particular page, and reads:

' "Now if my friend, Mr Wormold here, had invented you, you would have been a happier man. He would have given you an Oxford education, a name like Pennyfeather . . . "'

'Pennyfeather?' I ask, surprised to hear so familiar a name in this context.

Kate carries on reading:

' "What do you mean Pennyfeather? You've been drinking."'

'Pennyfeather?' I ask again, enjoying hearing myself echoing the name.

' "Of course I've been drinking. Drink blurs the imagination. That's why I thought you up in so banal a way: Miami and real estate, flying Delta. Pennyfeather would have come from Europe by KLM, he would be drinking his national drink, a pink gin."'

Kate looks up from the book, inviting reaction.

'What a lovely compliment to Waugh and his novel.'

'What a huge coincidence that the only other time I've dabbled with the crossover between reality and literary fiction, it turns out to have had a Barley Mow connection!'

I take hold of the book, note that it was written in 1958, thirty years after *Decline and Fall*, and read the Pennyfeather exchange for myself. Then I comment: 'I'm not sure Pennyfeather was a pink-gin man.'

'I suspected the train-spotter in you would say that. So to save you the trouble, I've skimmed through the Penguin copy of *Decline and Fall* that you generously donated to me. Ready for the drinks list?'

'Fire away.'

'In the Welsh-public-school section, Grimes and Pennyfeather drink beer together. At Margot's country house, everyone drinks cocktails. Prior to the wedding of Margot and Paul, Paul is drinking a toast to "Fortune, a much-maligned lady" with brandy, when the police arrest him. In Marseilles he savours a bottle of Meursault. In prison he is provided with brown sherry, courtesy of Margot. In her villa in Corfu, Paul enjoys a nameless aperitif as the sun goes down. And back at Oxford, he keeps whisky in his room.'

I top up our glasses with cool Chardonnay. I'm impressed with Kate's research. Not sure if she'll be blown away by the ditty I'm about to recite, but here goes:

' "Cruttwell dog, Cruttwell dog, where have you been?"
"I've been to Cuba to sleep with Graham Greene."
"Cruttwell dog, Cruttwell dog, what did you do there?" '

'Oh, don't say it,' urges Kate.

' "I bit off his penis and pubic hair." '

'Now that might have sounded gratuitous,' I admit. 'But I'm going to prove to you that it's not. About a year ago I sent you a copy of *The Loved One*, the Waugh novel written in 1948 that Evelyn dedicated to She-Evelyn's one-time housemate, Nancy Mitford. Throughout the copy I transcribed excerpts of letters between Waugh and Mitford concerning the book itself and other matters. So where have you shelved it?'

'Along with my other Waugh books, of course.'

Kate owns almost as many Waugh books as I do now. I link her collecting habit to the day we were walking together along the flooded river at Oxford and she first got inside my backpack. But I have to admit that long before then I was priming her with source material. I open the familiar blue-covered book, and read my own handwriting on the opening endpapers: 'Annotated edition, signed by the annotator, limited to five copies of which this is number two: Ms Clayton's copy.'

I guess I was aping what Evelyn wrote in his original edition, printed on special paper and limited to 250 copies. But that is half-forgotten now. I turn over until I have what I require, and read it aloud:

'Darling Nancy, So my friend Graham Greene whose books you won't read was sitting in a New York hotel feeling quite well when he felt very wet and sticky in the lap and hurried to the lavatory and found that his penis was pouring with blood. So he fainted and was taken to a hospital and the doctors said, "It may be caused by five diseases, two of which are not immediately fatal, the others are." Then they chloroformed him and he woke up two days later and they said: "Well, we can't find anything wrong at all. What have you been up to? Too much womanising?" "No, not for weeks." "Ah," they said, "that's it!" What a terrible warning. No wonder his books are sad.'

'I don't suppose for one moment a dog was involved,' says Kate, going to the heart of the matter. 'More likely a vacuum cleaner.'

We discuss what may or may not have happened to Graham Greene's privates in a hotel in Havana or New York. But at the back of my mind I'm left with the curious feeling – which I don't fully understand yet – that all roads ultimately lead to the Barley Mow.

VILE BUDDIES

Hard Cheese on He-Evelyn

1

Kate and I have arranged to meet near Green Park station, outside the Ritz. By good fortune we arrive simultaneously but soon realise we need to get off the crowded Piccadilly pavement. Round the corner we find what we need – a quiet spot and a ledge on which to sit down.

'This is Arlington Street,' I tell Kate. She looks blank. I remind her that in the sublime pages of *Decline and Fall*, Paul Pennyfeather is enjoying a pre-nuptial drink in the Ritz when he is told that Margot Beste-Chetwynde's second-best Hispano Suiza is waiting here at the side entrance to the smart hotel. Waiting to take him to the church where he is to get married to Margot.

'What is a Hispano Suiza?' asks Kate.

'Maybe it's just a white van,' I reply. In front of us, the greyest of white vans is sitting there with its engine running and a bloke sprawled across the passenger seat listening to the radio.

'What a vile body,' I suggest, if only to alert Kate to today's key phrase. I tell my partner that in the late spring of 1929 the Evelyns got back from their three-month cruise of the Mediterranean. It had not been a success, with She-Evelyn being ill from the beginning of the trip, causing a month-long lay-off in Port Said. Not a success for He-Evelyn either, with his plans for the trip to break out of the Mediterranean and into Russia having to be abandoned along with his plans for an ambitious travel book. But, back in England, after a month or so of re-acclimatising to their high-class friends, Evelyn took himself off to the tried and trusted Abingdon Arms in Beckley and began his second novel. How does *Vile Bodies* begin? It begins with the book's protagonist, Adam Fenwick-Symes, returning to Dover after having spent some time abroad.

'Adam is Evelyn?'

'Absolutely. After the Channel crossing, which allows Evelyn to introduce a cast of Bright Young Things and crusty old ones, Adam finds himself in trouble at customs. In fact, the customs official destroys the manuscript on which Adam has been hard at work in Paris for two months. Very handy for Evelyn, I suspect, that Adam is thereby reduced to his own condition of being an author who feels under pressure to come up with his next book.'

'How long since *Decline and Fall* was published?'

'Getting on for a year. Which isn't too long, on the face of it. But it is a fair time when you consider that the follow-up novel was not even started. So Evelyn did make a start. He brings Adam by train from Dover to London where he calls in on his publisher in Henrietta Street in the West End. As it happens, Evelyn's own publishers, Chapman and Hall, had premises in Henrietta Street. Adam explains that his book is lost and his devious publisher imposes on him an onerous new contract, which states that Adam can keep the fifty-guinea advance for the destroyed book. (He has to keep it because he has spent it and has no resources with which to refund the advance.) But as a result he has no choice but to agree to the same advance for each of his next twelve books.'

'Poor Adam.'

'Yeah, but you can tell by the jaunty way in which the scene's written that Evelyn was not really worried. He was still on top of the world at this stage. He knew he had got the makings of a classy novel in him – a satire on the morals of the age. Also, he has not lost his enthusiasm for Ronald Firbank's work. Let me recite a piece of dialogue from *Prancing Nigger*.'

'Oh, that title!'

'Actually, Firbank's own preferred title for the book was *Sorrow in Sunshine*.'

'Yes, let's go with that.'

'OK, compare these two quotes. This is from *Sorrow in Sunshine*:

> "Have you nothing, young man, to declare?"
> "'Butterflies!'"
> "Exempt of duty, pass."

'And this is from *Vile Bodies*:

> "Have you anything to declare?"
> "Wings."
> "Have you wore them?"
> "Sure."
> "That's all right then." '

Kate asks me to remind her what Ronald Firbank's influence on Waugh amounted to.

'He wrote books that alternated between wild extravagances and austere economy.'

'With conversational nuances?'

'With conversational nuances.'

We've crossed Piccadilly, walked north and have arrived at the junction of Hay Hill and Dover Street, which is where Adam checks into Shepheard's Hotel after the interview with his publisher. There is no hotel here these days. Nor was there in Evelyn's time. The Lottie Crump character who runs Shepheard's Hotel in the book was a lampooning of Rosa Lewis who ran a similar establishment on Duke Street, a little farther north. In fact, when the book came out, she threatened to sue Evelyn about the portrayal and banned him from the Cavendish Hotel for life. Anyway, at the end of Hay Hill, a chandelier is visible through a window. Enough to allow me to feel we are in precisely the right spot. I tell Kate: 'Lottie runs a unique institution. Champagne flows constantly, paid for by whichever millionaire-in-residence catches her eye. The hotel's Italian waiter is constantly pilloried by Lottie for being a fairy, because she once caught him powdering his nose. Rich and powerful men mix with glamorous young ladies, one of whom dies after falling from a chandelier which, according to the newspaper report, she was attempting to mend.'

'Sound like a sort of *Fawlty Towers*,' says Kate.

'That's not a bad point of reference.'

'As the actress said to the bishop while climbing the chandelier.'

'When Adam settles in there, another resident bets Adam £500 that Adam can't reproduce a sleight of hand with three halfpennies. Adam does it. The stranger gives Adam a £500 note. Next, they toss a coin – double or quits. Adam wins. And the loser gives Adam another £500 note and calls him a lucky chap. Adam then phones up Nina, who is dining at the Ritz, and tells her the good news – that now they have the money to get married.'

'Who is Nina?'

'Adam's girlfriend.'

'What is she like?'

'Like She-Evelyn. A bright young sociable butterfly.'

'What happens next?'

'At Shepheard's, a drunk major tells Adam that he should put the money he's won on a horse that's running in the November Handicap with odds of twenty to one. Adam thinks this is a jolly good idea and gives the thousand pounds to the major so that he can place the bet. But thinking more realistically about this after the major has disappeared with the cash, Adam phones Nina at the Ritz and reports that they may not be able to get married after all.'

We walk across Berkeley Square and turn into Hill Street. The relevance of this will soon become obvious to Kate, but first I must tell her that the next day Adam travels out of London, to Aylesbury, to visit Colonel Blount, Nina's father.

'The crusty old bounder is partly based on She-Evelyn's mother. And his portrayal certainly reflects Evelyn's grudging respect for the old woman who was so against the idea of penniless Evelyn marrying her Mayfair-born and -bred daughter. Adam explains about the lost thousand pounds and asks Colonel Blount if he could possibly give him some money. How much? Well, perhaps another thousand pounds would do the trick. So the colonel makes out a cheque for that precise sum. An elated Adam returns to London, finds out that Nina is having cocktails at Pastmaster House with Lady Metroland (Margot Beste-Chetwynde's new name) and orders a chauffeur-driven Daimler to report there while he saunters over on foot, the way we've come.'

'This is a lovely way to read *Vile Bodies*,' says Kate, squeezing my arm. 'I really feel part of the action.'

OK, now we must find somewhere that could pass for Pastmaster House circa 1929. Hill Street in the middle of Mayfair is still prime real estate, but the character of the place has changed over the intervening period. There are still some grand façades but most of the buildings are now divided into offices or flats. I'm looking for a house with a fine entrance hall dominated by a magnificent staircase.

Kate and I walk up the stairs of the most likely looking building and pass between the pillars of the entrance porch. The receptionist tells us that we cannot go any farther than his desk, and, on being asked, that there is no grand staircase in this building any more. We have an exchange whereby he stares expressionlessly at me every time I ask a question then responds warmly when Kate puts to him much the same enquiry. But the upshot is that, according to him, all the old staircases in Hill Street have been taken out and replaced with lifts. 'What about the Royal Navy place on the opposite side of the road?' I ask. 'Look, mate, I've told you, I'm just the receptionist here. I don't know what goes on throughout the rest of Central London.' Even Kate can't rescue the conversation this time around.

Immediately next door, number 15 Hill Street is in the process of being redeveloped. We walk through the entrance and there it is – a magnificent staircase complete with a royal-blue carpet that flows up on either side of a marble pillar. Kate and I stand just to one side, in an area of white marble featuring two slimmer pillars. It's a magical moment and what's more I don't think it need end just yet. Any activity seems to be in a side room and we've passed the entrance to that. Let's see if we can make the most of our luck. Let's just stand here while I carry on with my take on *Vile Bodies*.

'So Adam arrives here at Pastmaster House and sends word up to

Nina that he is in the hall waiting for her. When she gets to the top of the stairs she sees him down here having a little dance to himself.'

'Are you going to do a little dance for me?'

'That might draw attention to our presence. Just listen to my waltzing words. Why is Adam doing a jig? Because he has a cheque for £1000 in his pocket, which means that he and Nina can get married! But first they are to have a special meal to celebrate their future together.'

'Where?' asks Kate. 'The Ritz?'

'Adam and Nina go to the Ritz every other day. They consider a few places including Thame near Oxford (an old Harold Acton haunt). But in the end they decide on a hotel in Arundel, near the South Coast, even though they won't get there in the Daimler until nine o'clock.'

'What's that all about?' asks Kate, as a workman walks by without so much as glancing at us.

'That's what I wondered. Then I discovered that Diana Guinness, whom Evelyn got to know after his marriage to She-Evelyn – because She-Evelyn was very friendly with Diana's sister, Nancy Mitford . . . '

'Diana was one of the Mitford girls?'

'Yes, she's the one who ended up marrying the fascist Oswald Mosley. But first at nineteen years old she married Bryan Guinness, heir to the Guinness fortune. Just after this first marriage beautiful Diana and gold-plated Bryan owned, or had the use of, superb properties in the middle of Paris, in Central London and a house called Poole Place, a few miles from Arundel in West Sussex. What's more they used to go around in a chauffeur-driven Daimler. Now in *Vile Bodies*, Adam and Nina have a meal at the hotel in Arundel then, dispensing with the Daimler, they sleep together for the first time. There is a lot of scene-setting and Evelyn is clearly recalling an actual event in the Evelyns' shared history.'

'Sounds like the Evelyns stayed with the Guinnesses and borrowed the Daimler for a day or two.'

'Or something like that. Anyway, in the morning Nina has to puncture Adam's mood by revealing that his precious cheque has been signed "Charlie Chaplin" by her father. A joke that Adam is slow to appreciate, but in the end he does have to hand it to the old devil.'

Kate and I stand there, appreciating Colonel Blount's sense of humour. Kate tells me I should go back to number 13 and bet the receptionist a thousand pounds that right next door there is a magnificent marble staircase. Naturally, he would take me up on the wager. I would then win a thousand pounds and we would be able to get married at a London church of our choice.

'Trouble is he'll have signed the cheque "Diana Guinness".'

Back to *Vile Bodies*, the smart book cum A–Z lesson: 'On the way back to London, Nina seems thoughtful. Then she says that it's too bad that she'll never, as long as she lives, see Adam dancing like that again, all by himself.'

I hold Kate's hand as another workman goes past. This one does see us, but what does he see? A couple dressed up for afternoon tea at the Ritz. He chooses not to ask us what we're doing here. We clearly own the place. Or if we don't actually own it, then we are part of the team of architects who are trying to come up with a scheme of modernisation that retains the staircase in all its glory.

So we stay. It allows me to describe one of the great parties that take place in *Vile Bodies*, right here inside Pastmaster House. Margot is giving the party for Mrs Melrose Ape, an American Evangelist who is going round England with a band of Angels – ordinary young girls with false wings and even more misleading monikers – in order to raise money for her church. Margot has assembled a mix of bright young things and dim old lords and ladies for the event. She meets Mrs Ape at the bottom of the staircase and leads her and the Angels to a raised platform at one end of the ballroom, the rest of which is filled with gilt chairs on which are sitting the glittering guests. Standing separately are three distinguished men, the Labour Prime Minister Walter Outrage, Lord Metroland and a Jesuit called Father Rothschild. They are suspicious of a man in a beard – quite rightly because it's Lord Balcairn, who writes a gossip column under the byline of Mr Chatterbox in a daily paper. To safeguard their privacy, the three statesmen step into Lord Metroland's study for their conference.

This leaves the audience consisting of Margot (Lady Metroland); Lady Circumference (also from *Decline and Fall*); Adam and Nina; Mr Benfleet, Adam's publisher; Angela Runcible, leader of the Bright Young Things; Miles Malpractice, another leading member of the BYT; the Duchess of Stayle (from Evelyn's second published short story), and various others. Mrs Ape (surrounded by her Angels – vulgar adolescent girls called Humility, Chastity, Creative Endeavour and so on) begins by saying 'Brothers and sisters', then lets her eyes travel among the gilded chairs and the faces. Finally she speaks again: *'Just you look at yourselves.'*

She very nearly gets away with it. But not quite. 'What a damned impudent woman,' says Lady Circumference. Adam, Nina and Agatha Runcible begin to giggle. Lady Metroland realises she is actually quite glad that her guest of the evening is going to be a failure.

Good. That's as far as I wanted to get with the story *in situ*. Now we can get out of here.

'What happens next?' says Kate.

OK, let's push our luck.

'Mr Chatterbox goes into Lord Metroland's study to phone in his gossip to the paper. But there he falls foul of Father Rothschild, the Prime Minister and Lord Metroland, who, together, pull off his false beard and order him out of the house. Mr Chatterbox – Lord Balcairn – only lives round the corner in Bourden Street. He gets there and phones in his story, a tissue of outrageous lies. He makes out that Mrs Ape was a great success in the historic setting of Pastmaster House and that her "just you look at yourselves" line resulted in Agatha Runcible leading the subsequent American revivalist singing, tears streaming down her cheeks. He reports that the Countess of Throbbing rose to confess her sins, disclosing the true parentage of the present Earl of Throbbing. He reports that the Archbishop of Canterbury confessed that while at Eton he and the present leaders of the Conservative Party enjoyed a relationship that could not be considered proper. Finally, he reports that several titled ladies came up with "guilt offerings", throwing jewellery – pearls, emeralds and diamonds and even a blank cheque – on to the parquet flooring in front of Mrs Ape and her Angels.'

'Parquet flooring?' says Kate, as she considers the smooth white marble that we're standing in the middle of.

'Yes, but this is only the entrance hall remember. There's probably a ballroom with a parquet floor on the other side of that wall.'

We don't get to find out. As I'm telling Kate that Lord Balcairn gasses himself as soon as he's filed his copy, we both feel the urge for fresh air.

There's a pub in Hill Street, back towards Berkeley Square, so we pop into that. When we're sitting at a table with half pints in front of us, it's another pub – the Abingdon Arms in Beckley – that pops into our minds. Evelyn was staying there and halfway through the writing of *Vile Bodies* when he got a letter from She-Evelyn at Canonbury Square: 'He reads that She-Evelyn has fallen in love with John Heygate.'

'Who he?'

'A friend of the Evelyns from the previous autumn. He had been trusted with chaperoning She-Evelyn to parties during the week, while Evelyn himself would travel down by train from Oxford to London at the weekends. Anyway, this had gone wrong obviously, because She-Evelyn and Heygate ended up sleeping together, which is not normally part of the chaperone process. She-Evelyn was very confused about her feelings and was effectively asking He-Evelyn for help. So Evelyn abandoned his book and spent a fortnight in London by his wife's side, trying to rescue their marriage. But it didn't work out. Next thing he was faced with was trying to rescue his novel. A month or two after having abandoned the book he went back to it. Not at the Abingdon Arms – he couldn't face returning to the site of his honeymoon. Instead, most of the rest of the second half of the book was written, with great difficulty, in one or other of Bryan and Diana Guinness's houses, and in a pub in Devon. The book is dedicated to Bryan and Diana. The actual manuscript was given to the Guinnesses, which is why it hasn't ended up in Texas with most of Waugh's manuscripts. Rather, the manuscript of *Vile Bodies* is now in Leeds University Library, and although I haven't seen it myself I was able to ask the librarian a couple of questions about it.'

'How exciting. What did you ask?'

'I knew from Stannard that the manuscript was written in two blocks, and that some alterations were made to the first block. I wanted to know whether there were any alterations to two key scenes. There were indeed. In the scene where Nina and Adam are coming back to London from Arundel after their first night sleeping together, Adam asks Nina for confirmation that they'd enjoyed themselves. Nina's reply, not part of the original draft, is that she'd never hated anything so much in her life. But as long as Adam had enjoyed it, then that was something.'

'Oh, dear. Evelyn thinks he's been rejected sexually.'

'I don't think he was rejected for that reason, not primarily. The Evelyns were incompatible on a number of levels. He-Evelyn was an intellectual, when he wasn't in party mode, and an adventurer. I think She-Evelyn had trouble keeping up her end of the partnership in these respects. I think the whole marriage was an enormous strain for her. And she needed a way out.'

'I think that's a bit presumptuous. But go on.'

'Subsequent to the split, Evelyn also added a scene near the beginning of the chapter about the party at Pastmaster House. It includes this line of Nina's: "All this fuss about sleeping together. For physical pleasure I'd sooner go to my dentist any day." And when Adam quietly suggests that Nina will enjoy it more next time, she pulls him up for presuming there will be a next time.'

'Evelyn is not a happy puppy.'

'He's not a confirmed Casanova.'

In this new mood of disillusion, in a deeply perturbed state of mind, Evelyn attempted to finish *Vile Bodies*. He managed that. But of course it's a different book than it would have turned out to be if She-Evelyn hadn't dropped her bombshell.'

'In what way, do you think?'

'As things were at the halfway stage, the only thing standing between Adam and Nina getting married seemed to be their poverty. I think Evelyn would have liked to have written about Adam writing the equivalent of *Decline and Fall* and being able to set up house in Canonbury Square with money earned from the book and with no help from ludicrous windfalls or unsympathetic in-laws. I think he may have written about Adam and Nina as somehow surviving the hypocrisy and hedonism of the time. However, there was no chance of the book turning out like that following She-Evelyn's betrayal.'

I notice we've finished our drinks. It would be nice to have another one but fatal to the pattern of the day. So off we trot. It's Sloane Square Underground we aim for. We need to get on a Victoria Line train at Green Park then change on to the District or Circle Line at Victoria. When we arrive at Sloane Square we pause on the platform and I explain to Kate why we're here.

'With the death of Lord Balcairn, Adam takes over his old job at the paper. He fills the Mr Chatterbox column with stuff that he has no choice but to make up. Two of his claims are that bottle-green bowler hats are at the height of fashion and that the buffet at Sloane Square Tube Station is the latest hangout of the smart set.'

'Funny that the old tiles on the walls down here are bottle-green.'

'And there was indeed a licensed bar here on the westbound platform right up until the 1980s. However, I wouldn't push the auto-biographical link too hard in this case, because the bottle-green bowler idea may have been inspired by Ronald Firbank. In *The Flower Beneath the Foot*, a character is described as looking radiant in the palest of pistachio-green mashlaks, an item of clothing that was all the rage according to court diarist Eva Shnerb. Now, the social reporter in *Vile Bodies* is called Mr Chatterbox, but there is a bright young party-thrower in the book called Archie Schwert, a man so decadent that he *lives* at the Ritz.'

When we get to ground level we pass into Sloane Square itself. I can see red lights shining up through glass bricks in the ground. Turns out that an old toilet has been fitted out as a smart restaurant. True, there is nobody sitting down there at the moment, but presumably, come five o'clock it will fill up with bright young shoppers from the

King's Road. We give it a miss. Instead we take a seat at a café on the edge of Sloane Square that puts us more in mind of the one that Paul Pennyfeather uses for his chat with Potts in the *Decline and Fall* chapter titled 'Interlude in Belgravia'. We don't discuss that interlude, 'cos we really must stick with *Vile Bodies*, something that Kate seems to appreciate.

'What else does Adam write in his Chatterbox column?'

'He talks about the ultra-fashionable Imogen Quest.'

'Don't I know that name?'

'She's the love interest in "The Balance". The aloof girl that another Adam – Adam Doure – gets obsessed with. Imogen is the one that by the end of the story is expressing an interest in Ernest Vaughan.'

'I miss mad Ernest.'

'Do you? I think he's omnipresent. I think that Evelyn's got the Ernest in him working full-time on his behalf. I think he's got him pushing along *Vile Bodies* just as he pushed along *Decline and Fall*. In fact, I think he actually surfaced in *Decline and Fall* in the form of Grimes.'

'Is he there in *Vile Bodies*?'

'A new character is introduced in the second half of the book. But "Ginger" Littlejohn is no Ernest Vaughan. In fact, rather than an Evelyn Waugh altar ego, Ginger is a John Heygate surrogate. Little John Heygate, as it were.'

I explain to Kate that Adam and Nina meet Ginger at the race meeting where Indian Runner – Adam's horse – wins the November Handicap at odds of thirty-five to one. Adam spots the drunk major who should have – and as far as Adam is concerned may have – placed Adam's thousand pounds on the horse, but the major disappears before he can be collared about the money. It's at that exact point, when Adam is vainly pursuing the means to marry Nina, that he comes across her chatting to a ginger-haired young man sporting a moustache. The three of them spend the rest of the day together amicably enough. The next day Mr Chatterbox's readers learn that Captain 'Ginger' Littlejohn favours the new bottle-green bowler hat and is one of the wealthiest and best-known bachelors in Society.

'Is that Evelyn starting to set up a revenge on She-Evelyn's lover?'

'Sort of, but not exactly. Evelyn is very careful not to denigrate Ginger too much. It's a very subtle game he plays for the rest of the book, transforming his feelings of rage, impotence, jealousy, so that none of it shows on the surface. Instead, what comes over is a beautifully light touch. Evelyn is fully in control of his pen. And if Nina and her new lover are put down, then it's in the most carefully managed way. One would never know that Evelyn's blood had been boiling. Though of course it had been.'

'I suppose that's what he achieved by having the month or two's break from the book. How does the second half continue?'

'It gets going with two parties. The first is for the Bright Young Things and is held in a "captive dirigible".'

'A hot-air balloon?'

'Well, a large passenger balloon of some kind that's tethered in the suburbs of London. Ginger drives them there, but at the party Nina and Adam are alone together and exchange some cynical dialogue.'

I've got the book in my bag, but I don't need to pull it out. I can remember the lines near enough:

Adam: 'Nina, let's get married soon.'

Nina: 'Yes, it's a bore not being married.'

Adam: 'I don't know if it sounds absurd, but I do feel that a marriage ought to *go on* – for quite a long time, I mean. D'you feel that too, at all?'

Nina: 'Yes, it's one of the things about a marriage!'

But Kate has had enough of me talking to myself. ' "What a BORE it is not being married, Evelyn," ' she tells me. ' "LET'S GET MARRIED." '

' "And let's stay married for quite a long time," ' I reply.

' "Let's stay married until the marriage is literally killing me." '

I explain to Kate that on the same evening as the party is going on in the captive dirigible, a more well-to-do party is going on at Anchorage House in the middle of London.

'In the middle of London? I've come to expect more precision than that.'

'Mmm. It's one of those rare times in the book that Evelyn isn't street-specific. Anyway, Lady Circumference, the Duchess of Stayle and all of Establishment London are there. The topic of the Younger Generation spreads through the company like a yawn, as Evelyn puts it. Kitty Blackwater and Fanny Throbbing, two inseparable elderly ladies wonder what it is the youngsters get up to at their wild parties. Do they actually have *sex*?'

'Is that word used?'

'Only implied. Anyway, Lady Throbbing rather thinks that they do. Meanwhile, the three male statesmen are conferring again as at Pastmaster House. Father Rothschild, Walter Outrage (the PM) and Lord Metroland. This time they actually get a chance to say something, or at least the Jesuit does. He feels that the trouble with young people is that they are all possessed with an almost fatal hunger for permanence. A statement which he immediately seems to contradict by adding: "I think all these divorces show that." He goes on to say that the accepted wisdom used to be: "If a thing's worth doing it's worth doing well." He laments that Young People have turned the saying on its head, so that it has become: "If a thing's not worth doing well, it's not worth doing at all." '

'That's a bit abstract,' reckons Kate. 'What does he mean?'

'The old attitude would have been that as the Evelyns had got married, therefore they should have a go at making it work. Whereas what He-Evelyn thought She-Evelyn had decided was that as their marriage was never going to be perfect, they should just put an end to it.'

' "What a BORE it is being married, Evelyn," ' says Kate. ' "Let's get divorced." '

' "And let's stay divorced for quite a long time." '

' "Let's stay divorced until the divorce is literally killing you." '

'The party at Anchorage House ends with Lord Metroland walking home (we're told that Anchorage House is within five minutes walk of Pastmaster House). When he gets to the front door, Peter Pastmaster is letting himself in. Remember him from *Decline and Fall*?'

'The boy who insists on Paul giving him organ lessons at the Welsh public school because his mother, Margot, has paid for them?'

'That's it. Well, he's now a young man and he doesn't approve of his mother's second marriage to boring old Lord Metroland. So as he's walking up the broad Adam staircase, on being addressed in a friendly way by Lord Metroland, he tells his stepfather to go to hell. Metroland is phlegmatic about this. He's more concerned about the fact that Alastair Trumpington's top hat is lying on the table by the front door. Remember *him* from *Decline and Fall*?'

'Part of the crowd that got Paul sent down for indecent behaviour . . . Later, Paul's best man . . . And Margot's lover by the end of the book.'

'Well, he's still Margot's lover. And Lord Metroland both knows and accepts this. He doesn't want to pass his rival on the staircase, so he hides away in his study until he hears Alastair come down the stairs and leave by the front door.'

'Is this Evelyn still being cynical about marriage in general?' wonders Kate. 'Or is this an example of what He-Evelyn should be doing? Accepting his wife's infidelity, like Lord Metroland. Putting up with She-Evelyn having John Heygate as a lover?'

'I don't think Evelyn's quite ready for that.'

We've been talking on the move. However, we're now emerging from the tube network again, this time at St James's Park. Why are we here? Because close by is a mews called Buckingham Place (Buckingham Street as it was in Waugh's day). And number 10 is the house where Bryan and Diana Guinness lived when they were up in town. Judging by the front door, the house is still under single ownership.

We cross the street to get a better view of the house front. Four floors plus a basement. Six windows across, with a fancy bit of arching over the front door. The whole thing is just a stone's throw from Buckingham Palace in one direction, Victoria Station in the other.

'What a piece of real estate!'

'Agreed. But let's go back to the summer of 1929. There were a lot of parties in town. A costume ball just about every night according to Diana's sister, Nancy Mitford. There was the Catalan Party in Lowndes Square, the Baby Party in Rutland Gate, the Bath and Bottle Party at the St George's Swimming Baths, and the Heroes and Heroines Party at Claridge's. John Heygate . . . '

'Evelyn's rival?'

'The Basement Boy – as Evelyn described him in letters to friends, because he lived in a basement flat – threw a Party Without End, during which people could come and go as they pleased, with sandwiches always available. And on 25 June, Diana and Bryan gave an 1860s Party in the house we're looking at.'

'An 1860s Party?'

'It must have been a midweek affair, because Waugh missed it, which is a shame as he could have dressed up as Rossetti in his prime. Harold Acton reported in a letter, sent to Waugh at Beckley, that he danced blissfully with She-Evelyn that night.'

We watch as a man arrives at the front door with what appears to be a tray of sandwiches.

'Look,' says Kate, 'the Party Without End is still going on. I suppose they'll have a ballroom in there.'

'If you had a house that size, then, yes, you'd want a grand entrance hall, a fabulous staircase and a bloody great ballroom . . . But there was another fancy dress party that took place the same night as Diana's and Bryan's 1860s Party, a Watteau Party held aboard the *Friendship*, a boat permanently moored at Charing Cross and a regular party venue. *The Bystander* reported the presence together of John Heygate, Nancy Mitford and the Hon. Mrs Evelyn Waugh whose husband had isolated himself in the country in an effort to produce a second novel to excel his first.'

'Was that the night the affair started?'

'No, the affair began a few days later. On 20 June Evelyn had written to his novelist friend Henry Yorke saying that he'd come up with twenty-five thousand words of a novel in ten days. That must have taken him to about the halfway point in the book. But on 10 July or so he got the letter from his wife saying that she had fallen in love with another man.'

'I'm in love with John Beaver,' says Kate, who read *A Handful of Dust* with me a few months ago. But I mustn't go to that party until this one's finished.

'The night of the adultery is an interesting story in itself. John Heygate had taken Eleanor Watts to a party and proposed to her. She turned him down and left the party early. Heygate stayed on, and at the end of the evening he took She-Evelyn home to his flat in Cornwall Gardens, Kensington, and slept with her.'

'The rascal.'

'When He-Evelyn came to London to try and find out what had been going on, and to try and save his marriage, he accompanied She-Evelyn to parties. There's a photo of the pair of them dressed for a Tropical Party aboard the *Friendship*, where the press caption states that the author of *Decline and Fall* looked somewhat scared, though there were no fierce Zulus on board.'

'How perceptive of the press.'

'Waugh looks like a ghost in that photo. She looks pretty glum too. After a fortnight of increasing tension between the Evelyns, Waugh went to Cheshire for a few days with none other than Eleanor Watts, a sympathy having arisen between them due to mutual unhappiness.'

'Wasn't she glad to be shot of Heygate?'

'Apparently she was quite keen on him, and had some regrets at turning him down. Especially the way things turned out. According to Eleanor's subsequent testimony, she kept telling He-Evelyn that he must put the events of the summer out of his mind. *"I can't, I can't,"* was Waugh's constant refrain. Meanwhile, She-Evelyn was sharing the flat at Canonbury Square with Nancy Mitford, as she had been since He-Evelyn's departure to write in Beckley. When a new photograph of She-Evelyn and John Heygate together at a party appeared in a paper, She-Evelyn was distraught. Nancy's advice was for She-Evelyn to say to He-Evelyn that it wasn't her fault and that she loved him. "But I don't love him," She-Evelyn replied, going on to confide that she'd only married him to escape her own home, and in particular her domineering mother.'

'Oh, dear.'

'Hastings is very good on the break up of the marriage, just as Stannard is very good on the effect the break-up had on *Vile Bodies*. According to Hastings, She-Evelyn had disclosed to a girl friend that He-Evelyn was "bad in bed". Given how little sexual experience with women Waugh had at this stage in his life, that does not come as a surprise. Also, given that he'd learned his sexual techniques from intimacy with men, I don't think it can come as a shock that She-Evelyn found He-Evelyn to be limited in the sack.'

' "Oh, stop, Evelyn, dearest. That's not the right place," ' says Kate.

' "Oh, but darling, that's what Alastair used to like," ' I reply. But my heart's not in it. This whole exchange is primarily about misery, not sex.

He-Evelyn seems to have decided that the best thing would be for Heygate and She-Evelyn to live together, and he telegrammed Heygate, telling him to come back to the UK from a motoring holiday he'd embarked on with Anthony Powell. This Heygate did, and the new pairing moved into Heygate's flat, later living together in the Evelyns' former flat at Canonbury Square.'

'Really?'

'He-Evelyn no longer wanted to have anything to do with the place.'

'I'm surprised that she did. Obviously she didn't want to preserve the memory of their time together. She preferred to over-write it with another relationship.'

'Hastings ends her chapter on the debacle by comparing the two Evelyns' attitude to what had happened. When She-Evelyn received a solicitor's letter telling her that her husband was suing for divorce, she said to a friend in her little girl's voice: "Well, you can't call life dull." Meanwhile, He-Evelyn was writing to Harold Acton in words that bring to mind the despair he expressed to Eleanor Watts: "I did not know it was possible to be so miserable and live."'

'I'm sorry for them both.'

'Me too. But life goes on. In August, Evelyn went to Ireland, possibly with Alastair Graham and Richard Plunket Greene. They went to motor races in Belfast and then stayed at Diana and Bryan's house near Dublin.'

It takes me quite a while to say this because Kate and I are on the move again, negotiating the tube network. But by the time we emerge from the underground at South Kensington, I have it clear in my mind what I want to say next.

'Evelyn was desperate to get the book finished. And although he had a structure of sorts to fall back on – meaning he could carry on with the Chatterbox stuff, he could describe more parties and Adam could visit Colonel Blount again in Aylesbury – basically Evelyn was pedalling hard for the finishing line. He intended to stop as soon as he could present something that publisher and public would recognise as being of book length.'

'What happens when Adam revisits Nina's father?'

'Adam goes there to get his agreement to his marrying Nina now that he's got a job at the paper. When Adam arrives at Doubting Hall, he discovers that a film is in the process of being made by a Mr Isaacs, keenly assisted by Colonel Blount. For this chapter, the colonel is effectively Evelyn's father, and the chapter is an exploration of the time that Waugh and pals made a film at Underhill about the Dean of Balliol's attempt to undermine the Royal Family. Effie La Touche is the female lead at Doubting Hall, while at Underhill the star's name had been Elsie Lanchester. For *Vile Bodies*, Evelyn made the film be about John Wesley, which is what he was planning to write about in the autumn of 1928, following the publication of *Decline and Fall*. The biography was abandoned when Evelyn discovered that his mother-in-law knew more about the subject than he did. The only way that the plot of *Vile Bodies* is truly progressed by the chapter is that while Adam is at Doubting Hall for the day, Nina and Ginger are putting together the Chatterbox column for him. Alas, they say more about the green-bowler hat nonsense that Adam was specifically told by the newspaper's proprietor not to mention again. The upshot is that Adam loses his job, and his prospects of marrying Nina recede.'

'Again.'

'Again.'

We're on our way to Peter Harrington's antiquarian bookshop in the Fulham Road. In stock are the two most expensive copies of *Vile Bodies* currently advertised on the web, at £1,250 and £6,500, and I want to see exactly what I'd get for my money should somebody give me a big fat cheque out of the blue. In the meantime, I should carry on with my reading of the book for Kate.

'Chapter Ten is the longest in the book at thirty pages. Adam is again Ninaless. This time he goes to the motor races with Miles Malpractice and Archie Schwert (stand-ins for Alastair Graham and Richard Plunket-Greene). There are several pages about trying to find somewhere to sleep for the night, though there is little accommodation to be had because of the big race meeting. No doubt the material is autobiographical, relating to the summer of 1929, and therefore of interest, but it's pure padding as far as the novel is concerned. At least that's what I thought until I read it more carefully. Then I noticed the part played by a Mr Titchcock, a local man who has to sleep on the floor so that Adam and his party can all sleep in beds at the Royal George.'

'Poor Mr Titchcock,' says Kate.

'Mr Titchcock maintains it's all the same to him whether he sleeps in a bed or on the floor.'

'Just like it's all the same to He-Evelyn whether She-Evelyn is in love with John Heygate or not.'

'For sure there is a complex coding going on throughout the book. Evelyn may be heartbroken by the split with She-Evelyn, but he's too sophisticated a writer for that to show in any obvious way. Sub-text, Evelyn was fucked. But line-by-line throughout *Vile Bodies* you would be hard pushed to notice that. If Waugh expresses contempt for Mr Titchcock, who is so easily displaced from his rightful bed, what does he feel about himself who has suffered the same fate?'

Kate's got her arm round my waist as we walk along Fulham Road. She's not used to walking in high-heeled shoes and is endeavouring to slow our progress. That's fine by me, we're in no hurry and have been making sound progress all day. I tell her: 'As I said, in *Vile Bodies* Adam and his party sleep at the Royal George. Well, the Royal George, Appledore, on the coast of north Devon is the pub that Evelyn eventually settled in to finish the novel. For all I know there was a long-term resident there, name of Titchcock, who had to give up his room so that Evelyn could have it. Settled into a suite at the Royal George, Evelyn resumed writing his long chapter. He made sure that the drunk major is at the motor-race meeting. The major acknowledges that he now owes Adam thirty-five thousand pounds, yet manages to borrow a fiver from Adam before disappearing again. The notion of speed is then explored, society being out of control. It comes as no surprise that Agatha Runcible, who has been steering close to the wind all through the book, ends up being the replacement driver of car No. 13 which she drives faster and faster until it crashes.'

'Where does all that motor-racing stuff leave Nina and Adam?'

'The relationship is placed on hold for the whole chapter. However, The next very short chapter consists purely of phone-call dialogue between the pair. She tells him she is engaged to Ginger. He tells her that he never wants to see her again.'

We've reached the shop. Every book in here costs a fortune and I've no intention of buying one. But because I'm with Kate, and because we're smartly dressed, and above all because I really want to see these books close up, I'm pretty relaxed about browsing. Soon the choicest of *Vile Bodies* are produced for our delectation.

The copy that I would certainly buy, if Charlie Chaplin or Diana Guinness were to give me a thousand pounds towards it, is a first edition, from January 1930. It's been rebound by the Chelsea Bindery in pillar-box-red leather. This bright red matches the flaming red of the dramatic title-page which is a woodcut (I think) by Evelyn (definitely) showing Agatha Runcible crashing in an old-style racing car.

'It looks more like a tractor,' observes Kate.

'It looks like Margot Metroland's second-best Hispano Suiza.'

OK, so that's the less expensive book given the once-over. The other is also a first edition. The original dust-jacket is protected by a transparent plastic cover which is why I feel totally at ease in handling the book. The jacket has been professionally repaired, so that one would hardly know it had been chipped and torn. The image on it is of the crashing car, which Kate loves because of the drawing's vivacity and despite the vehicle's tractor-like qualities. I peel back the dust-jacket to reveal the original boards of black-and-red snakeskin effect. The book is gorgeous. But let's be clear about this – only a nutter would pay £6,500 for it. A nutter like Adam Symes, perhaps. And he's broke.

As I stand there with the book in my hand, and with the bookseller pretending to take no interest in the wellbeing of his asset, Kate flicks over the pages until she gets to Chapter Eleven, the one which consists entirely of terse dialogue.

'*Does* Adam see Nina again?' she asks.

'Yes, there's a party at Agatha Runcible's bedside in her Wimpole Street nursing home. They meet there. Nina and Adam then go back together to his room at Shepheard's Hotel. But Nina decides that Adam isn't enjoying himself and leaves him in the middle of the night. A

WITH LOVE FROM EVELYN

CHRISTMAS 1927

Christmas cards.
Above: Waugh's 1927 card, sent months after meeting Evelyn Gardner.
Below: his 1929 card, sent months after she'd left him.

The Evelyns in the grounds of Barford House in the summer 1928.
Photographs by Alastair Graham. Courtesy of Alexander Waugh,
Waugh Family Archive, Milverton.

Above: The grounds of Barford House, photograph by Alastair Graham.
Courtesy of Alexander Waugh, Waugh Family Archive, Milverton.
Below: The Evelyn Waughs by Olivia Wyndham, 1928.

17a Canonbury Square.
Above: dining room, with three paintings or sketches of the Evelyns by Henry Lamb.
Below: living room, with Waugh's painted cover for *Vile Bodies* on mantelpiece.
Alexander Waugh, Waugh Family Archive, Milverton.

AS A CHILD IN THE YEAR 1860: THE HON. MRS. EVELYN WAUGH.

The Canonbury Square flat was empty on the evening of 25 June 1929.
She-Evelyn was with Nancy Mitford and John Heygate at Bryan and
Diana Guinness's party at 10 Buckingham Street, dressed as a Victorian girl in
trousers. She went onto another party later that night (see overleaf).

On the *Friendship* moored at Charing Cross for the Watteau Party aka
Embarkation For Cythera, 25th June 1929.
Above: John Heygate wearing a boater in the middle of the picture.
Below: She-Evelyn and John Heygate lying together in the background.

The Evelyns together on the *Friendship* for the Tropical Party, 16 July 1929, during their fortnight's reconciliation.

"A nip in time saves nine".

John Heygate, courtesy of Richard Heygate. Taken by Evelyn Heygate?

curious thing is that Waugh never states where Nina lives, in a novel that is otherwise chock-a-block with geographical information. I suspect that's because before She-Evelyn and He-Evelyn went down to the South Coast together for the writing of *Decline and Fall*, She-Evelyn and Pansy Packenham lived in several different flats in fashionable parts of West London. So the location of her base had become a little blurred in Waugh's mind, and he chose to keep it that way.'

'Where did the race meeting take place?'

'The November Handicap horse race was at a meet near Manchester. But Evelyn doesn't tell us where the motor race was. Obviously the autobiographical equivalent of the race took place in Ireland, but he has no compelling reason to take the action of *Vile Bodies* out of England, so he stays quiet about its location.'

'Why does Nina leave Adam in the middle of the night?'

'Partly to clear the way for the next scene at Shepheard's Hotel. Ginger comes by in the morning to try and warn Adam off from seeing Nina any more. Adam cynically agrees to comply in return for Ginger's paying his hotel bill.'

'How much?'

I have to flick though to the relevant page of the book, which is quite a bit thicker than the editions of *Vile Bodies* I've previously handled, before I can definitively announce: 'Seventy-eight pounds, sixteen shillings and twopence.'

'Isn't that what this book is selling at?'

'A little more than that, darling,' I say, both to satisfy the pride of the bookseller and to allow him to feel that a sale might still be on the cards.

'What happens next?' asks Kate. I think she wants to finish her reading of *Vile Bodies* right here. Certainly, that's what I want to do.

'Nina and Ginger get married.'

'Where?'

'Evelyn doesn't say. Let's assume in the little church on Portman Square just to the north of Oxford Street, the one where the Evelyns got married. Waugh *does* say where Nina and Ginger spend their honeymoon – in the Mediterranean.'

'Same as the Evelyns?'

'The Evelyns actual honeymoon was spent in the Abingdon Arms, Beckley. But they thought of the Mediterranean cruise that they took a few months later as their real honeymoon. Nina and Ginger spend their honeymoon at a golf course near Monte Carlo. That's where the ship that the Evelyns sailed in, the *Stella Polaris*, both started and finished its cruise. So, yes, that is an Evelyns reference, though of course Waugh was not a golfer.'

'I suppose being a golfer was an insult in Waugh's eyes?'

'As an adult he was consistently disparaging about sports.'

Chapter Thirteen stares up at us. Now that too is quite a long chapter, and it's the penultimate one, so I do a very clever thing. I put down the expensive book and pick up the relatively cheap one, as if still comparing the two. I turn to the coloured title page.

'I've got a Chapman and Hall hardback from 1948, printed eighteen years after these first editions, that includes this bright beauty. It's not the same though. The paper in my book is thinner, and the publication details from the title verso can be seen when you're looking at the title page. This edition is made with lovely thick creamy paper. There's a horizontal texture to it that reminds you that what's going on here is ink being laid upon paper.'

'It is lovely.'

Kate has maybe said that for the bookseller's ears. I'm hoping it's bought us some more time. I turn past the dedication to Bryan and Diana Guinness and then pause to observe: 'You see that the book begins with two quotes from *Through the Looking Glass*. Basically about speed and the nature of reality. I told you about those when we were walking along the river at Oxford. On the typescript itself, these quotes aren't there. Instead, Waugh wrote something to the effect that bright young people and others should note that all the characters are wholly imaginary. And that you get far too much publicity already whoever you are.'

'I prefer the Alice quotes.'

Fine, but I'm flicking away from them and towards the start of Chapter Thirteen at a speed that would have impressed the Red

Queen. Before I get there a line of italics catches my eye and stops me dead in my tracks. 'Here's the bit that Diana Guinness read out in the 1983 TV programme about Evelyn. The reading made for a magical piece of television. By then Diana would have been in her seventies. She was still striking to look at, tall, with high cheekbones and big blue eyes that shone with the wisdom of her pedigree. From a Penguin paperback, she read out the exchange that took place between Kitty Blackwater and Fanny Throbbing at the party at Anchorage House.'

I point out the passage on pages 140–1 of this edition, but don't stop speaking: 'Fanny asks Kitty what the young people actually *do* at their parties, and Kitty suggests that they do rather a lot. " 'Oh, to be young again, Kitty,' " read Diana, one-time beauty queen, getting every ounce of pathos out of the line. And after Kitty's response which ends with " '*Si la jeunesse savait*,' " Fanny has the last word when she says, " '*Si la vieillesse pouvait*, Kitty.' " After saying that, Diana takes off her reading glasses, stretches her neck, and, smiling at the interviewer, says, "Marvellous." And it certainly was.' The memory of it moves me. But I feel composed by the time I've flicked on to the beginning of Chapter Thirteen.

'It's Christmas. The newlyweds are staying with Nina's father. Only it's Adam who is accompanying Nina, having passed himself off as Ginger who has been called up by his regiment. Agatha Runcible has died, so there is a note of mourning in the background. In the foreground there is hilarity. Colonel Blount has a copy of the finished film: "A BRAND FROM THE BURNING: A FILM BASED ON THE LIFE OF JOHN WESLEY". The film is shown at the Rectory. It is badly acted, produced for an American audience and hopelessly boring as far as everyone except the Colonel is concerned.'

Evelyn was on top form in the writing of this chapter. I select a passage and read it out aloud in the premises of Peter Harrington, while keeping the place with my index finger so that Kate, if she chooses, can be reading the brightly printed words as well as listening to my quietly spoken ones:

'When the reel came to an end everyone stirred luxuriously.
' "Well, that was very nice," said the Rector's wife, "very nice and instructive."
' "I really must congratulate you, Colonel. A production of absorbing interest. I had no idea Wesley's life was so full of adventure. I see I must read up my Lecky."
' "Too divine, Papa."
' "Thank you so much, sir, I enjoyed that immensely."
' "But bless you, that isn't the end," said the Colonel. "There are four more reels yet." '

Back to paraphrasing. I tell Kate: 'During the second reel, there is a crackle and the projection goes out. In fact, the lighting throughout the Rectory has blown, and there is no possibility of an electrician turning up until after Christmas. Colonel Blount is not at all pleased that his film night has ended so abruptly, but does see that it must be just as disappointing for the Rector and his wife. Adam and Nina and the Colonel return to Doubting Hall for a traditional Christmas, complete with a turkey, carol singing and a bowl of punch. The

Rector does get the last word, however, when he comes round on Christmas Day to announce that he's heard on the wireless in his darkened house that war has been declared.'

That takes us to the last chapter. So I put the £1,250 copy of *Vile Bodies* down on the desk of Peter Harrington and take up the £6,500 tome. 'Only five reels to go,' I say to Kate, whose chin is resting on my shoulder as we both take in the title of the last chapter. 'Happy Ending'.

I paraphrase: 'Everything has turned upside down again. Ginger is at home with Nina. She writes to Adam – who has been called up and posted to the front line – that she is expecting a baby. Luckily, Ginger has made up his mind that the baby is his. Adam tucks the letter into his battledress pocket and stumbles out on to the biggest battlefield in the history of the world. (This is written in 1929, remember, so it's prophetic of what is to happen ten years down the line.) Adam runs into the drunk major, now a general, who gladly acknowledges the money he owes Adam, a sum that's been made worthless by rampant inflation. They head towards the general's staff car where they find a young lady asleep in the corner.'

'It's a Daimler,' Kate observes, reading over my shoulder.

So it is. I realise that Kate is reading this last section as well as me, so I leave her to it. By which I mean I keep reading, but stop reading aloud.

The girl in the Daimler was known as Chastity earlier in the novel, when she was one of Mrs Ape's Angels. But she's been around the block a few times since then, her wings have been well and truly clipped. The general opens a bottle of champagne and she tamely submits to his advances. Adam doesn't embarrass the couple (who are effectively Ginger and Nina). Instead, tired by the wine and the accumulated fatigue of two days fighting, he goes to sleep in the back of the car.

Kate takes the book from my hands in order to read aloud the last line: ' "And presently, like a circling typhoon, the sounds of battle began to return." '

She closes the book. The racing car on the cover looks more like an armoured car on a battlefield now, we agree. One which has just been bombed. From the distress of her silhouette it looks very much like Agatha/Chastity/Nina/She-Evelyn has copped it.

Before we leave the shop, the bookseller asks us if we've ever seen a copy of *Vile Bodies* that's been inscribed by the author. Well, of course we haven't. So he tells us that when Waugh's second novel came out in 1930, Evelyn was writing on the copies that he personally presented the words: '*That to which you refer as your Vile Body, our Lord Jesus Christ died for.*'

It's a curious moment as we leave the shop. We feel – how do we feel? – kind of humbled. But whether by the generosity of the bookseller or by the penmanship of Evelyn neither of us can say.

2

Afternoon Tea at the Ritz. Actually, the only time that was available when I booked this treat a month ago was the 7.30 to 9.00 p.m. slot. So it's a high tea in place of any dinner for us tonight.

Tea starts with champagne. We clink glasses and drink a toast: 'To Fortune – a much-maligned lady.' I wait for someone to arrest us or chuck me out for not wearing the right clothes. It doesn't happen. So I begin to relax.

Gold and yellow are the colours of the Palm Court, a circular dining-room raised a little from the ground floor. The room is decorated in the French style, Louis XVI or some such period. Evelyn used to come here all the time. I mean that in 1930 he used to come here *all the time.* I've made a list of occasions, which I wave in front of Kate's nose.

'20 May 1930: Evelyn had tea here with Inez and Peter Rodd.'

Kate says nothing, just sips her champers and looks like Lady Metroland.

'6 June 1930: Evelyn gave what he reckoned should have been an amusing luncheon party in one of the private dining-rooms here, but there was a horse race that day and everyone chucked. Of course, when Evelyn says "everyone" he really means Teresa "Baby" Jungman, his latest loved one.'

'When did he meet her?'

'Sometime in the Diana Guinness period. Plenty more about Baby in due course. For now let's go forward to 18 June 1930. While at tea here with Nancy Mitford, Evelyn explained to her about sexual shyness in men.'

'What's going on there?' asks my partner.

'Nancy fancied Hamish Erskine, as they got on so well together. I don't know why Evelyn raised the matter of sexual shyness in the way he did though, as Hamish was decidedly gay. Evelyn probably left Nancy thinking she still had a chance with the man, when in fact she didn't.'

'Poor deluded girl.'

'Doubly so. In due course, she married the aforementioned Peter Rodd, a notorious womaniser who made her miserable for years.'

How's the champagne going? It's all I can do not to down the tiny glass in one. But I want this meal to last. I want it to punch its weight. So let me place the glass back down on to the white tablecloth and carry on with my list of Evelyn's assignations at the Ritz Hotel: '21

June: Lunch with Olivia Plunket Greene . . . 7 July: Lunch with Noël
Coward . . . 11 July: Lunch with Richard Plunket Greene . . . 22 July :
Lunch with David Cecil . . . '

'What about lunch with Ronald Firbank?'

'Mmm, Evelyn would have loved that. Alas, Firbank died in
1926, aged forty-one. There are some funny stories told by Firbank's
publisher about lunching at posh restaurants with the author. Alas
again for Evelyn, Grant Richards – who published Alec Waugh's *The
Loom of Youth* – went bust in 1927, otherwise his list would have been
ideal for Evelyn's early books. Much more appropriate than staid old
Chapman and Hall.'

'Tell me one of the lunch stories.'

'Firbank invited Richards to lunch at the Savoy then ordered only
strawberries and Chablis. When the waiter went off, Firbank decided
to change tables. It took a while for the waiter to catch up with them,
by which time Firbank had gone off the idea of Chablis, which he
asked the waiter to give away to someone, and ordered a bottle of the
most fashionable brand of champagne.'

'Don't even *think* of behaving like that here.'

'I couldn't even if I wanted to. You have to be Eton-educated and
the heir to some serious money before you can consider behaving
like that.'

'Did Evelyn lunch here with his father?'

'Chapman and Hall? Course not! But let's get back to July, 1930 . . .
Let's see . . . 23 July: Lunch with Olivia . . . 25 July: Dinner with
Audrey.'

'Who was Audrey?'

'Evelyn's girlfriend.'

'Oh!'

'Well, not really. Audrey had fancied Evelyn in post-Oxford days
when Evelyn had been in love with Olivia. On being rejected by
Evelyn, Audrey had married someone else. But with the end of
Evelyn's marriage clearly his attitude to women had changed. He
would sleep with any willing woman. Certainly, if Audrey wanted to
sleep with him then Evelyn would oblige her, though she still didn't

mean much to him. I'm sorry to say that every time she's mentioned in his diary it's in an offhand manner.'

The very moment that I notice we're out of champagne, a deferential waiter comes round and asks us what kind of tea we'd like. Kate goes for Rooibos, which is a daft choice as it's the caffeine-free stuff that she drinks every day of the year. I go for Darjeeling First Flush, because it's the Champagne of teas, don't you know, from the Himalayan foothills. But just as the waiter bows and turns to go, I change my mind. What I really want is Ritz Royal English, because surely that's the *real* Champagne of teas, the one that Evelyn liked to be seen drinking in here with his upper-class chums. Gosh, I'm feeling f-f-frisky! Is it me sitting here in my smart clothes or Ronald F-F-Firbank, darling?

I need to put over to Kate just how the publication of *Vile Bodies* changed Evelyn's life. It was a best-seller in a way that *Decline and Fall* hadn't been, and it put his name on everyone's lips. The book came out in January 1930 and had to be reprinted twice that month and three times in February. Everybody was reading it! The Bright Young Things was a phenomenon that fascinated society, and Evelyn had caught the essence of gilded youth in his novel. Meanwhile, Evelyn was holed up in Paris at the Guinnesses' house.

'Tell me about that, d-d-darling.' Kate fancies herself as Anthony Blanche, who, according to the pages of *Brideshead Revisited*, was wont to receive the novels of Ronald Firbank, complete with fervid inscriptions penned by the author's own hand. Indeed, it is so very *Brideshead* in here. I suppose I could be persuaded to settle into the more-down-to-earth Charles Ryder's narrator's role. Just as Jeremy Irons, who was pencilled-in to play Sebastian in the Granada serial, eventually played Charles Ryder, the more serious part. But where was I?

'Actually the set-up *chez* Guinness was not so dissimilar to that in Dorset when Henry Lamb and Pansy and the Evelyns had been living in close conjunction, with three of them writing novels. In this case, Evelyn, Nancy Mitford and Bryan Guinness were writing books, while Diana Guinness was entering the final months of her pregnancy.'

'What was He-Evelyn writing?'

'*Labels.*'

'The travel book from the Mediterranean trip with She-Evelyn?'

'By February of 1930 he finally felt he had the distance to approach that material. One of the longest sections is set in Paris, from where they set off by train in February of 1929 and where he was writing the book a year later. Another big chunk is set in Port Said, of all places, where he was forced to spend March of 1929 while She-Evelyn was lying ill in hospital. In *Labels*, Waugh refers to this situation by inventing a couple called Geoffrey and Juliet, whom he travels around with. Juliet is sick in Port Said, Geoffrey is concerned about his sick wife, and Evelyn sticks around for no convincing reason. While Evelyn was stuck there in 1929, Alastair Graham visited from Athens, and that visit is recorded in *Labels*. What Evelyn doesn't mention is that he sent for Alastair in a state of some distress, so worried was he about She-Evelyn's health at the time.'

'What a peculiar book that must be,' says Kate.

'When she was well enough to travel . . . '

'She-Evelyn?'

'Well, Juliet. When Juliet is well enough to travel, the three visit Cairo and the Pyramids together, having rejoined the *Stella Polaris*. But neither Geoffrey nor Juliet contributes much to the chapter and at the end of it Evelyn has himself go his separate way. Interesting timing, because next stop for the Evelyn of *Labels* is to drop in on his friend Alastair in Athens. In reality, She-Evelyn *was* part of that visit. And you can't help wondering what a recovering She-Evelyn would have made of the alternative lifestyle that Alastair and his gay colleagues in the diplomatic service enjoyed in Athens. Not something that He-Evelyn felt comfortable even alluding to, I guess. Hence, no Juliet in the sanitised version of the Athens visit.'

'You don't like *Labels* much, do you?'

'It's desperate. Evelyn tries to be a sophisticated commentator, a bluff man of the world, and it doesn't work. On the way back to England, the *Stella Polaris* stops for a couple of nights in Naples, a day or two in Barcelona, and Waugh tries to make that be enough to come up with enthusiasms about artists, insights about architecture and an overview on European culture. It doesn't even come close to working. And when you know the turmoil that's gone on behind the scenes, both during the trip and in the aftermath of the "honeymoon cruise", you realise why it doesn't work. I'm surprised he wrote it.'

'He would have been contracted to write it, I suppose. He might have had to pay back his free passage otherwise.'

'*And* he needed the money. Or he thought he did when he started to write it. I don't think he yet had any idea that *Vile Bodies* was going to be such a success.'

Tea arrives in curvaceous, long-spouted pots, shortly followed by things to eat. Sandwiches are fitted into the lower tier of a three-layer stand, while pastries are simultaneously placed on the top. What about the middle layer? That must be for the freshly baked scones that are mentioned on the menu, Kate reckons. No doubt these will appear when we've made inroads into the sandwiches. I think I'm getting the hang of this. Kate goes straight for a smoked salmon sandwich. I'll have mine later; in the meantime I plump for ham. Three bites and it's gone but I'm truly enjoying chewing things over in this luxurious room.

'When Evelyn gets back from Paris, having written *Labels*, a marvellous thing happens. He goes back to keeping his diary after a gap of eighteen months. His motivation for beginning to write it again may well come from the fact that *Vile Bodies* has entered its ninth impression and has been so successful that *Decline and Fall* has been reissued too. So at the time Evelyn resumes his diary there are two red-and-black-snakeskin books of his in the shops, one with the crashing-car title page, the other with half a dozen of his line drawings. Proud Evelyn doesn't mention this in his diary. Instead, the diary reveals indirectly how his life has been transformed by his literary success and how he has been hardened by what's happened to him in his personal life.'

'Tell me about it,' says Kate, picking up a tuna-mayonnaise sandwich just as I do the same. 'I want to know all the delicious details.'

'He's based at Underhill, but he eats out all the time. Not just here at the Ritz, but at Quaglino's and the Savoy Grill. He's regularly invited to cocktails at Harold Acton's massive house at 108 Lancaster Gate . . . '

'We haven't been to that one.'

' . . . And, even more often, he's invited by Diana Guinness to Buckingham Street for cocktails, or lunch, or dinner, or a fancy-dress party. In fact, eating on his own at Underhill is such a rare event that he makes a note of it in his diary. Read the entry for 29 May 1930.'

I pass The Thirties Diary over to Kate, but it's been put together from my dismantled paperback copy of the whole *Diaries*, and the print size of the original Penguin is too small for her to read in this artificial light. The Palm Court is lined with mirrors, which almost disguise the fact that there are no windows. But that's fine, I can paraphrase the entries for my companion.

'29 May. The proofs arrive of *Labels*. Evelyn lunches alone at North End Road. But shed no tears for Evelyn all-alone, because that's followed by a delightful cocktail party at Lancaster Gate. He stays there drinking all evening with Harold and his guests. Diana is there but not Bryan. Audrey tells Evelyn that she thinks she's going to have a baby. Evelyn writes that he doesn't care either way really, so long as it's a boy.'

Kate sniffs. 'I don't like this new side of Evelyn that I'm sensing.'

'Two weeks later, he's lunching by invitation at a women's club. Then tea with Olivia and her mother. Cocktails with Sachie Sitwell. Dinner with Richard Plunkett Greene and Elizabeth. After that, there is a small party. Evelyn sleeps with Varda but both of them are too drunk to enjoy themselves.'

'Who was Varda?'

'One of several women who seemed to decide that Evelyn was attractive once he'd written a best-seller.'

'Suddenly Evelyn seems four inches taller!'

'A week later, Diana hosts a huge cocktail party. Before that Evelyn has lunch in the City. After cocktails at Buckingham Street, he goes to dinner at Quaglino's with Audrey. She is not going to have a baby after all, Evelyn reports, so all that was bogus.'

'He's really up himself now,' says Kate, thanking the waiter for neatly slotting the scones into place.

'In May there is a diary entry where Evelyn writes that he went from dinner at the Waldorf with his American publisher to the Savoy Theatre and said, '*I am Evelyn Waugh. Please give me a seat.*' And they did.

'Oh, Evelyn's spoilt now! The success has gone to his head,' says Kate, tucking into a scone, but not before covering it with clotted cream and jam.

' "*I am Evelyn Waugh. Please give me a scone.*" '

Kate doesn't, so I have to reach over for it myself.

'In this period Evelyn is invited to all sorts of places. He has tea with the Prime Minister on the terrace of the House of Commons and pronounces Ramsay MacDonald a nasty and inadequate man. But perhaps he does that because he has already portrayed Walter Outrage, the Labour Prime Minister in *Vile Bodies*, as a sexual obsessive. And you see *Vile Bodies* is such an *excellent* book in so many ways, darling. Simply *everybody* who is *anybody* says so, don't you know.'

' "Adam, how much is this tea costing you," ' says Kate.

' "Seventy-eight pounds, sixteen shillings and twopence," ' I tell her, which is pretty close to the mark.

' "That's all very well, but I can't believe you didn't b-buy me that book," ' pouts Kate, eyelids flickering in time with her stutter. 'The one I r-r-really wanted." '

' "The cheap one" '

' "No, not the cheap one. The one with the combine harvester on the cover. Simply too earth-shattering, darling." '

'In May 1930, Evelyn got an invitation to dine at Marlborough House. That's the London house of the Duke and Duchess of Marlborough, who lived most of the time at Blenheim Palace. Evelyn got placed next to Edith Sitwell. However, he must have been within chatting distance of his hostess as well, because he reports in his diary being taken down a peg by the duchess. She tells him that he has a very mundane mind, just like her husband. According to her, Marlborough would go to any party for which he was sent a printed invitation.'

'That's funny. Good for the duchess.'

'Evelyn also got his pick of weekends in the country, of course.'

'He wasn't stuck at Underhill with Colonel Blount then?'

'Lord, no. Evelyn was hobnobbing full-time with lords and ladies. First there was the Guinness house. Poole Place, near Arundel.'

'He would have got a lift from the station in the Daimler.'

'Then there was a visit to Sezincote. It's a Regency house, in the style of the Brighton Pavilion, only everything is made of Cotswold stone instead of plaster. According to Evelyn, from the house you get the best view in England.'

'This is getting too much. I'll need to have a little respite before going on to the cakes.'

'There's no rush. I don't see anyone else bolting their food.' We look around at our fellow guests. Some are easing scones down their necks, others are chatting before getting stuck into the cakes. *'Just you look at yourselves,'* I'd like to say. But I'm too busy trying to see just how much clotted cream I can get on to this pleasantly warm scone . . . OK, that'll do. Back to work: 'Then Evelyn went to Jim Laurence's house for the weekend.'

'Who he?'

'Don't know. Just another of the million people that our Evelyn found himself in with once he'd cracked it.'

'What was this Jim's place like?'

'A fine old house, very large and well furnished. But there was too much sport that weekend for Evelyn's taste. So he hid in his bedroom most of the time, emerging for meals. By Sunday evening he couldn't stand it any more so fled back to London for dinner with Audrey here at the Ritz.'

'He would have summoned her by phone.'

'That's exactly what he would have done.'

'Did he spend the night with her?'

'The diary says he spent the *evening* with her. He may not have spent the night with her because this comes at the end of the month in which he joined the Savile, a gentlemen's club, which would certainly not have allowed members to sleep with women on its premises.'

'Why would he have joined such a club?'

'Well, I've been there before, and after today's jaunt I can see exactly why he would want to be a member. It's only five minutes walk from the Ritz. Evelyn doesn't want to come out of dinner at the Ritz, or any of his other Mayfair haunts, and have to travel via the tube to Underhill. Sod the Northern Line! Far better to get his agent A. D. Peters and his chum Harold Acton to put his name forward for the Savile. Though both Alec Waugh and Arthur Waugh were also members, so he wouldn't have been short of ways into the club once he'd decided that it was the right place for him. He was only a member for a few years though. He got expelled for kicking a waiter.'

'Oh, that's terrible!'

'I'm not so sure. I got the urge to kick our waiter here when those scones still hadn't arrived and I was beginning to want one.'

'Kicking waiters is a complete no-no. No wonder the Savile turned round and kicked Evelyn out.'

'Yes, but that was a few years down the line. Let's return to the summer of 1930. Back from Jim's place, Evelyn has dinner with Audrey at the Ritz. He dismisses her, and strolls along to the Savile Club for a night's rest in the middle of Mayfair. The next day he gets a taxi to Charing Cross and a train south to the Lambs' house in Coombe Bissett.'

'Henry and Pansy's place?'

'Yes, he was still friends with them. Most of the friends of the Evelyns sided with He-Evelyn when the split came, though the Lambs remained friends with both. Anyway, He-Evelyn had their house as his base for a month or so while they were abroad. First, he had his mother down there for a break from Colonel Blount and Underhill. Next he went over to Forthampton Court, the house of Henry Yorke and his wife. A very agreeable weekend doing nothing, with copious conversation, according to the diary. Back at Coombe Bissett, Audrey was waiting for him and they had four days together. "Audrey left", is all he says at the end of her visit. Christopher Hollis and Douglas Woodruff, Catholic friends, arrived for a boozy weekend. When they departed, Richard and Elizabeth Plunket Greene took their places. After that Olivia arrived, and once Richard and Elizabeth had gone, Olivia and Evelyn had a slightly drunken night talking about religion.'

'No sex?'

'I doubt it. I don't think Olivia had changed her mind about Evelyn just because he was now a big-shot author. Independence of outlook was one of the qualities that Evelyn admired in her. I think their chat about religion was significant, though. Earlier in the summer Waugh had asked Olivia to find a priest to help his conversion to Catholicism. Father D'Arcy had been recommended, and Evelyn had been meeting him regularly in Mayfair as that was where Father D'Arcy was based. So Olivia would have been briefed about how that was going. In fact it was going very well. After all, Alastair and Olivia were Catholics. Baby Jungman was a Catholic. Harold Acton too. Almost every important person in Evelyn's life was Catholic. Except the now despised She-Evelyn.'

'What about Diana Guinness?'

'Oh, she didn't matter for long. They argued at the beginning of July during a weekend house party at Poole Place. According to the diary, on the Saturday, Evelyn and Diana quarrelled at luncheon, then at dinner and also after dinner. On Sunday, Evelyn decided to leave, quarrelled again with Diana, and then did leave.'

'Why all the arguing?'

'Maybe the dispute was about religion. I don't think Diana would have had much time for Evelyn's stance on that. She would have seen it as backward looking. However, according to Evelyn, the bad feeling was caused by something else. Evelyn tried to explain to her at the time, but only obliquely. Decades later, he did explain frankly in a letter. He found he was jealous of Diana enlarging her circle again after having had her baby, much preferring the exclusive intimacy of their time together while she was pregnant. I suspect also that he fancied her, but that Diana made it clear that there was going to be no affair between them.'

'Didn't she fancy Evelyn, star author of *Vile Bodies*?'

'She was about four inches taller than him. And, like Olivia, she knew her own mind. Diana and Bryan Guinness only became important to Evelyn after the break-up with She-Evelyn. He dedicated both *Vile Bodies* and *Labels* to them in return for their hospitality, but after July 1930 he hardly ever saw them again. Though one lasting thing that came from the year-long flaring of friendship was another friendship – with Randolph Churchill. Apparently, Evelyn and Randolph first met at the christening of Diana's baby. But Randolph is a treat that must wait for another time.'

Meanwhile, cakes. I think I can manage three if I eat just half of each. Kate has already eaten a whole cake and is now finished. Or at least she's having another respite. A waiter asks if she wants any more tea. She does. The waiter opens up Kate's teapot and takes a deep sniff. 'Rooibos?' he asks. Kate confirms his suspicions with a smile of complicity, but wouldn't it have been easier just to ask her? God, you just can't get the service these days. I'm certainly not having the waiter sniff my pot. If he tries to do that he'll get a kick up the backside for his trouble. 'Ritz Royal,' I tell him regally. 'You know, the stuff that Evelyn Waugh used to sup.'

The waiter goes on his way, his buttocks winking at me.

'Shall I tell you about Renishaw?'

'What's that?

'Another country house for Evelyn to rest upon his laurels within. The home of the Sitwells. Evelyn describes the house in the diary. The north front is castellated and made of discoloured Derbyshire stone. There is a very dark hall and many other rooms of great beauty, fine tapestry and Italian furniture. There is a finely-laid-out terrace garden with a prospect of undulating hills.'

'The finest view in England?' asks Kate.

'Well, maybe not. From the terrace you can see pit-heads, slag heaps and factory chimneys. Which brings to mind a page in Osbert Sitwell's ludicrous sequence of books, *Left Hand, Right Hand!*'

'Great title.'

'In my opinion it refers to Osbert's habit of wanking with alternate hands from one day to the next. The first volume has got a weird frontispiece showing the author, age three, looking the spitting image of Stewie out of *Family Guy*. And at the back of the book there is a family tree showing that one of Osbert's ancestors was called Sir Sitwell Sitwell.'

'Maybe that was Stewie's real grandfather.'

'Maybe. Anyway, this page I want to tell you about is an appendix to the fourth volume, *Laughter in the Next Room*, and is a letter from Evelyn that was solicited by Osbert. In the letter, an older Evelyn dutifully thinks back to an early visit to Renishaw, and recalls standing next to Osbert's father who looks out from the terrace over the mining community that huddles in the valley. Sitwell senior says nothing at all then suddenly comes up with, "There is *no one* between us and the Locker-Lampsons." '

'Oh, the snob!'

'I wonder if Osbert would have given Evelyn's recollection a place in his book if he had known that in a letter to Nancy Mitford a few years before, Evelyn had written that Osbert was as bad at writing as Charles Ryder was at painting.'

'Nice.'

'OK, back to Evelyn's 1930 visit to Renishaw. Unimpressed by his entertainment, Evelyn summoned Alastair who had returned to this country.'

'Does he use the word "summoned"?'

'He does in this case. Evelyn reckoned the Sitwell household to be full of private jokes and that people were deliberately misrepresented to each other. It was said that Alastair played the violin. In other words, Alastair was completely unmusical. According to Evelyn, Sachie Sitwell liked talking about sex, Osbert was very shy and Edith wholly ignorant. Almost everything was a secret and most of the conversations engineered in prosecution of a private joke. It was unsafe to mention any living author as the Sitwells and their guests were all so vindictive about them.'

'Sounds like fun: meet the Shitwells. I'm surprised to learn that Alastair was still on the scene though.'

'Evelyn was very loyal to his old friends. Just because he had become a literary lion, it didn't mean he was going to drop Alastair or Olivia or Richard. He's been through a lot with his old muckers. The diary stops there for a couple of months. But I know that after ten days at Renishaw, Alastair and Evelyn went on to Pakenham Hall, the country house in Ireland with Pansy connections. Evelyn and Alastair stayed there for ten days, during which period a significant conversation took place in the library over an atlas. Evelyn was talking about a journey he proposed making to China and Japan. Alastair, who was on leave from where he now worked in Cairo, mentioned entertaining two visiting crown princes from Abyssinia. The princes arrived wearing silk capes and bowler hats that they kept on throughout the lunch. Also they didn't speak any of the languages expected of them, so the meal turned into a comic occasion.'

'I wonder if the African princes wore bottle-green bowlers.'

'No doubt it was a chance for someone at Pakenham Hall to try and get on the right side of Evelyn by making a reference to Mr Chatterbox's column. Anyway, Alastair's advice was that Evelyn should go to Abyssinia for the coronation of Haile Selassie, as it was bound to give him lots of material for a new book. And so that's what Evelyn did, dropping his vague plans to go to the Far East. On 29 September, he was received into the Catholic Church. And within a fortnight he was travelling to Africa. A double whammy that Alastair had achieved immediately after Oxford, a few years before, if you remember.'

'He didn't become a Catholic just to repeat a pattern.'

'I think he became a Catholic because – as the diary attests – he'd just had three months enjoying absolutely everything that a secular society had to offer. And it wasn't enough.'

'These cakes at the Ritz not enough? Don't be ridiculous.'

'I think the move towards God was Evelyn's considered response to the break-up of his marriage. I think the vacuum that She-Evelyn's leaving created inside him just had to be filled with something of substance. Writing didn't fill the hole. The luxurious hospitality of the Savile Club and the Ritz didn't fill it. Sex with Audrey didn't fill it. Evelyn came to the conclusion that the only thing that could make him whole again was the Holy Roman Catholic Church.'

'Remind me: is there a Catholic character in *Vile Bodies*?'

'Yes. Father Rothschild, the Jesuit.'

'And is he not mocked along with everyone else?'

'I'd say he gets an easier ride than most characters in the book. Although he is portrayed as being too standoffish, letting Mrs Ape and her ridiculous brand of American Evangelism hog the centre-stage on religious matters. But generally, when he's in conference with the Prime Minister and Lord Metroland, he is the only one able to present some kind of overview of what's happening in the world, and to take a moral position about it.'

Kate can't eat any more. Well, perhaps she can manage a raspberry from my third cake.

'I should add that at the start of *Vile Bodies*, immediately after Adam Fenwick-Symes first appears, Father Rothschild is quick to introduce introduce himself. He doubts whether Adam remembers him, but they met at Oxford five years ago at luncheon with the Dean of Balliol. He tells Adam that he will be interested to see his book when it appears – an autobiography, he understands.'

'Oh, no!' says Kate.

'What?'

'Any moment now you'll be announcing that the Dean of Balliol sleeps with Jesuits.'

I am indeed about to suggest something along these lines, but Kate stops me. She really can't take any more in. Well, maybe she can manage a second raspberry from my third cake. She lifts the berry to her lips, then pauses with it held in front of her mouth: ' *"That to which you refer as your Vile Body, our Lord Jesus Christ died for."* '

The words make more sense than they did a couple of hours ago. Evelyn, when inscribing his book for a friend, would seem to have been apologising for much of what had been printed in his sensationally successful second novel.

The next thing I'm aware of is Kate coolly ordering two more glasses of champagne. Why has she done that? A glass of champagne here costs fifteen quid! I haven't budgeted for an extra thirty pounds.

'That's not all you haven't budgeted for, darling,' says Kate enigmatically. 'Let me tell you about my new correspondent. His name is Sir Richard Heygate.'

'Sir Richard who?'

'Son of Sir John Heygate.'

'I don't follow you.'

'Oh, come on, Preco! All that cake has put you to sleep. Ah, here we are . . .'

The waiter pours Kate a glass, carefully topping it up. Then he does the same for me. The drink tastes incredibly dry after so much sweetness. But I'm sure my taste buds will adjust to the new situation. What is Kate up to?

'Sir Richard Heygate is the son of Evelyn's hated rival and happens to be a friend of a friend of mine.'

'Are you going to persist with this "sir" business.'

'No, that was just to annoy you. Richard knows that we are working on a book about Evelyn Waugh. He thought we might like to put the record straight about his father.'

'When did this happen?'

'Earlier in the week,' says Kate smiling. 'I thought I would save the story for our treat tonight. I even pretended I didn't know who John Heygate was earlier on in the day. Impressed?'

I take hold of my drink, which I haven't recovered the taste for yet. So I confine myself to the merest sip. 'OK, so what has Heygate got to say?'

'Richard points out that over the last few decades his father has been vilified by the literary establishment and labelled as some sort of creepy-crawly. The "basement boy", who lived with his mother, and who toadied around parties, preying on hapless society ladies. Richard reckons the truth was that his father was an Etonian of good family (unlike Waugh), of great personal good looks (unlike Waugh), and a highly amusing companion (unlike Waugh). He was well known and liked by all sorts of bright young things at that time.'

'Unlike Waugh! This is clearly a biased view you've been fed. But please do go on with it.'

'Richard, who writes charming e-mails, admits that his father did become very friendly with the two Evelyns and that they used to drive around southern England together as a threesome, roughing it in working-class pubs.'

'I suppose he means back in 1928, either side of the Evelyns' marriage.'

'Why She-Evelyn ever married Waugh, remains a complete mystery to Richard. But by his account she had a taste for the bizarre. She soon realised what a bore He-Evelyn was in the flesh, however good a writer he was. The trouble came to the boil when He-Evelyn went off to write *Vile Bodies* after the cruise in 1929.'

'Yes, well we know *that*.'

'Just be content to do some listening for a change.'

'I'm trying.'

'According to Richard, He-Evelyn left John Heygate in London to look after She-Evelyn, whom he describes as a highly sexed, not-particularly-satisfied young wife. His father used to tell Richard that She-Evelyn complained to him that Evelyn was "homosexual and very bad in bed". One thing led to another and after various illicit meetings in nightclubs the affair came to light. There was a messy divorce and Richard's father was given the sack from his job as a news reader at the BBC by the puritan regime there.'

' "Evelyn was homosexual and bad in bed." Have you followed that up?'

'I asked Richard about the gay thing, pointing out that Evelyn's affairs with men at Oxford were well documented, but that as far as we were aware, He-Evelyn's sexual attachments after that were to women.'

'And what did Heygate say?'

'Nothing about that. And nor did Richard have anything to add when I asked him to expand on the "bad in bed" quote.'

'Not much use to me then. In Selina Hastings's book she uses that very phrase, crediting it to She-Evelyn in a conversation she had with a woman friend about He-Evelyn. Bad in bed, indeed. It's probably a misquote. She-Evelyn was probably trying to communicate that He-Evelyn used to joke that he liked a pint of Badger in bed before getting down to it.'

'LISTEN,' says Kate, perhaps spotting that I'm losing patience with her source of new information. 'John Heygate married Evelyn Gardner in August of 1930, you didn't mention that in your summary this evening. In other words, they married just before He-Evelyn made a combined dash for the Catholic Church and darkest Africa.'

I have to admit that I hadn't noticed that conjunction. Kate continues gleefully: 'I looked up August 1930 in Waugh's *Diaries*. As you were saying, Evelyn spent most of the month in Pansy and Henry's house in Coombe Bissett. But I think the marriage must have taken place towards the end of the month, because in Selina Hastings's book . . . '

'Do you have your own copy, then?'

'Of course. I got it from a charity shop in Southend for two quid. I told you that, but I expect you weren't listening.'

I'm listening now.

'In that stout volume there is just a tiny bit about the second wedding. Selina Hastings describes how the day before John Heygate and Evelyn Gardner got married Evelyn was supposed to be at Chapman and Hall's premises in Henrietta Street for an important luncheon given for Amy Johnson, the world-famous flyer, who was the subject of a new book. Evelyn, the firm's star author, didn't turn up for the party and didn't tell anyone where he was.'

'Looks as if he might have been sulking.'

'Looks as if his whole conduct around this time was affected by feelings of jealousy and anger. Anyway, Richard's main point seems to be that She-Evelyn had a happier time of it with his father than with He-Evelyn. She was encouraged in her own creative writing and was able to join in with her partner's career far more than she would have been as Evelyn's other half.'

'What did he mean by that?'

'In 1930, that same year you've been going on about all night from a strictly Evelyn Waugh perspective, John Heygate published a novel of his own.'

'Did he?'

'It's called *Decent Fellows*.'

'Not *Vile Bodies*?'

"*Decent Fellows,*' says Kate, clapping her hands.

'Don't tell me it can hold a candle to *Vile Bodies*. What the hell is it about?'

'It's a first novel and it's about John Heygate's time at Eton,' says Kate, dipping a hand into her bag and coming out with a well-creased fawn paperback. This only arrived yesterday. I've just about managed to read the first couple of chapters.'

I tug it out of her hands. The front cover features the title in a red box high up on the page. The back cover has a bigger red box taking up the whole page, bar a margin, in which are the words: 'JOHN HEYGATE, the author of this book, is an Old Etonian, and is now in the middle twenties.'

Fascinated, I turn the book over again. Under title and author, in the middle of the front cover, in very large print, is: PRICE 3ˢ NETT. It prompts me to ask: 'How much did you have to pay for this?'

Kate shrugs. 'The same as a glass of champagne sets you back here. The same as you paid for your early edition of *Decline and Fall*.'

At the bottom of the front cover are details of the publisher. Victor Gollancz is mentioned. But the actual imprint of the publishing house is Mundanus. The word is written with a ludicrously extended vertical line for the 'd'. This gives emphasis to the part of the word that follows the long ascender, namely: 'anus'. When I point this out to Kate, she tells me that I'm only jealous on Evelyn's behalf.

'But Evelyn's book was printed many times in 1930 and became a runaway best-seller. The reason you had to fork out fifteen quid for this creased paperback is because there was only one edition of maybe two thousand copies.'

'Actually, I think the book did rather well. Richard mentions a figure of fifty thousand books sold.'

Interesting that it's a paperback first edition. There's been a thing reported in the press just this week about how Picador are only going to publish paperback first editions of literary novels from now on. Hardbacks don't sell enough to justify their existence – all they do is flatter authors' egos. A similar argument is made on page 1 of this book, published all these years ago. Nothing much changes, then.

I turn to page 5, and there is the author's note. 'Every character in this book is drawn from life.' Such a statement could appear quite correctly at the start of *Vile Bodies*. Heygate goes on: 'I have, however, taken such anatomical liberties with all my subjects, dividing and joining at pleasure, that a reconstitution and comparison with the originals must prove an entirely unprofitable, if pleasurable, exercise.' Yes, that sentiment too, and the style, could almost have come from Waugh's pen. It prompts me to tell Kate that I may read the book.

'I've got a better idea,' says Kate, finishing her champagne. 'Why don't you carry on with Evelyn's story, leaving me to follow up on the Heygate side of things.'

'Any reason for suggesting that?'

'I think Richard will communicate more fully with me than you. You're too obviously on Waugh's side. Whereas Richard and I are as one in thinking that Evelyn could at times be a BORE, a CREEP and a SNOB.'

I hate to hear Evelyn being put down in that way. Strange – why should I care?

'The truth is, Richard and I are already enjoying a bit of a laugh.'

I'm not sure what to say. Kate may pick up on my sense of unease, because she leans towards me and tells me that today's been really special. The walk from Piccadilly to Pastmaster House, then over to Buckingham Street, then across town to the bookshop and now back here to the Ritz. She concludes: 'But I've just been following in your footsteps. I want a slice of the action.'

There is a soupçon left in my champagne glass. I pour half of it into Kate's. Barely enough to wet the top of her tongue, but it's the symbol that counts.

'To the Party Without End,' toasts Kate.

As I swallow the last drop from my glass, I get a flash of Evelyn, happily beavering away at Beckley, on the receiving end of a certain communication from She-Evelyn. Could it be that I've painted myself into a *Vile Bodies* corner?

'To the Party Without End,' I concur, as I place my empty glass on the table.

A week later, Kate and I meet again in Central London. We walk along the Strand and enter the Savoy Grill. Perhaps I'm getting blasé about chandeliers, because 'understated chic' is how I'd describe the interior. Once we have ordered our braised turbot, I tell Kate about my tour of Madresfield, the hundred-and-twenty-room country house in Worcestershire where Evelyn stayed as the guest of Lady Mary and Lady Dorothy Lygon, Blondie and Poll respectively. The chapel at Madresfield was eventually transferred wholesale to the pages of *Brideshead Revisited*, but it was while staying at Madresfield in 1931 and 1932, following his return from Africa, that Waugh wrote much of *Black Mischief*. Perhaps I go on a bit about darkest Africa and brightest Madresfield. In any case, Kate eventually says: 'Never mind all that. Aren't you going to ask how I'm getting on with *my* research?'

'How are your Basement Boy studies coming along, Blondie?'

'Sir Richard had told me that *Agents and Patients* contains a portrait of She-Evelyn and John Heygate as man and wife.'

'*Agents and Patients?*'

'An early novel by Anthony Powell. Well, his fourth, published in 1936. I bought it via the web, turned to the opening page, and in the first sentence came across the name Maltravers. Does that ring any bells?'

'Should it?'

'It's only the name of Margot Beste-Chetwynde's second husband in *Decline and Fall* and *Vile Bodies!*'

'Hang on, she married Lord Metroland.'

'Lord Metroland is his *title*. But Maltravers is his surname,' says Kate, flashing a superior smile. 'So by giving his main character the name Maltravers, Powell was subtly signalling who he really was – the second husband of someone who can be closely associated with Evelyn Gardner. John Heygate, no less.'

'An Evelyn Waugh trick that.'

'Well, you did say that Powell, when he was a junior editor, had been read aloud by Waugh the beginning of *Decline and Fall*. He would have known that book well and he obviously admired it.'

'True.'

'Near the beginning of *Agents and Patients*, Maltravers drives to his flat. He travels north from Bloomsbury then passes a statue of someone called Sir Hugh Myddleton before turning off down a lane that leads to a wide treeless square. I looked up the statue and discovered that it's on Islington Green. Which makes sense if the flat that Maltravers lives in with his wife is the one in Canonbury Square.'

'Hey, this is interesting! So you have learned a few tricks by trotting along after me.'

Kate sips her wine, then continues in as composed a way as before. 'Powell describes the flat. It contains a wide sofa and two chromium-plated chairs. The seats and tables are piled high with typescripts and records. I was looking out for any mention of furnishings inherited from the Evelyns' marriage but couldn't detect any. He's been superseded. Maltravers's wife – Sarah – is at home with their two cats. The Maltraverses' relationship is portrayed as combative. He's trying to type, while she tells him she's going out that night. He tries to express indifference as to her movements. In fact the whole time he's in the flat he's distinctly offhand with her. When he finds out that she's going out with someone called Nipper, he forbids her to go, but it's obvious that she will do as she likes. Then, while she's running a bath, he's asking her if there's any food in the house. She has to keep turning off the taps in order to hear his nagging, selfish questions. They argue again about whose turn it is to go out in the evening. In the end she tells him to leave her in peace to have her bath. He slams the door on the way out of the building.'

'A feisty relationship.'

'Very different from the relationship between the Evelyns, is what I thought.'

'I'm trying to remember what that earlier relationship was like . . . Waugh destroyed his diary covering the time they were together.

But Harold Acton and Cyril Connolly, who visited the Canonbury Square flat when the Evelyns were a couple, reported experiencing a "nursery" atmosphere. This Heygate set-up seems more grown-up, for all the bickering.'

Kate agrees: 'There's the suggestion that theirs is an open relationship, with both of them taking other lovers. This is confirmed later in the book, though in 1936 that kind of morality has to be hinted at rather than overtly stated.'

'What is the book about?'

'Paul Pennyfeather.'

'How do you mean?' I ask, conscious that she's already done this to me once, with the help of *Our Man in Havana*.

'A character called Blore-Smith, just down from Oxford, is taken in hand by Maltravers and his wily associate.'

'Sarah?'

'No, she isn't really central to the story. Maltravers is in the experimental film business and Blore-Smith agrees to finance his activities. In return, Blore-Smith gets to experience a bit of the lifestyle that Maltravers and his sophisticated set take for granted. Travel, sex, drugs, adventure. Each dose of which leaves poor Blore-Smith anxious to get back to a quiet life.'

'And does he?'

'At the end of the book, Blore-Smith is back at home, his only remaining link to the high life being an invite to spend summer in a little house near St Tropez, the invite being from someone who is . . . *obviously gay, darling!*'

'Poor old Blore-Smith, presuming he's straight.'

'Straight-laced and boring. There's another scene set at the Maltravers flat that is very revealing. Blore-Smith is visiting, so you see the place from his perspective as well as the narrator's. What leapt out at me was the connection with the scenes concerning Charles Ryder early on in *Brideshead*. Just as, after visiting Sebastian's idiosyncratic rooms at Christ Church, Charles feels ashamed of his own conventional student tastes, so when Blore-Smith arrives at the Maltravers flat he feels ashamed of the Medici prints on the wall of his own flat, which is in Belgravia. Blore-Smith decides there and then that when he gets home he'll move his copy of Van Gogh's *Sunflowers* out of sight, and he won't ever spend another evening reading *Vision and Design*.

'Is that by Roger Fry?'

'Yes,' says Kate. '*Vision and Design*, *Sunflowers* and the Medici Press are all specifically mentioned in connection with Charles Ryder before his visit to Meadow Buildings, Christ Church.'

'Are they?' I say doubtfully.

'I did check, darling! *Brideshead* is a much later book. Waugh must have read *Agents and Patients* and either consciously or subconsciously made use of its motifs to suggest the innocent young man.'

I consider this: 'Waugh was an admirer of Anthony Powell's books, even though Powell remained a close friend of Heygate. Actually, I'm glad that the initial impetus to do away with *Sunflowers* came from Powell and not Waugh. Yes, I'm much more comfortable with that perspective.' But I'm in danger of missing the main point here. 'It's fascinating that Powell stole from *Decline and Fall* for some of the elements in *Agents and Patients*, and that Waugh returned the compliment when writing *Brideshead*.'

Kate is itching to get back to the scene at the fictional Canonbury Square. I tell her to go for it.

'OK, so Powell's She-Heygate, Sarah, turns up at the flat wearing green leathers. Her hair is cut short and her collar turned up. I bet she looked chic and cool. She's been out with Nipper, the racing-car driver, who developed a headache that evening, which is the reason she's home early . . . I wouldn't have made much of that, but Richard told me in an e-mail that She-Evelyn was partial to "car mechanics with grimy fingernails". "Rough trade" as he also put it.'

'I wonder if that is why Sarah's mysterious friend is called Nipper. Perhaps he likes to dig his dirty fingernails into her pure white flesh. Maybe she likes him to dig his dirty fingernails into her bubble bottom . . .'

'Don't get carried away,' urges Kate. 'Sarah's not a one-dimensional girl. She goes off to her room and can be heard typing. Meanwhile, in the lounge, Maltravers begins to go through with Blore-Smith the film script he's working on. But soon Maltravers realises he's hungry, and calls for Sarah to make them bacon and eggs.'

The bacon and eggs fight against the turbot that I'm consuming. But I mustn't worry about that, I must just listen to my colleague.

'Sarah's about to go to sleep, but she's obviously used to complying with such demands for food. Later, while they're all eating, Blore-Smith asks Sarah what she's writing. Maltravers answers for his wife, saying that it's a novel and that he's the hero in it. Now as you told me, She-Evelyn was writing a novel of her own when He-Evelyn was writing *Decline and Fall*. I think it's interesting to learn that she was still trying to write novels during her time with Heygate.'

'Mmm.'

'Sarah denies that Maltravers is the hero, stating that Maltravers is no longer even in the book as he turned out to be too boring a character. Then she admits that Maltravers *is* mentioned right at the end of her book, but only as a half-mad tramp who comes into a public house and frightens some commercial travellers.'

'So there's some subtle putting-down going on?'

'I'd say so. Maltravers complains about the bacon and says that Sarah must learn to cook better. Then, spontaneous as ever, he marches off to bed, leaving Sarah and Blore-Smith alone together. She tells him that she is the motoring correspondent for *Mode* magazine and asks if Blore-Smith is interested in cars. He's not, but – limply, he really is pathetic – he supposes *she* must be. She then delivers the ice-cool line: "*I go down on my knees to them,*" which takes her visitor aback. "To cars?" he asks. "They're my religion," she explains. She offers to take him out in her car sometime. Indeed, he must phone her up to arrange this, she tells him. Which would be quite forward behaviour for a young woman in those days. Anyway, Blore-Smith quickly makes a getaway from the flat. Sarah is altogether too much for him.'

' "*I go down on my knees to them,*" ' I say, trying to get the same innuendo that Kate managed to extract from the line.

'Ha! – you go down on your knees to He-Evelyn, boy!'

'I go down on my knees to She-Evelyn, now that I know a bit more about her.'

Kate uses her napkin to wipe her lips, then tells me: 'After finishing with *Agents and Patients*, I went back to Richard's e-mail, and as he mentions the Powell autobiography, I got a copy of that as well. At least I got the volume that deals with the late twenties and early thirties. There's an anecdote about Waugh in there that I know you'll like.'

'Oh yes?'

'According to Anthony Powell, when the Evelyns were together, there was a musical called *Blackbirds* that was very successful in the West End, with the coloured cast getting invited everywhere. So much so that when issuing an invite to a dinner party that season, He-Evelyn would write on the card: "It's not a proper party. There won't be a black man there." '

That is quite funny.

'Powell's autobiography makes it clear that he was pally with John Heygate for many years. And at the time of writing, in the late seventies, he was still very friendly with She-Evelyn, who by then had settled down with her third husband. Powell emphasises that she was, and always had been, a woman of warmth and charm. Though I have to say that I found this book a bit lacking in both these qualities.'

'I don't think Auberon Waugh was trying to be complimentary when he described Powell's writing as being like knitting.'

'However, there's another lively anecdote dating from just before the Evelyns split, in June of 1929. Waugh was writing at the Abingdon Arms. Powell was with Heygate, She-Evelyn and a few others at a dinner party. However, the night before, Heygate had been at a party on the boat that was permanently moored at Charing Cross. You know, that regular venue for the parties of Bright Young Things.'

'Yes, the *Friendship*.'

'Well, Heygate had stayed on the boat, partying until dawn. The result was that at the evening dinner party later the same day he just couldn't keep his eyes open. And he went to sleep in between courses.'

'Actually fell sleep at the table?'

'According to Powell, it was quite an affecting sight.'

'Maybe that's when She-Evelyn fell in love with him.' Which gives me an idea. I let my forehead rest on the cloth covering our table.

'Oh, are you exhausted, you poor darling?' says Kate. 'Well, don't think I'm going to order you a pudding.'

'Tell me, I've got to know.' My voice sounds strange to my ears, bouncing up from the tabletop. 'Are you sleeping with Richard Heygate?'

'Well, of course I am, darling,' says Kate. I have a hunch she's smiling more brightly than she has smiled all night. 'I'm lying on my back for this book of yours. I know that you need a surrogate for John Heygate.'

Forehead pressing against tabletop, I speak once more into the white linen: 'No I don't.'

'Yes, you do. You need to feel He-Evelyn's sense of outrage at the loss of "his" woman. Just as you needed to feel his self-satisfaction when he got to stay at Madresfield. Now pull yourself together and soldier on, just like He-Evelyn had to.'

This is going quite well, so I remain with my head on the table and await further developments.

'*McLaren dog, McLaren dog, where have you been?*' chants Kate.

I can't help wondering if our fellow diners are paying any attention to the goings on at our table.

' *"I've been to Madders to sleep with Evleen,"* ' she answers on my behalf.

'*McLaren dog, McLaren dog, what did you do there?*'

' *"I bit off his penis and pubic hair."* '

I'm up like a jack-in-the-box to refute these scandalous lies. Besides I've no intention of falling asleep at the Savoy Grill. '*It's not a proper party,*' I find myself saying in a sarcastic voice to Kate. '*There's not a Heygate here.*'

THE AMAZON JUNGLE

Du Côté de Chez Cooper

It's Saturday morning and I've made it from Essex to Victoria in time to catch my train to Bognor Regis. Why am I travelling to the resort on the South Coast of England? In a roundabout way because Evelyn Waugh went on the journey of his life – a four-month trip to the heart of the Amazon jungle – in the winter of 1932–3. I'm hoping my own journey will begin to make sense by about lunchtime.

I'm alone because Kate has hatched some plot of her own for this weekend. Maybe that's for the best, since Evelyn was on his own as he boarded the ship at Tilbury in Essex. He was still very chummy with the girls at Madresfield; he'd made a new friend in the form of the actress Diana Cooper; he was in the midst of an affair with a glamorous older woman, Hazel Lavery. But as he boarded the boat he felt all alone because Baby Jungman wasn't with him. She'd accompanied Evelyn as far as the docks though, and given him a gold St Christopher on a chain, a gift that had deeply moved him. Then Baby had been driven off in her mother's car for lunch in London, leaving Evelyn with a heart of lead, according to his diary.

Three questions come to mind as my train pulls out of Victoria. One: Were things any different for him as he embarked on this expedition than two years before when he set sail for East Africa? He still loved Baby. He was still a Roman Catholic. He was still a well-respected author who was yet to get over the failure of his marriage to She-Evelyn. So things were effectively the same.

Second question: Why was he making such an ambitious journey? Well, because since finishing *Black Mischief* he'd been enjoying himself in Venice, Madresfield and London, but felt he needed a break from such an exhausting social life.

Third question: Why British Guiana? Answer: For no good reason that I can make out. Perhaps simply because he knew he would be a million miles out of his home territory. He had the vague intention of penetrating to the interior of the continent but was making no specific arrangements until he arrived in Georgetown and met a few locals. Christ, what a plan!

He resumed his diary for the trip, then later wrote that up as a travel book called *Ninety-two Days*. I bought a second-hand Penguin copy, but in the end I had to spend £30 on an original hardback because of the superior map and the twenty-odd photographs that decorate the book. The photographs aren't any good – Evelyn admits as much. But the map is something I keep going back to. As I open it out on to the table in this more or less empty carriage, I feel sure it will help me get stuck into Waugh's ninety-two days in South America.

The ninety-two days of the title don't include the length of the ocean voyage. He boarded ship on 4 December and arrived in Georgetown on 22 December. What did he do during the eighteen long days at sea? Well, the bar was open. And apparently he did a lot of reading about the place he was visiting. And he had his St Christopher to rub between finger and thumb when the urge came, thinking of Baby or She-Evelyn. So I dare say the days passed.

Neither do the ninety-two days include the time spent in George-town, where he stayed alone until 3 January. Evelyn had a note of introduction to a Jesuit missionary who lived on the Takutu River, hundreds of miles inland. Without any real thought, he made paying a visit to the Jesuit his goal. With that established, Evelyn was advised to go and see a Mr Haynes who was the commissioner of the relevant district and who happened to be in Georgetown for Christmas. Mr Haynes (Mr Bain in *Ninety-two Days*) is described as middle-aged and emaciated, a Creole with some Indian blood. By Haynes's reckoning (Waugh dryly reported), Rupununi was the most beautiful place in the world and anyone with a gift for expression should be able to make a book about it. He was returning to the jungle in a day or two via a cattle trail and was sending a boat of stores by river. Evelyn was invited to take advantage of the boat for his own stores and travel with Mr

Haynes. Evelyn readily agreed to this and ordered essentials. First, a hammock, mosquito net and blanket. Second, flour, sugar, corned beef, potatoes and bottles of rum. Facing the jungle was one thing, facing the jungle without his daily quota of alcohol quite another.

The first leg of the journey was by train along the coast to New Amsterdam. Mr Bain (I've switched my attention from the diary to the travel book) never stopped talking and by this time Evelyn had realised that his companion for the next week or so was half cracked. The second leg of the journey was a lazy uneventful day in a paddle steamer up the Berbice River being served gin-swizzles at regular intervals. Before the third leg, Evelyn got a chance to sleep in a hammock. But as Bain was troubled with asthma for much of the night and there were two others sleeping in the same draughty room, and as all four hammocks were attached to the same frame-work, so that one body moving had consequences for all four, Evelyn got little sleep.

The next stage was to be negotiated on horseback. Evelyn

THE WRITER AT TAKUTU RIVER.

DISCARD

Ninety-two Days

*The Account of a Tropical Journey
Through British Guiana and Part
of Brazil • • • By* EVELYN WAUGH

FARRAR & RINEHART, INC.
Publishers   *New York*

observes in passing that he had never yet approached a new horse without a sinking of his self-esteem. Mr Bain and a black man named Yetto had to give Evelyn advice ('Loosen de reins!') as to how to ride his horse, as these Amazonian horses ('Loosen de reins!') were not like Madresfield horses. It took them six days, at fifteen miles a day, to reach the ranch at Kurupukari. In so doing they only passed one other human being. Evelyn describes the forest, known locally as bush, as a relentless wall of tree-trunks through which a path as wide as an English lane had been cut. The life was all confined to the treetops, hundreds of feet up, leaving Evelyn with nothing to look at on the forest floor. But if there was little to see there was plenty to hear. From sunset to dawn, the eleven hours or so that were spent in their hammocks, the bush was alive with sounds. One day Mr Bain pointed out a particularly interesting noise – that of the six o'clock beetle. It was so named because it always made its distinctive noise at exactly six o'clock. 'But it's now a quarter past four,' protested Evelyn. 'Yes, that is what is so interesting,' said Bain. Waugh reports dryly that in the course of his expedition he heard the six o'clock beetle at every hour of the day and night.

Kurupukari was marked large on the map, and had figured constantly in Mr Bain's conversation for a week. When they got there it consisted of a single wooden house standing in a clearing on a slight hill. In a very different way, the first sight of Kurupukari must have been like Charles Ryder's first view of Brideshead – astonishing.

Unhappy news for Mr Bain and Evelyn both at bountiful Kurupukari: the boat with the stores had not arrived. Mr Bain, who had previously been unreasonably confident of the welfare of their stores, immediately became deeply depressed at the prospect of never seeing said stores again. For days there was no sign of the boat and the inhabitants of Kurupukari were reduced to a basic diet of farine and tasso, respectively a grain and a meat product, both of which staples of the Indian cuisine Evelyn had contempt for. Evelyn conceived that it just might be possible for a newcomer to stomach a little farine with a rich aromatic stew; or a little tasso with plenty of fresh vegetables and bread. Unhappily, the food of the savannah was farine and tasso AND NOTHING ELSE. Never mind, Evelyn, you'll soon be back at the Ritz. And as a joke you could suggest a Party Without End for Buckingham Street in which farine and tasso would be served on a silver platter until the last guest keeled over from food frustration.

On the fifth day the boat arrived with the stores intact. Evelyn was able to make plans for the next stage of his journey. He was going on alone – or at least without Mr Bain's companionship. Mr Bain's parting gift was to advise Evelyn, when he eventually got to the Jesuit's mission at Bon Success, to go on by canoe to a town called Boa Vista. Mr Bain painted a very splendid picture of the town. He knew it only by repute, but by the end of his description, Evelyn felt that it was a singularly fortunate man who ever made it to Boa Vista. As the alert reader, you feel like saying, 'For Boa Vista, think Kuru-pukari, Evelyn.' But that would be prejudging the issue. Let's be as patient and as optimistic as brave Evelyn was. Let's just wait and see what Boa Vista has in store for us all.

I get out of the train at Bognor Regis and make my way down to the shore. There I turn right and am walking west towards the first of what I might as well call my base camps for today. The sun is high in the sky over the sea to my left. I've got neither sun-block nor hat to deal with the rays of the sun. But what I do have to reduce their impact is knowledge of what Evelyn had to put up with over the next few weeks of his ninety-two days. That should put my own discomfort into perspective.

For the next stretch of the journey, Evelyn was accompanied by a team of three, two of whom were of African extraction. Most of the individuals whom Evelyn writes about in *Ninety-two Days* are either white or black or half-caste. Evelyn didn't have much time for Indians and they seem to have kept their distance from him. An observation that he makes early on in the book is that the Indians are a solitary people and that it takes several hours heavy drinking to arouse any social interests in them. I'd have thought that qualified them to be bosom buddies of Evelyn, but apparently not.

God, I'm hot. And although the pack on my back is heavy, it doesn't include the weight of any water. Just books. Never mind I can carry on quite happily, providing I can tag along beside Evelyn's party. They were out of the jungle and in the savannah by this stage. The heat was intense, glaring up off the earth so that Evelyn's face was skinned under the shade of a broad-brimmed hat. Exhaustion was infectious, Evelyn felt it seeping up from the stumbling horse. Constant urging was necessary to keep it at a trot. At five o'clock one afternoon, Evelyn arrived ahead of the others at the ranch of a man named Christie. It was a building of dilapidated thatch, open on all sides, with a plank floor raised a couple of feet from the earth. Christie, a negro with white moustache and white woolly head, was sipping cold water from the spout of a teapot. This exotic individual told Evelyn that he had been expecting him, that he'd been warned in a vision of his approach. More practically, he pointed out the footpath that led to the water hole. Evelyn and the horse drank their fill. Evelyn sluiced down the horse and turned him into the corral. Then he slung his hammock under a shelter near Mr Christie's house and fell asleep for the two hours that passed before the rest of Team Evelyn arrived. Their arrival meant Evelyn could change clothes, have a bath and a mug of rum. Evelyn drank a lot of rum that evening as he listened to Christie's quasi-religious, mystical patter. The night had a profound effect on Evelyn. The Mr Christie of *Ninety-two Days* is translated into Mr MacMaster for *The Man Who Liked Dickens*, and he reprises the sinister role under the name of Mr Todd in *A Handful of Dust*. Which is what all this is coming to. But it's important to get there via ninety-two days in the Amazon. And, as I hope to show, via Bognor Regis.

More days in the saddle followed, more nights in the hammock. Evelyn was bitten by countless small flies. He found a tick on his body, with its head buried deep in his flesh and with its abdomen swollen to the size of a pea. Evelyn reckoned that in the weeks from leaving Kurupukari until some time after his return to Georgetown there was not a two-inch square of his body that was not itching at some moment of the day or night.

At the next ranch, Evelyn was introduced to the only mechanical vehicle for thousands of miles around. Leaving the horses behind, Evelyn's party was given a lift in the vehicle to Bon Success, covering the twenty miles in a third of the time it would have taken by horse. From Bon Success they were then driven the last two miles to his arbitrarily chosen first destination, the Jesuit Mission of St Ignatius, where Evelyn was to spend ten days as the guest of Father Mather. Evelyn paid off his team and set about the serious business of recovering from his long hard journey on the road to nowhere.

Father Mather lived alone, though there was a servant boy and pets – a misanthropic bush turkey, a mischievous mocking bird and a giant toad. The Jesuit would conduct mass each day in the little church where sometimes half a dozen Indian boys would appear. Then Father Mather would go off to his workshop and Evelyn would sit and read Dickens in a long chair in the windswept gallery. After supper they smoked and talked about Guiana or England, while Father Mather sorted out photographs or insects or feathers. During those evenings, Evelyn learned to smoke the local tobacco and wrote one letter from St Ignatius that is published. It was to Diana Cooper and is dated 28 January 1933. That is, day twenty-five of the ninety-two. Evelyn reports that he has stayed with a black man who in a vision saw the Love of God and pronounced it to be spherical in shape and slightly larger than a football. He goes on to say that he is presently staying with a priest who has never had a visitor before and couldn't sleep for the first three nights of Evelyn's visit out of sheer excitement.

I like the fact that the only letter I know about that was written from St Ignatius was to Diana Cooper. This is because I am now just a stone's throw from her holiday house, which was lent to Evelyn in October 1933 so that he could write up *Ninety-two Days*. Evelyn went with Baby Jungman to see a play starring Diana Cooper in April of 1932, just a few months before Evelyn went off on his South American trip. Waugh didn't like the play much, but very much enjoyed the looks and wit of Diana when he was introduced to her. Diana, at thirty-nine, was eleven years older than Evelyn, happily married, and a widely adored actress. But she loved being with Evelyn. At some deep level they satisfied one another's needs.

So let's find the building that kind of justifies today's exertions. It's on Barrack Lane, which I should be able to access from the pebble beach. OK, this is the right street. I'm looking for West House, which is 151 Barrack Lane and should be close to the shore. Here is number 151. I consult the painting by Rex Whistler that is reproduced in *Mr Wu and Mrs Stitch*, a clumsily titled hardback containing the correspondence between Evelyn Waugh and Diana Cooper. Yes, this would seem to be the house, a substantial two-storey white-walled dwelling. Aspects of the frontage have changed, but there is a Gothic window near the front door that is exactly the same as in the painting. And the general set-up is consistent. This is the house, I reckon. Still, I might as well find out for sure.

I walk up the drive and press the bell. To my left is a bow window; inside, on the ledge of the alcove, I can see a number of books on nature and painting. That bodes well for my being able to strike up a conversation with the present owners. What in fact am I going to say? Am I going to ask if I can see what Evelyn Waugh refers to as 'the deserted nurseries', where he sat down and wrote his travel book in just over a month? Evelyn might as well have called the book *Thirty-two Days*, that being about the length of time he spent in this house writing it. But that won't do for an opening remark to whoever lives here now . . . The absence of an answer to my ringing almost comes as a relief.

I walk past the part of the ground floor that has a roofed area outside it, creating an extended porch, as it were. But I'm not comfortable going round the back of the house uninvited. Besides, what am I going to achieve by doing so? I retrace my footsteps and I sit down with my back against the substantial wall that separates what was West House from the quiet road that leads to the beach.

The prospect of a chat that I wasn't really looking forward to has distracted me from something pretty obvious. I'm hungry. Alas, I have only got the equivalent of farine and tasso in my bag, meaning a scotch egg. It tastes like cardboard, as I knew it would. I also have an orange and a banana. No doubt Evelyn ate some fruit in the jungle, indeed he does mention bananas and mangoes. Anyway, let's leave him resting up at Father Mather's, reading and map-tracing to pass the time, and concentrate on what he subsequently did *here*, in the holiday house at Bognor Regis.

The first letter to Diana at her main home in London, in October 1933, tells her that he was a little drunk when he boarded the train at Victoria and so felt low on arrival in Bognor. The housekeeper was welcoming and kind but Evelyn still felt low. The reason for this is that he had been rejected again by Baby. He'd found out that there was a chance that the Catholic Church might annul his marriage to She-Evelyn. Therefore, he'd proposed to Baby, only to be turned down. So, yes, he was low. But Evelyn intended to put a stop to that. He was in Bognor to do a job of work.

The next letter tells Diana that things are a little better. That is, the book has begun – five hundred words the first day, fifteen hundred the second day, and two thousand so far on the day of writing the new letter. Evelyn is encouraged by the fact that he is getting a little interested in his travel book. Not much, but when he is not writing he thinks of it sometimes instead of never. He reports that he's found a fairly empty place called Pagham, with some mud that stinks, and

that he walks there every day. I intend to walk to Pagham today and find this mud that stinks. I've looked at Pagham Harbour on the map, and if the low-lying swamp area stank in 1933 there is a good chance it will stink still. We'll soon see. In the meantime, I do a counting exercise in my Penguin copy of *Ninety-two Days*.

In the first five hundred words on day one, he tells the reader that the previous evening he arrived at the house he has borrowed by the sea and established himself in absolute solitude in the deserted nurseries. Just as I arrived at the house half an hour ago and have established myself in solitude hard against the perimeter wall. He then talks of the difficulty he has getting started on the book, but concludes that he is a writer by trade, and, in common with most in his profession, wouldn't choose to do anything else. Nevertheless, he asks himself :'Who in his senses will read, still less buy, a travel book of no scientific value about a place he has no intention of visiting?' Evelyn's own answer is that man is a communicative animal, and what was worth several months of his own time may be worth a few hours to others. Evelyn concludes what I take to be his first day's writing by stating that for the next month or so he shall be reliving his journey in Guiana and Brazil. Not that it's ever been out of his memory in the intervening months. But now, in the seaside nursery, the story will be laid out, like the maps and photographs that are already spread over the writing table.

The fifteen hundred words written on the second day at West House would have got Evelyn well out into the Atlantic. And by the end of the two thousand words of his third day he'd be reporting the smell of 'Flit' in his Georgetown hotel room. Interestingly, in that third day's block of writing, with his ship making a stop at Trinidad, there is the following exchange:

We had a round or two of swizzles and then one of my new friends said, 'I say, your name is mud in this joint.'
　'It stinks,' said the other.

It can't be coincidental that when writing a letter to Diana the same day he wrote these sentences in his travel book; he talks of walking each day to Pagham with its 'mud that stinks'. These daily walks clearly did the business as far as blowing away cobwebs in Evelyn's mind went, because in a later letter to Diana, dated 4 November, he boasts that he has broken all records with a four-thousand-word day. He believes the book will be finished in the next week and so asks Diana: 'Shall we make a date for the evening of the Dunn-Lynn party and have fun first?' I wonder what he means here by having fun, since his relationship with Diana – who was married to Duff Cooper, the politician – was certainly platonic. I suppose anything would seem like fun after a month's solid writing. But that's underestimating their relationship. It's undervaluing the importance of flashing words and smiles and laughter.

I am itching to get to Pagham. Just as, after ten days at Father Mather's retreat, Evelyn was itching to get to Boa Vista. But I must stay here a bit longer, visualising Evelyn sitting in the house behind me with his maps and photographs. At the end of *Ninety-two Days* he tells the reader that he had taken two dozen rolls of photos while in South America. Evelyn explains that many of the films got spoiled during the journey. A large number of those developed were failures as pictures, he admits. Without exception all photographs taken in the jungle were pitch dark with glaring spots of light. Those taken in the savannah aren't much better, the hills being flattened out and the trees unrecognisable. As for his portraits of Indians, well they made elusive subjects and most of them appear not so much ill-at-ease as terrified of Evelyn's lens. Of the hundred and ninety-two exposures, barely fifty were of any real interest, states Evelyn. Well, of the twenty-three actually printed in the 1934 edition, only two are of interest to this reader. Evelyn's photo of Father Mather is not well composed and the subject seems tense. Father Mather's photograph of Evelyn, on the other hand, is expertly composed, and Evelyn seems comfortable being the centre of attention, standing at Takutu River in his sun hat and shorts, whose absurdly high waistband harks back to the distant days of Preters at Lancing. It's no surprise that this is the photograph selected to be the book's frontispiece.

Time to go. Evelyn to Boa Vista; me to mud that stinks. I guess this is the way that Evelyn would have walked to Pagham every day, mulling over his Amazon trip of nine or ten months earlier. There is no road, so you walk along the shore. High up on the beach, the pebbles are laid down in a thick layer, and are difficult to walk over, so you edge down until you find sand that is hard enough to allow you to plod along without leaving deep footmarks. It's even hotter now. The left side of my forehead and nose and the top of my neck are getting burnt. But let's not dwell on that.

On horseback, accompanied by David, the rancher that kept the cattle at St Ignatius, Evelyn rode towards Boa Vista. On the fourth day they reached the bank of the Rio Bravo at an empty hut immediately opposite Boa Vista. Were his expectations still as high as Mr Bain had left them? Father Mather had only been once to Boa Vista and then in a state of malignant malaria, so he had been unable to pass on an opinion on the place. But David spoke of it as a town of dazzling attraction. So let's savour Evelyn's description of his entrance into town. Having been ferried across the river, he hauled his possessions up the steep bank and found himself in the main street. It was very broad, composed of hard mud, cracked into wide fissures in all directions and scored by dry gulleys. On either side was a row of single-storeyed, whitewashed mud houses with tiled roofs. At each doorstep sat one or more of the citizens staring at Evelyn with eyes that were insolent, hostile and apathetic. The remains of an electric cable hung loose from a row of crazy posts, or lay in coils and loops about the gutter. The description conjures up something that might be found in *The Simpsons*, with Homer having worked himself into ecstasies about the attractions of a place only to be brought crashing down to earth by reality. Poor Homer Simpson. Unhappy Evelyn Waugh.

Halfway up the street was the Benedictine priory, where Evelyn hoped to stay. Built of concrete, with a modestly ornamental façade, it was at least more imposing than anything he'd seen since leaving Georgetown. There was a German-Swiss monk in residence who spoke to Evelyn in halting French. Evelyn could stay there if he liked. But Evelyn was already thinking of getting the hell out of Boa Vista.

A new prior would be coming from Manáos sooner or later, and the boat that brought him would presumably return to the city someday.

'Will it be a question of days or weeks?' Evelyn asked the monk.

'A question of weeks or months,' was the reply.

Meanwhile, David had been making enquiries of his own and came back with the more reassuring information that a Boundary Commission boat was expected in four or five days. And a week after that there would be a trade launch passing through. With that good news, the cheerful David bade Evelyn goodbye and returned with the horses to the other side of the river.

Evelyn was left to get what he could from Boa Vista. Apart from the main street there were two smaller streets running parallel and four or five more running at right angles. All petered out into straggling footpaths. There was one fair-sized store, a barber's shop and two cafés. Two cafés! With any luck he could rum-swizzle his time away. So let's see. One of the cafés was on the main street, a little shed selling farine, bananas and fish, and there were three tables in front of it, where a few people collected in the evening to drink coffee. The second café, in a side street, was more attractive. It had a concrete floor (in the jungle concrete has more glamour attached to it than in a city, I'm supposing) and a counter where one could buy cigarettes and nuts. There were dominoes for the use of habitués and, besides coffee, Evelyn could drink warm and expensive beer. Concrete, cigarettes, nuts, dominoes, warm beer – things were looking up.

Well, not really. Let me trawl the Boa Vista chapter for more titbits, just as Evelyn trawled the place itself. There was only one English-speaking person in the town, a charmless youth. Most of the thousand-odd inhabitants spent the day lying indoors in their hammocks, and the evenings squatting on their doorsteps. It's fair to say that Evelyn was bored out of his mind in Boa Vista. But because he had been criticised for saying in print that he'd been bored beyond belief at certain stages in his African journey, he made a point of not going on about it in print this time. However, in his diary, and in letters written from Boa Vista, he makes no bones about it.

I need to consult my books again. But first I need to check where I am. The lagoon that I've just walked around doesn't stink. I thought it might because the stretch of water is cut off from the sea and must be jaded at best. But the bed of the lagoon consists of pebbles, and the water is clear. I'm now heading for the great stretch of muddy estuary that is known as Pagham Harbour. There is a slight whiff in the air, so surely it's only a matter of walking the perimeter until I find a bit that truly stinks. As I'm walking along I'm suddenly stopped in my tracks by a smell that hits me right between the eyes. Gotcha! So I look for a place out of the sun and I take the pack off my back and I sit down on some pebbles within a few yard of the boggy seaweed-covered mud that pongs. I'm downwind of it, so I can still sniff the stuff. I need something to distract me from the heat and the stench. No problem there – my pack is full of distraction.

In the main *Letters* volume there is a single letter written from Boa Vista, dated 12 February, which is two days after a diary entry which states baldly: 'Four days of degrading boredom.' Unsurprisingly, this was written to Blondy and Poll at Madresfield. The whole letter is ferociously facetious and might well have been composed after a few pints of warm Amazonian beer. 'Perhaps you are dead and will never get this. How sad. How sad.'

Not sad is the fact that there is also a letter from Boa Vista in the *Mr Wu and Mrs Stitch* volume. It is also dated February 10 (day 37 of 92), but the tone is much franker. 'Goodness the boredom of Boa Vista,' reads his first sentence to Diana. He reports that he's been there for a week and will be there for at least another week. He is already nearly crazy. No one speaks English. There are no books except for an ant-eaten edition of sermons by Bossuet. He can't get drunk as the only liquor in the village is some very mild beer that he must drink at a table in the store while being plagued by a cloud of flies and stared at by Brazilians dressed in pyjamas and boaters. There are no cars or boats and nowhere to go in them if there were. Jungle on one side, pampas on the other. Everyone is asleep most of the day. No café or hotel life of any kind. Poor, poor Evelyn. I feel I can put myself in his position. The feeling of self-consciousness that came near to overwhelming him as he sat on his own in the claustrophobic cloud of flies and locals, vainly trying to get pissed.

Then comes a key paragraph where Evelyn states that no amount of fun compensates for the kind of misery he is enduring at Boa Vista. He is utterly homesick and will return home direct, as soon as he gets to Manáos. He doesn't believe there will be a book in his experiences to date. The funny thing is that just when he got to that lowest point, he did find the inspiration that he was looking for. He doesn't mention it at all in the travel book. But in the diary entry for 12 February (two days after the letters), he mentions that he's thought of the plot for a short story. And two days after that he notes in his diary that he's finished the story. The tale in question is 'The Man Who Liked Dickens'. It draws on Evelyn's period holed up with Father Mather at St Ignatius, reading Dickens. It draws on his night as the guest of Mr Christie who in the story becomes his jailer, the man who insists on Evelyn's protagonist staying in the jungle and reading Dickens. But most of all it draws on Evelyn's boredom, his sense of being trapped in Boa Vista, the horror of never getting back to England. Most significantly in the long term, something that would take root in his mind, Evelyn's protagonist in the story is in Brazil for a very particular reason. He's there because his wife has committed adultery.

I'm on my way back now. Job done. Just as Evelyn was on the way home from the day he finished his short story. But it wasn't that easy to get out of Boa Vista. Having been refused a place on the Boundary Commission boat that passed through on 10 February (further fuelling his sense of being trapped), Evelyn decided to return across the river and go back to Georgetown via Guiana, by horse and on foot. But even for this there were arrangements to be made. He needed a guide, a mule, a horse, some stores and a boat to get him across the river. It was 19 February (day 45 of 92) by the time he got away. Bye-bye, Boa Vista. *'Bye-bye, Baby. Baby, bye-bye.'* Who's that song by again? The Bay City Rollers. Well, as a variation, let's have The Boa Vista Rollers singing *'Bye-bye, Evelyn. Evelyn, bye-bye.'*

But Evelyn was not thinking straight. He mistook where he was on the map. With staggering stupidity (and not a little arrogance) he decided certain hills were other hills and that such a river was such-and-such another river, overruling his puzzled guide. Moreover, he decided to take a short-cut on his own, and having mistaken where he was he soon found himself lost in the middle of nowhere. Soon his horse was on its knees, he was starving and exhausted. All of this he would be able to make use of when he came back to the short story, expanded on it, showed how the protagonist got to the Amazon jungle in the first place, and turned the short story into a novel. But first he had to survive his experience. According to his own reckoning, he was saved by a miracle. Evelyn stumbled across a hut where the Indian spoke English, had food to spare (the Indians didn't usually store *any* food), and was himself going to Bon Success later that same day. And on the way to St Ignatius they even came across Evelyn's guide, who was delighted to be hooked up again with his master. In *Ninety-two Days*, Evelyn reckons the odds against all those lucky things happening were millions to one, and gives the credit for his rescue to the St Christopher that Baby had given him. But really all he needed was to stumble across an Indian settlement of any kind and he'd probably have been saved. He was only a day or so's walk from the Jesuit mission of St Ignatius, after all.

Ten days in the hammock reading Dickens again. Perhaps this was a strange thing for Evelyn to elect to do so soon after being holed up at Boa Vista and writing 'The Man Who Liked Dickens'. Actually, it's only at this stage in the diary that the Dickens reading material is mentioned for the first time. However, it's clear from the short story that Evelyn must have spent some of his first sojourn at St Ignatius reading these books. This time he reads *Dombey and Son* while in residence and takes away *Martin Chuzzlewit* to read *en route*.

I'm walking along the beach again. The heat of the sun is less fierce than it was on my outward journey, but because the sun has moved round in the sky it's in danger of shining on that part of my face that got a good toasting this morning, damn it. But by turning slightly so as to look out to sea as I walk, I can avoid this happening. Mind you, I can't do that all the time because I don't want to miss West House on the way back. I want to rest against its perimeter wall one more time.

I see it as my St Ignatius mission and my St Christopher's medal rolled into one.

Here we are. There is a car in the drive now. I'm less presentable than I was this morning, even less in a state to pay a social call, but ring the bell I do. A man answers. I try and state the purpose of my cold call. I'm writing a book about Evelyn Waugh and would like to know if this is the house that was once known as West House under the ownership of the Duff Coopers. He calls a woman's name. Apparently, this is something that she will be better able to help me with.

The woman of the house confirms that the property was once owned by Diana and her husband Duff Cooper, though they didn't know that when they bought it. Am I familiar with the painting by Rex Whistler on the cover of the Diana Cooper book? I do indeed know the Whistler picture, but from an illustration inside the volume of correspondence between Diana Cooper and Evelyn Waugh. She nods curtly and I follow the present owner of what was West House out into the drive where she points out the disparities between the house in the painting and the house now. Basically, the drive approaches from the opposite direction than in the Coopers' day, and what had been a prominent chimney has been removed. Before, the grounds of the house stretched down to the beach, which is where the Coopers had a piggery. Now there are two or three houses separating 151 Barrack Lane from the beach itself. There is not much more to say, since I'm not prepared to ask to look around the house with a view to identifying 'the deserted nurseries' and recreating the workplace where Evelyn set about reliving his trip on the other side of the world. I'm just too tired successfully to communicate my desire to do that. My host fills a short silence with the observation: 'I hate to think of Evelyn Waugh having been in my bed.' That seems an odd thing to say. Because Evelyn Waugh, seventy years ago, would surely not have been sleeping in any bed that was currently in use. He may have slept in the same *bedroom* though. Perhaps that's what she means. We chat about Ronald Knox, the subject of a biography by Waugh towards the end of his career, a religious figure whom the lady I'm talking to knew personally. And after an exchange of views about Duff Cooper, whose sleeping around was something that this lady of high ideals has disdain for, we go our separate ways.

On the beach once more. Two miles back to Bognor where I have a B&B booked. Evelyn's own journey back to Georgetown wasn't incident free, but nor was it as interesting as his journey out. When Waugh came to edit his travel books in order to publish *When the Going was Good* in 1946, condensing four travel books into one, he only took the reader as far as Boa Vista. Yes, the going gets rather turgid on the way back. Still, I vividly recall the bit where a djigga got inside Evelyn's boot and under his toenail to lay its eggs. The sack of eggs was seemingly removed successfully by his guide, but perhaps one egg was left in the foot because pain was crippling Evelyn the next day. Riding the horse soon got too painful – the encroaching vegetation brushed against his bad foot – and walking was agonising. Limping and lurching, limping and lurching. And in the process, Evelyn would be conscious that he was holding back the party that he had joined and thus causing great inconvenience to everyone. Poor Evelyn: a burden on others and an excruciating pain to himself.

He left behind half of *Martin Chuzzlewit* at one of his stopping-off places, as his host had run out of reading material of his own; from that point he carried on by canoe. He was travelling with a 'useless' Indian family by this stage, along with two blacks who did all the paddling and the carrying of the canoe when rapids made movement through the water too dangerous. Then he was carried along by a bigger boat. And, finally, he reached Georgetown. I know I'm chopping my way through whole chapters here, in single sentences of my own, but I am tired. In fact, I am going to stop now so as not to miss 17 Nyewood Lane, which lies not much farther from the shore than 151 Barrack Lane does, so I couldn't really have more appropriate lodgings for tonight.

One thing is clear though: as soon as I get in there, I'll be getting into the nearest thing to a hammock that my room contains. Evelyn explains the technique early on in *Ninety-two Days*. And once ensconced I will not be stirring for an hour or more. Later in the evening, I might be found in the middle of Bognor in a cloud of flies with a warm pint in front of me, being ogled by locals. On the other hand, I might have to stay in my hammock in order to take this exercise a stage further.

2

It's only now, after a full Bognor breakfast, that I've got my sense of self back. It was weird sleeping here last night, probably because it was a Friday. I went to bed at eleven, after a couple of pints in a nearby pub. At one in the morning a group of four came back to a room on the floor above mine and woke me up with drunken noise. I lay pretending I was in my jungle hammock, listening to the monkeys and the parrots high in the treetops. It was soothing to do that. So much so that when a male member of the foursome shouted an obscenity at the top of his voice, a sound that must have penetrated the consciousness of everyone in the building, I just thought: 'Ah, that's interesting, the six o'clock beetle.'

I'm able to stay here until early afternoon. The second bed in the room is handy to lay out the books I'll need. The ones already open are Stannard and Hastings and the two volumes of letters I was using yesterday. Not so handy is that there is no proper desk, just a tiny bedside table, which I can't use, and a chair, which I'm sitting on. I've got highlighter pens and ordinary pens and pencils, so I'll just work away within the books themselves and put together the text later. But whatever I ultimately write is being composed here and now.

When Evelyn got back to Georgetown he wrote to both Diana and the Lygons. His relief is palpable. To Poll and Blondie he writes that he is back in Georgetown and that all the world is Highclere. Highclere being the home of Lord Carnarvon, where Lady Sibell Lygon had once stayed and had thereafter always referred to its remarkable splendour. Out Madresfielding Madresfield, as it were. The phrase became widely employed throughout Waugh's set, or at least his opening comment to Diana suggests as much, when he declares that he is out of the wild wood at last and everything is Highclere.

Back in London at the beginning of May 1933, Waugh paid a short visit to Underhill to see his parents and pick up five months of mail. He went from there to Bath, explaining in another letter to Diana that he was in Bath because after so much forest it was a relief to be surrounded by good architecture. At the beginning of September, Waugh accompanied his rich friend Alfred Duggan on a cruise, the idea being to keep the alcoholic Duggan off the hard stuff and maybe get him back to the religion from which he had lapsed. Judging by Evelyn's letters to Diana Cooper from the SS *Kraljica Marija* (Queen Mary) there were lots of well-connected people on board. From Portofino he wrote her a letter containing pen portraits of thirty-odd fellow passengers. The letter from the ship to the Lygon sisters tells them that Hazel Lavery missed the ship. That would partly explain his observation that there was not much rogering on board. But given that, 'Don't tell Hazel I'm back,' was something that he had said to another correspondent immediately on his return from South America, it's pretty obvious Waugh was trying to keep his distance from her. As for Baby Jungman, Evelyn urged Lady Mary and Lady Dorothy to give her his love and a kiss on the arse, taking one each for themselves too.

Which gets us to October. And Evelyn settling in to his B&B a couple of miles from where I sit now, battening down the hatches for a prolonged bout of writing up his Amazon experience. The trip itself lasted five months, December to April. Recovery from the trip took another five months, May to September. And although he wrote up *Ninety-two Days* in little more than a month, with daily walks to the mud that stinks to help him pull it off, that was not the end of the story.

Something else happened in October. Encouraged by fellow believers, Evelyn had put in motion an attempt to have his marriage annulled in the eyes of the Roman Catholic Church. Selina Hastings indicates there were five sittings of the tribunal in a building adjoining Westminster Cathedral during October and November. I don't know how many of those Waugh had to attend, but he was there on 18 October, breaking off from his Bognor sojourn. He had lunch with She-Evelyn and told her what she must expect to be asked, and how she might most usefully answer the questions. He similarly prepared

Pansy Lamb for interview, probably on another occasion, as Hastings states that Pansy and She-Evelyn didn't meet during the tribunal. His brother Alec was another witness that Evelyn called to testify on his behalf. It would be another three years before Waugh heard that his marriage had indeed been annulled, leaving him free to marry again as far as the Pope was concerned. But of significance in the meantime, surely, was the conjunction of writing about his spirit-crushing trip up the Amazon, on the one hand, with speaking in public about his soul-destroying marriage, on the other.

So what next? Waugh wrote to his agent in the middle of November to say that *Ninety-two Days* was finished. Stannard reckons he probably spent Christmas at Madresfield, but on what evidence he doesn't say. On 28 December, after lunching with his parents at their new, smaller house at Highgate (Underhill having proved too large for the now elderly couple), he boarded a boat for Tangier. Diana Cooper saw him off. Evelyn now liked to feel the sun on his back once he'd had enough of the festive period, a preference that would never leave him. But he also wanted to get straight into the novel that he felt ready to write. On a personal recommendation, Evelyn was going to try to settle down to write his new novel in Morocco.

I take a break to walk round the room and make myself a cup of tea. I seem to be in fine fettle this morning, despite Kate's absence. I've been moving easily between all these books that remain open on the bed in front of me. I feel I've got the momentum to go straight through the composition process of *A Handful of Dust*. Should I check out the mud that stinks first? No, I think I must stay here and make the most of my energies.

As Diana had seen him off, it feels right that she got the first letter from Fez, from Hotel Bellevue (translation: Hotel Boa Vista?), dated 4 January 1934. In it, Evelyn tells her he's been to the brothel and bought a girl, but didn't enjoy her much. He's quite ready to write his book. A second letter, this time to Lady Mary Lygon, states that he has formed an attachment to a young lady at the brothel called Fatima who is 'not at all Dutch [uncooperative] in her ways'. Evelyn and Fatima don't speak the same language, so their association is

kept to what Evelyn again calls rogering in a January letter to Madresfield. In the same letter to Lady Mary he tells her in the first paragraph
that he has written eighteen thousand, five hundred words of his
novel. He thinks his work excellent though grim. But it's in the third
letter, again to Diana and still written in January, that he is most
informative about his book's progress. He's reached a pausing point
having written nearly fifty thousand words. And as *Black Mischief* is
only seventy thousand words in all, Evelyn is tempted to say that his
new book is nearly finished, though he knows it isn't. Again he states
that what he has done is excellent but gruesome. He mentions a fine
scene where a bereaved father plays animal snap with an unknown
American woman all afternoon while his little boy lies dead upstairs.
He mentions that there is also a brilliant scene at the '43' Club in
London and a divorce expedition to Brighton with a tart. According
to Evelyn, the general architecture of the novel is masterly.

At that point Evelyn doesn't know where to go with his book, and
it's March before he writes the remaining third of it back in England.
So let's take a look at what he wrote in Fez. Architecture is a key
word. Three of the seven chapters are called 'English Gothic'. The
protagonist, Tony Last, lives in Hetton Abbey, which, like Madresfield,
was entirely rebuilt in 1864–5 in the Gothic style 'rendering it devoid
of interest'. The terrace commanded a fine view. The spires of six
churches could be seen from Hetton. The house was surrounded by
a moat. The fact that he's effectively talking about Madresfield is
significant in certain ways, but not in others. Waugh wanted his novel
to live and breathe, so he chose a place that he knew well and which
could be made to contribute thematically. Tony and Brenda Last are in
some ways based on Lord Peregrine Brownlow and his wife (Perry
and Kitty), whose country house Evelyn had been a guest in. Brenda
Last has an affair with John Beaver, who comes to stay with the Lasts
for the weekend at Tony's invitation. Waugh states that Beaver is
drawn from an acquaintance called Murrough O'Brien ('Sponger') who
was notorious for taking advantage of people's hospitality. But, as with
the use of Madresfield, all Waugh is really doing is getting into his mind
something whose external attributes and superficial characteristics he

can write about with ease. For all important purposes, Tony Last is Evelyn, Brenda Last is She-Evelyn, and John Beaver is John Heygate.

Quick summary of that part of the novel written in Fez: Tony loves Hetton Abbey. Brenda, bored with Tony and his deplorable house, sleeps with worthless Mayfair gadabout John Beaver, whom she falls in love with. The affair is carried on in London and in secret, though everyone knows about it except Tony, isolated at Hetton. Tony and Brenda's son dies in a riding accident in the grounds of Hetton, so there is no longer anything to bring Brenda back there. At first, following the death of his son, heartbroken and bemused, Tony is compliant when he learns of his wife's adultery and her wish for a separation. But when he realises a divorce is going to mean him losing his beloved Hetton, he suddenly stops cooperating with the convention of the process whereby the woman divorces the man. Tony lets it be known that he is going abroad for six months and that when he gets back, if Brenda wishes it, he will divorce her without any settlement.

Does that shadow Evelyn's experience? Effectively, it does. For Hetton Abbey read the Abingdon Arms. For Brenda's love of John Beaver read She-Evelyn's besotment with John Heygate, the 'ramshackle oaf'-cum-'basement boy' who 'cuckolded' Evelyn, but of whom I'm beginning to form a revised picture thanks to Kate's correspondence with his son. And the six-month trip that Tony takes will be to the Amazon, of course. Up the jungle! But Evelyn has to take a deep breath and a pause for thought before finishing his book. Why? Because he was going to weave together the two most miserable experiences of his life.

But let's stick with the Fez fiction. If the general architecture of the first half of the book is masterly, where does the son fit in? The boy is introduced to show how English society gets it wrong in educating its young. The boy is given inadequate and contradictory moral guidance by his tolerant father, lazy mother, working-class groom and prim nanny. In particular, John Andrew (John Julius was the name of Diana and Duff Cooper's only son) is raised to be a sacrifice, unable to defend himself against the wiles of *femmes fatales*. Raised in a spirit of romance, the boy falls for the exotic woman that Brenda arranges to visit Hetton to seduce Tony. Obsessed with horse-riding and hunting and desperate to be 'in at the kill' during his first hunt, he is in at the kill all right – his own death. The death itself, from the hoof of a horse whose female rider has lost control, is a complete accident, but that doesn't change what's going on here. The death of the boy prefigures the fate of the man. What is to be the fate of the boy's father? He is to be stranded in Brazil, cut off from everything he loves. But how is Waugh to make that believable and appropriate?

Waugh returned to England and retreated to the Easton Court Hotel in Devon, the place where he knew he could concentrate when he didn't have a free country house to stay in. There he once more settled down to write about his trip to South America. He wrote again about the voyage out from England across the Atlantic, introducing Dr Messinger who is partly based on Waugh's companion when he was in Africa – Professor Whitehead – and partly on Mr Haynes (aka Mr Bain in *Ninety-two days*). On ship, with Dr Messinger prostrate in his bunk with seasickness, Tony goes over in his mind how he met him in a London club and was impressed with the plan to go to Brazil and find the lost city of the Pie-wie Indians. Messinger's joke credentials are established when he describes how he became the blood brother of a Pie-wie on his previous visit to Brazil. He tells Tony that the Indians had an interesting ceremony. They'd buried him up to his neck in mud and all the women of the tribe had spat on his head. Messinger's blood brother it was who told him that the wondrous City lay between the head waters of the Courantyne and the Takutu. Both these rivers are marked on the map that Waugh drew for *Ninety-two Days*, emphasising that he was on familiar un-familiar ground. As for that spitting-on-the-head business, women really are given a hard time in *A Handful of Dust*.

During the voyage, Tony has a romance with a fellow passenger called Thérèse de Vitré. She is eighteen years old, small and dark with grave eyes and a high forehead. In certain respects she is that glass Teresa, Teresa Jungman, that Evelyn calls Baby. Thérèse's father is Catholic and has one of the best houses in Trinidad. She is going home to be married although she has no one in mind as yet and there are so few men she can marry because they must be Catholic and of an island family. Soon Tony and Thérèse are on first-name terms and playing deck games with each other. When they reach the first of the Caribbean islands they bathe together, Thérèse swimming badly with her head held ridiculously erect out of the water. They lie on the silver beach and then drive back to the boat where Tony kisses her for the first time. They bathe again at Barbados and drive round the island visiting churches. They dine at a hotel high up out of town and eat flying fish. Thérèse wants Tony to visit her in Trinidad when he returns from his expedition. In the ensuing conversation, Thérèse asks why Tony never got married. Tony tells her that he *is* married, but that he and his wife have fallen out. And that is the end of that. Thérèse doesn't want to know what the row was about or how final the rift was – the fact that Tony is a married man is the thing that matters to the good little Catholic girl. She cuts off all contact with him.

The way I interpret those half-dozen pages is as follows. Even at such a late stage in the expedition's planning, Tony could perhaps get over his rejection by Brenda if another suitable mate came along. Messinger has been observing the growing friendship between the pair with the strongest disapproval. But Dr Messinger can relax. Even if Tony *was* up for making a new start with Thérèse after a suitable period of penance, she will not be giving him that option. So it's on with the self-sacrifice.

Tony and Dr Messinger land at Georgetown, disembark their stores, and then start on stage one of their journey to find the lost City. For ten days they chug up the Demerera River in a broad shallow boat manned by six black men. By so doing, Waugh was reversing the direction of his actual journey. But it looks to me that, after a day or two, the boat would have had to veer off Waugh's return course and, after fifty miles or so of southward progress, cross the course of his original outward journey. The north-south river would then take him into unexplored territory along the river that is by this stage called the Rupununi. In the novel, Waugh takes the opportunity of using various details from his own jungle adventure. For example, Dr Messinger thinks he is able to tell the hour by the succession of bush sounds (just as Haynes/Bain thought he could). Tony's face and neck are burned by the sun reflecting up from the water, and there is no part of his body that is wholly at ease. The explorers are pestered by cabouri fly, and djiggas have to be dug out from under their toenails. As Tony scratches in his hammock he shakes the framework from which both hammocks hang, eliciting repeated complaints from Messinger.

'First Base Camp' is established. There is an Indian camp a couple of miles away and contact is made. One of the Indians, a woman called Rosa, speaks English. This is fortunate, because the tribe doesn't speak Wapishiana, the language Messinger speaks, but Macushi (both languages are mentioned in *Ninety-two Days*). Tony and Messinger have to wait for the men of the tribe to get back from a hunting trip. Two days later they do return and a feast begins during which all the natives get so drunk that Messinger reckons it will be a week before they sober up. This is one of the very few things Messinger calls correctly. When negotiations do begin, the Indians are reluctant to act as guides to Pie-wie country. But three days later a caravan involving twelve men, seven accompanied by their wives, one of whom is Rosa, sets out. They walk for a fortnight, averaging fifteen miles a day. They seem to pass from one river watershed into the Amazon itself. Messinger has an exchange with Rosa about what the new river system is called. 'Waurapang,' she replies. 'No, not the river where we first camped, this river here.' 'Waurapang,' confirms Rosa. '*This river here*,' repeats Messinger, getting rattled. 'Macushi people call him all Waurapang,' says Rosa. It's one of several verbal skirmishes with Messinger that she wins hands down.

At the end of the two weeks they come to another wide river, flowing deep and swift to the south-east. They are on the border of Pie-wie country and Dr Messinger establishes 'Second Base Camp'. Meanwhile Waugh has been inserting short scenes set in London. These follow another thread – the increasing distance between Brenda Last and John Beaver. First, at a party with Beaver at Anchorage House, Brenda tells another friend that unless Beaver gets a taste of such highlife once per week he shows signs of restlessness. Second, we overhear a phone call between the lovers where Beaver blames Brenda for not pulling strings in order to get him into Brown's club. Third, we discover that Beaver is going to spend the summer in California with his mother. That is, separated from Brenda.

Back in the Amazon, it takes the Indians three days to find suitable trees from which to make canoes and another four days to make the canoes. Then the problems really start. Rosa makes clear, 'Macushi peoples no go with Pie-wie peoples.' Messinger tries to explain that no one is asking the Macushi to *go with* Pie-wie people. All they need to do is take Messinger and Tony as far as the Pie-wies, then they can go back to their own territory. But Rosa will not give an inch. It's a stalemate, one that Kate and I particularly enjoyed when we were reading the book together a few days ago. Kate (the epitome of Rosa) would raise her arm in an embracing circle, which I knew was intended to cover our Westcliff camp and the road travelled behind us all the way to the Barley Mow. 'Macushi peoples here,' she said. Then she raised the other arm and made circles in a direction I took to mean towards the yet to be explored country post-Mayfair. 'Pie-wie peoples there,' she said. Frowning, she then said: 'Macushi peoples no go with Pie-wie peoples.'

I tried to explain to Kate that everything would be fine. All I needed was a guide until contact with the Pie-wie people was made in or around Bognor. Kate pointed at herself. 'Macushi peoples,' she said. She pointed at me: 'Pie-wie peoples.' Then, frowning, she spat out: 'MACUSHI PEOPLES NO GO WITH PIE-WIE PEOPLES.'

Christ, I wish she were here today. I'm having a productive time on my own in a B&B on the South Coast of England. And perhaps this bit of the work really has to be done this way. But I wish she was sharing it with me instead of doing her own thing. 'Pie-wie peoples miss Macushi peoples,' I say into the empty four walls of this lonely room. 'Pie-wie peoples miss Macushi peoples. Big-time.'

Dr Messinger has another go at persuading Rosa to get her people on board for the next stage of the journey. Rosa's excuse this time is that the men must return to their own territory because it was time to dig the cassava. Messinger argues that they will only be delayed a week or so. But there is no moving Rosa: the cassava must be dug before the rains come. Messinger resorts to bribing the Indians with some of the flashy trash that Tony and he bought together from a shop on Oxford Street. The natives are interested, but the bottom line comes again from their spokeswoman: 'Macushi peoples dig cassava field now.' So Messinger reluctantly resorts to his most expensive gimmick. These are clockwork mice, the size of large rats, with green and white spots, and when Messinger winds one up and sets it running across a clearing towards the Indians they look horrified and scarper. Messinger admits that this was more of a response than he had expected, but *he knows the Indian mind* – they'll be back soon enough from the depths of the jungle. They don't come back. Well, they do come back, but only in the middle of the night to retrieve their own possessions and what was due to them. 'The situation is grave,' says Dr Messinger, 'but not desperate.'

Well, pretty soon it gets desperate. For four days they paddle downstream, then Tony develops fever. In his delirium he sees Brenda. Over the days she comes and goes, as Tony, nursed by Messinger, drifts from hallucinations to a normal state and back to hallucinations again. Messinger establishes 'Temporary Emergency Base Camp'.

After three days there, with Tony's condition not improving, Messinger decides to go downstream on his own for a day in the hope of finding help. He sets off, soon encounters rapids that lead to a waterfall with a ten-foot drop, and that is the end of Dr Messinger. He's done his job though. The same dreadful job that all Tony's guides and father figures through life have done. He's led Tony astray.

Tony lies in his hammock all day, fitfully oblivious of the passage of time. He tries to eat some of the food that Messinger has left out for him, but is too dizzy. At night he lights the lamp successfully, but has to return giddy to the hammock where he begins to cry. After hours of darkness he realises he should refill the lamp with oil. In trying to do so, he has another giddy turn and not only spills the oil from the lamp but knocks over the keg, which empties itself into the mud. When he realises what he has done he lies awake in the darkness, crying.

Meanwhile, in London, Brenda wakes up alone. She has been told there will be no money from Tony's estate even in his protracted absence. The previous evening she came back to her flat with a meat pie that she found she could not eat. Beaver is in California and all her friends are out of town. She reads in the morning paper that August in London is the gayest time. She breaks down and buries her face in the pillow, crying.

It's worth pausing at that point, with Tony-Evelyn, lost in the middle of the jungle, lying in the darkness, in tears; and Brenda-Evelyn with her tears wetting the pillow in a city half a world away. A good place, perhaps, to introduce the quote from *The Waste Land* that Waugh chose to place on the title page of *A Handful of Dust*, no doubt thinking of Evelyn Gardner as he did so:

> 'I will show you something different from either
> Your shadow at morning striding behind you
> Or your shadow at evening rising to meet you;
> I will show you fear in a handful of dust.'

The next day Tony and Brenda are together, in his mind. She is wearing the same ragged cotton gown that Rosa wore. She has come to tell him that members of the County Council are gathered at Hetton awaiting him. The subject under discussion is the Green Line bus. Yes, the subjects under discussion are the Green Line rats that have so scared the villagers that they have evacuated their cottages. The meeting continues with Tony in attendance. Things get confused for a while, but then Tony realises that something is being put to the vote. The question is whether the contract for the widening of the corner of Hetton Cross shall be given to John Beaver's mother, who was complicit in Beaver and Brenda getting together in the first place. Of the tenders submitted, hers was by far the most expensive. Nevertheless the motion is passed. Brenda is so glad that Mrs Beaver has been given the job. You see she's in love with her son.

'I'm in love with John Beaver.'

Three times Brenda says this line loud and clear. It reminds me of something I heard yesterday. Or at least a variation of it: 'I hate to think of Tony Last having been in my bed.'

Ambrose, the trusted old butler at Hetton, appears and states that *he*'s in love with John Beaver. Which reminds me that Kate must have whispered in my ear a dozen times during the course of our reading *A Handful of Dust* that *she* was in love with John Beaver, precursor of Richard Heygate in her teasing mind. But Tony doesn't make the mistake of saying that he's in love with John Beaver as well. Just as I never even once said to Kate that I was in love with the basement boy.

So that's Brenda, Kate and Ambrose in love with John Beaver. Leaving Tony, Evelyn and myself begging to differ.

'I'm in love with John Beaver,' says Tony.

The situation is grave, I realise, but not desperate.

Actually, Evelyn would have been feeling pretty pleased with himself when he got to this point in the book. Now he can simply slot the short story that he wrote at Boa Vista into place. He does amend it slightly, but not much. Tony goes walkabout and comes across the house of Mr Todd rather than Mr McMaster, the character based on the Mr Christie that Evelyn stayed one night with on his outward journey through Guiana.

Mr Todd, on finding the weak, hallucinating Tony, urges him to rest in his hammock. 'That's what Messinger said,' says Tony. 'He's in love with John Beaver.' Mr Todd bids Tony drink from a potion and soon he falls deeply asleep.

Tony is put on the road to recovery. But once recovered he is trapped reading the novels of Dickens, whose novels Waugh came across at St Ignatius's Mission, both before and after his miserable stay at Boa Vista. Tony hopes that a search party will someday come. But when that day arrives, Mr Todd has already taken care that Tony will be drugged and out of sight. The search party go away with Tony's watch and photographs of a cross that purports to mark his grave.

Does it work for Waugh to have slotted a short story written while at Boa Vista into the resolution of the novel he wrote about a year later?

Before I address that question I should just clarify something. Selina Hastings makes a mistake in her analysis of Waugh during this period. On page 278 of her consistently readable 723-pager, she states that it has wrongly been supposed that 'The Man Who Liked Dickens' was the story that Waugh wrote at Boa Vista (even though Waugh made a note in pencil to this effect on the typescript of *A Handful of Dust*). Her first argument is that the story is too long to have been written in two days. Well, as the story is no more than six thousand words, this is not a telling point. Evelyn was quite capable of writing at the speed of three thousand words per day and reached a maximum of four thousand while writing up *Ninety-two Days* at Bognor Regis. Her main argument is that there are episodes in the story that had not happened at the time Evelyn arrived at Boa Vista. She gives two examples. Dr Messinger takes with him a selection of trade goods including some mechanical mice. These mechanical mice are mentioned in the inward part of Evelyn's journey, *after* his stay at Boa Vista, when the diamond prospector, Mr Winter, talks about going to Georgetown and coming back with novelties, including some mechanical mice. The trouble with this example is that the green-and-white-spotted mice do not occur in 'The Man Who Liked Dickens' or its equivalent chapter in the novel, 'Du Côté de Chez Todd'. They occur in that part of *A Handful of Dust* that is set in the Amazon and working *towards* the point where Waugh can slot in his short story. Her only other example is the pivari drink that Henty / Tony is given by McMaster / Todd. Well, true, Evelyn only records getting a taste for cassiri, a local drink that he tells us is similar to pivari, on his inward journey, after Boa Vista. But that doesn't mean that he was unaware of the native drink during those times when either he had his own supply of rum or the option of the warm beer of Boa Vista.

OK, back to my question. Does it work for Waugh to have slotted a short story written while at Boa Vista into the resolution of the novel he wrote about a year later? In the short story, it's entirely appropriate that it was Dickens who had to be read *ad nauseam*, because to some extent Waugh is writing about the boredom and frustration of the life he'd led at his own father's house, Arthur Waugh being the man who published Dickens and read Dickens aloud during Evelyn's childhood. But in the novel?

In the novel, Tony-Evelyn has lost Brenda-Evelyn. He has journeyed to the other side of the world to escape the devastation of his loss. And what he finds there is a vision of Brenda tormenting him with the repeated line: 'I am in love with John Beaver.' Rock bottom for Tony. Rock bottom settles down to be a prison peopled by Tony and Mr Todd. Should Tony's jailer not be John Beaver? No, because Beaver is with Brenda. Or if not with Brenda, having sucked her dry, then sunning himself in California.

Tony must be by himself, therefore Todd must effectively be an altar ego of Tony. Todd has chosen to isolate himself, centring his life on one thing. Just as the love of Tony's life was a Hetton containing Brenda, so the love of Todd's life is a hut full of Dickens. Hetton was rebuilt in 1864. In that year Dickens was writing and publishing *Our Mutual Friend* in monthly parts. Tony is condemned to live out the rest of his days in a mud hut that has a deeply ironic relationship to Hetton. This is what you wanted, Tony? This is what you bloody well get.

Another book lying on the spare bed in my room is *The Picturesque Prison: Evelyn Waugh and his Writing* by Jeffrey Heath. It's a conventional book of literary analysis that was published in 1982 and is well thought of in Waugh studies. The cover shows a picture of Waugh looking old and sedentary, writing a letter in his library, dressed in a three-piece hound's tooth check suit and tie. Appropriately, the book was once library stock and came to me from AbeBooks with a misty transparent plastic cover on it. There is a twenty-page chapter on *A Handful of Dust*, just as there is a chapter on every other novel that Waugh wrote. Almost every line in the chapter has been underlined in pencil by a particularly keen student who was clearly intent on following every step of the argument in the slippered footprints of Jeffrey Heath.

The book's thematic assertions are thoroughly argued. While it's obvious to me that the fundamental driving force behind Waugh's writing is autobiography, the desire to transform experience into art, Heath's book is a reminder that Waugh was also driven by ideas. According to Heath (and Stannard), *A Handful of Dust* sees Waugh trying to show that secular happiness is not possible. According to their analysis, Waugh is suggesting that a house like Hetton Abbey, which is effectively without God, is doomed to decay over time. Tony may enjoy going to church on Sunday, but he doesn't listen to the sermon, which is preached by an inadequate Church of England vicar. Tony goes through the motions of standing, singing and kneeling while thinking of bathroom fittings at Hetton. Alas, Tony must suffer the consequences of setting up a rival to God – consisting of Hetton and Brenda – in the sense that time will reduce his material wealth – his house and his lady – to a handful of dust.

How did I put it before? Tony is condemned to live out the rest of his days in a mud hut that has a deeply ironic relationship to Hetton. But is Dickens an appropriate choice for his daily humiliation? In 'The Man Who Liked Dickens' there is this exchange between Henty and McMaster:

> (McMaster:) 'Do you believe in God?'
> (Henty:) 'I've never really thought about it much.'
> (McMaster:) 'You are perfectly right. I have thought about it a
>   *great* deal and I still do not know . . . Dickens did.'
> (Henty:) ' I suppose so.'
> (McMaster:) 'Oh, yes, it is apparent in all his books. You will see.'

The conversation is repeated verbatim in *A Handful of Dust*, except the sentence, 'You are perfectly right,' being superfluous, is omitted. When McMaster/Todd says, 'Dickens did,' he means, of course, Dickens believed in God. Would it not have been more suitable for the theme of the books to be atheist? Let's face it, the reason that it is Dickens that Henty/Tony is condemned to read over and over again is that it was Dickens that Waugh was forced to read in the jungle. Even at the expense of a little thematic confusion, he wanted to be loyal to his experience. That's my conclusion anyway.

Time to look at the way the novel ends. 'English Gothic III' consists of five pages set at Hetton, a year or more down the line. Tony's cousin Richard has inherited the house, which he runs with a 'skeleton staff' indoors (of five servants rather than the fifteen that were employed in Tony's time). The dining-hall and the library have been added to the state apartments as rooms that are kept locked. The family live in the morning-room, the smoking-room and what had been Tony's study. But fundamentally things are still not right at Hetton, the clock strikes fourteen at half-past eight in the morning.

Richard and his wife have four children. The oldest son, Teddy, is twenty-two and lives at home where he is breeding silver foxes. Peter is still at Oxford. Molly keeps angora rabbits and drives a two-stroke motorcycle. Agnes is twelve, and is sometimes a few minutes late for the family breakfast. A happy family? A Godless one, rather, and each individual has in store for him or her the same fate as Tony, Brenda and John Andrew – a handful of dust.

In the book's last paragraph, Teddy surveys his silver foxes. The farmed beasts are intended (ironically) 'to restore Hetton to the glory that it had enjoyed in the days of his Cousin Tony'. In the early thirties, fashionable ladies would wear coats made of silver-fox fur, or even have the whole pelt – head, feet and all – draped around their shoulders. So what is Waugh implying? Perhaps that a business plan based on the vacillations of fashion and the vanity of women might not be the soundest.

Teddy goes to his foxes from a dedication ceremony in memory of Tony Last held in the grounds of Hetton. Brenda does not attend, but her mother does (possibly a touch of respect from Evelyn to the fierce mother of She-Evelyn who had tried to prevent their marriage in the first place). Following a few words from the same inept vicar that presided over church matters in Tony's day, a stone monolith is unveiled. The inscription reads, hilariously:

ANTHONY LAST OF HETTON
EXPLORER
Born at Hetton, 1902
Died in Brazil, 1934

These are the same years, more or less, in which Evelyn was born and in which he found himself *in extremis* in the jungle.

I stand up in order to pack my bag. As I'm about to put away my copy of *A Handful of Dust* I recall that it's an edition that contains the alternative ending that Waugh wrote for an American periodical.

He wrote it for copyright reasons. In other words, a rival American magazine had already printed 'The Man Who Liked Dickens'. The periodical version of the book is effectively the four chapters written in Fez plus just ten new pages. The story cuts from Tony saying he is going abroad for six months (and that when he gets back, if Brenda still wants a divorce she can get one, but on his terms) to the new scene with Tony arriving back into the harbour at Southampton. Brenda is there to meet him. She has been humbled by events and is hoping for a reconciliation. She tries to talk to Tony, but Tony is tired from his journey and falls asleep in the car that is driving them to Hetton. In the event, Tony/Evelyn does take Brenda/Evelyn back. But, unbeknown to her, he also keeps on her flat in London, the implication being that Tony has set up his own little nest of adultery in Mayfair.

Last to go into my pack is the volume of letters between Evelyn and Diana Cooper. That's because there is one more letter that I need to relish. It was written in September 1934, the month in which *A Handful of Dust* was first published by Chapman and Hall. Diana tells Evelyn that she's read '*Handfulers*' aloud to Barbie Wallace, Joan Guinness and Sheila Loughborough, and that the success has been dynamic. The book was now being fought over by their husbands. The footnotes on the page tell me that these women were, respectively: Barbara Wallace, age thirty-six, daughter of Sir Edwin Lutyens, married to the Right Honourable Euan Wallace since 1920; Joan Yarde-Buller, age twenty-six, married since 1927 to Lionel Guinness, part of the brewing dynasty; and Sheila Loughborough, Australian born, married since 1915 to Lord Loughborough. All titled, all rich, all eminently presentable, no doubt. I'm sure Evelyn would have been over the moon to know that his book had gone down so well with these glitzy Ritz regulars.

As for herself, Diana declares that she cannot tell Evelyn how beautiful she thinks *Handfulers* is because she is not educated, she is inarticulate and she is uncoordinated in thought. What she does manage to say – in a way that shows she is the opposite of how she modestly describes herself – is that she read the whole of the second half with a lump in her throat, produced by the chapter and the verse. I can't resist playing and replaying aspects of this letter as I make my way towards Bognor Regis Station:

Barbara Wallace: 'I'm in love with Evelyn Waugh.'
Joan Yarde-Buller: '*I'm* in love with Evelyn Waugh.'
Sheila Loughborough: 'I'm in love with *Evelyn* Waugh.'

Take your pick of the lovely ladies, Ev. More *Blind Date*-style introductions required? Let's see if these supplementary statements help you make up your mind:

Lady A: 'Let us read *A Handful of Dust* again. There are passages in that book I can never hear without the temptation to weep.'
Lady B: 'Let us read *Decline and Fall* again. There are passages in that book I can never hear without the temptation to laugh.'
Lady C: 'Let us read *Vile Bodies* again. There are passages in that book I can never hear without the temptation to Party Without End.'
Lady DC: 'Let us read *Handfulers* again and again and again. With lumps in our throats. Produced by the chapter. And the verse.'

3

When I'm in the train heading back to London I remember something. Kate gave me a package that she told me not to open until I got to Boa Vista. It did flit through my mind when I was sitting by the mud that stinks in Pagham, but I was following a particular line of thought then and it didn't seem appropriate to break off from that. I've taken my own analysis as far as I can now. So what has Kate got to add?

It's a book, of course. But it's one whose existence was previously unknown to me: *Motor Tramp* by John Heygate. There is a frontispiece showing the author at the wheel of his car. He's facing to the right, towards the bulk of the book that follows. Just as Evelyn, dressed for the jungle, is on the frontispiece of *Ninety-two Days*, facing right towards the bulk of his book.

The book has been lent to Kate by Richard Heygate on condition that she takes very great care of it. Kate tells me this via a pencil note on a blank page that follows the title page. So we'd better say nothing of yesterday's journey at the bottom of my rucksack to the mud that stinks.

As I flick through the book I realise what Kate's pointing out via her notes. It seems that at the same time that Waugh was experiencing adventures abroad, then writing them up in a travel book, so was John Heygate. The book starts in May 1932 with Heygate collecting a new MG sports car from the Abingdon works near Oxford. The vehicle had to be run in, so Heygate spent a summer month cruising up and down the streets of London. He'd arranged to go on holiday to Berlin with a friend called Rightlaw (Anthony Powell, Kate tells me in the margin). They drove to Berlin, but after two weeks of a three-week holiday, Rightlaw had to return to England as a result of an affair of the heart. In a note, Kate explains that Heygate is probably conflating two experiences here. He did go to Germany with Powell in 1932. But he also went there with him in the summer of 1929, just when Heygate's affair with Evelyn Gardner had exploded in their faces. It was Heygate (not Powell) who had to return to Britain after two weeks and this was as a result of a telegram from Evelyn Waugh

to Powell which said: 'Instruct Heygate return immediately.' Heygate did as he was told and returned to England to shack up with She-Evelyn, ultimately in Canonbury Square, as Anthony Powell describes in *Agents and Patients*.

I look out of the window. But not for long, *Motor Tramp* has little difficulty in drawing my attention back to it. During the winter of 1932, the winter in which Waugh spent his ninety-two days in the Amazon, Heygate lived and worked at a film studio in Berlin. In the spring he drove south into Austria, to an alpine part of the country. He picked up an Austrian passenger and they ended up at the top of a pass, snowed in. Indeed the Pass Inn at the head of Rolle Pass was Heygate's Boa Vista. Not that it was boring or unpleasant there, with splendid ski-ing during the day and eating and drinking at night. But he *was* trapped.

An Italian army officer was also in residence, and both he and the Austrian fancied the waitress. After several days of mounting tension, the Austrian it was who became chatty with her. The romance – if romance it was – was short-lived, because the next day the pass was free of snow to the extent that it was again navigable by road. Before heading off, Heygate had a chat with the waitress which climaxed with her saying suggestively, 'One thing I would like above all to do before I die. I would like to see England.' Heygate took fright at this implied come-on, and off he sped with his Austrian chum. But what's significant here, as Kate points out in the margin, is that while in Prague the next year, Heygate found himself playing the same role in a triangle consisting of a Czech man, his girlfriend and himself. In that case, the girlfriend made it clear to Heygate that she was open to his advances. Given what happened with the Evelyns, what we would seem to have is a repeating pattern: John Heygate befriends a couple and, in due course, the woman makes an advance towards him. So don't blame yourself, He-Evelyn. It was just nature taking its course.

Back in England, Heygate gets the car serviced in May of 1933, just when Evelyn was recovering in England from his trip up the Amazon. That summer, Heygate covered six thousand miles in England. He seems to have been living on the South Coast, near Southampton, and driving regularly to London on film business. Winchester, the Test

Valley, Brockenhurst level-crossing, Camberley are all places that crop up in the text. This lifestyle extended into the autumn. Bognor Regis isn't far from the house on the Solent in which Heygate was based. Waugh and Heygate were South Coast neighbours, then – until Waugh went off to Fez to write *A Handful of Dust*, while Heygate took his car across to continental Europe again.

Heygate notes in *Motor Tramp* that Germany had changed now that Hitler had got into power. He didn't feel as at home surrounded by signs of militarism, though he does mention his admiration for Hitler, something that reads strangely now. He revisited alpine Austria and had a fleeting moment of passion with 'a woman in a brown woollen beret' in northern Italy. He travelled on to Czechoslovakia and ended up in Prague, where he rented a room and spent a few months writing a book, probably a film script. In the summer of 1934, by which time Evelyn had finished *A Handful of Dust*, Heygate took leave of his bar-man friend and the barman's girlfriend and returned to Italy to look for the girl with the brown beret. He found her easily enough at the top of the zig-zagging Stelvio mountain road, despite its forty-eight hairpin bends. Kate has used red highlighter on a key sentence, which reads: 'So I kissed her, and as I lay on my mattress my brain revolved the thought that this was the sort of girl men came to like and laugh at common things together until any life without her would seem poor and lifeless.'

Kate notes in the margin, in black ink this time, that Richard has suggested that the girl with the brown beret is a reference to She-Evelyn. Apparently, She-Evelyn accompanied him on some of his European travels in the MG, even though *Motor Tramp* doesn't admit as much. According to Richard, at one point they stopped in northern Italy, where She-Evelyn acquired two lovers – a local smuggler and a customs official. John Heygate left his highly-sexed wife to it, but returned in the MG months later and took up briefly again with her.

What *Motor Tramp* itself tells the reader is that on the morning that Heygate left the mountain for the last time, he and his brown-bereted girl listened to Italian racing cars climbing up the forty-eight hairpin bends. The girl, a sports-car fanatic, could tell which car was which just by listening to the engine. And when the drivers got to the top of the mountain, she was there to meet them with shining eyes, as she had been many times before.

I look up from the book. This brown beret thing has my attention. Was She-Evelyn keen on berets? I've seen a photo of her wearing one but don't know what colour it was. In *Black Mischief*, the male protagonist discovers a pillar-box-red beret which is all that's left of his lover who has been eaten by the chiefs of an African tribe. Nice touch, He-Evelyn. Kate was wearing a similar red beret the day we went to the Barley Mow. So perhaps she was seeing herself in a She-Evelyn role even at the *Decline and Fall* stage of our investigation. Nice touch, Kate.

I return to the book in hand. *Motor Tramp*? It's Heygate's name for his wife, I reckon. It's a touching tribute to Evelyn Heygate. If only He-Evelyn had had half as much understanding of She-Evelyn's nature as John Heygate seems to have had! But in that case *A Handful of Dust* wouldn't have been written, so I'll settle for the position as it stands.

I've reached the last page of *Motor Tramp*, but I turn over and take in what would appear to be some kind of shrine that Kate has made over a couple of blank endpapers. 'MOTOR TRAMP' is writ large on the left-hand side. Underneath that, a photo of Evelyn Gardner has been glued. In the picture, which is badly out of focus, She-Evelyn is staring intently at a kitten, which she holds in both hands close to her face. According to a scrawled arrow, the kitten is called Maltravers, Anthony Powell's name for Heygate. On the facing endpaper, Kate has written the following dialogue:

> Maltravers: 'A novel. I'm the hero.'
> Motor Tramp: 'You're not. I had to take you out. You were such a boring character.'

Kate's jest goes on, but I shut the book and close my eyes and let the train rush me back to whichever main-line station in London it's headed for. I feel I've been all round the world this weekend, yet all I've got is a T-shirt in my bag that states I LOVE BOGNOR on it.

That's Bognor, not Beaver.

Repeat: Bognor, not Beaver. Or Gardner.

CHAGFORD

Out of the Wild Wood and
Everything is Heygate

1

This place is a couple of miles from Chagford, Devon, and a couple more from the edge of Dartmoor. Evelyn used to come here to write, starting from the time in 1931 when he was told by his brother that the American landlady was particularly supportive to writers. It's still a superb place to concentrate, it seems to me. Though now it's no longer a hotel, just a thriving B&B. Where Kate has promised to rejoin me tomorrow afternoon.

The house has changed a bit since the thirties, but not much. There are six rooms in a wing attached to the original block, and it was in one or other of these, probably several of them over the years, that Evelyn did his writing. I've been given a chance to look around the whole building, and the grounds, but for now this desk in my own spacious double room feels like the right place to be.

Evelyn wrote the second half of *A Handful of Dust* here. But when that book came out in September of 1934, when he wrote to Lady Mary Lygon telling her that he was going to spend a studious autumn writing the life of 'a dead beast', his plan was to stay at his parents' new house in Highgate. In the same letter he tells Blondie that his alternative was to stay at the Savile Club, but that when he did that he was likely to go out whoring and make himself ill. The plan to stay at his parents' small home, if genuine, fell through, and he travelled out west again to the silence and seclusion of the Easton Court Hotel.

It took him from September 1934 to May 1935 to write the not particularly long *Edmund Campion*. The biography was written mostly here, but a note at the end of the book mentions only the three secondary places that the book was written, namely, Mells, Belton and Newton Ferrers. In *The Letters*, for the period covering the book's composition, there is exactly one letter written from each of these home-from-homes, all of which make for amusing reading.

But back to basics. Why was Waugh writing a biography of Edmund Campion? After all, his earlier biography of Rossetti had not been a great success and nor had he enjoyed writing it. Well, partly because Campion Hall was being rebuilt, 'on a site and in a manner more worthy of its distinction' than it's old home in St Giles, Oxford, and Waugh wanted to celebrate the occasion. The new site was up a lane from the main street, St Aldate's, that runs along the front of Christ Church College. Indeed, Ernest Vaughan, when crashing a car in 'The Balance', may inadvertently have been marking the new site of Campion Hall. Part of Waugh's motivation would have been that he was writing an *Oxford* book. More important than that though, the book was to raise his stock within Catholic circles. Despite himself, he had taken to heart criticism of *Black Mischief* in the Catholic press. Most important of all, Father D'Arcy, who had smoothly overseen Evelyn's entry into the Catholic Church, was Master of Campion Hall at the time of its flit across Oxford. He gets the formal dedication at the front of *Edmund Campion*. So the book was a gift to him for seeing Evelyn safely home.

When I first read *Edmund Campion* as a teenager I found it the dimmest of books. I could not believe it had been composed by the same mind that had come up with the irrepressible *Decline and Fall*. While reading *Edmund Campion* again today, I've begun to enjoy it, because I now know some of the coding. For Catholicism read the continuity of civilisation. For Edmund Campion – Scholar, Priest, Hero and Martyr – read Evelyn Waugh – Scholar, Priest, Hero and Martyr.

It must have been boring for Evelyn doing the historical research. The reader feels the author's pain as he sets the scene in 1566. Queen Elizabeth visited Oxford, one of whose finest scholars was a twenty-six-year-old fellow at St John's, who made an impressive speech to

the royal entourage. Edmund Campion was nominally a member of the Church of England but his intellectual sympathies with the Catholic Church grew. To the extent that when he was asked to make a public proclamation of his faith to the Church of England, his conscience wouldn't let him, and he was forced to leave Oxford for Dublin, where he began to write a book about his adopted country.

So much for the first part of *Edmund Campion*, the Oxford bit. In Chagford, say in this very room, part two got underway: the 'Priest' section. Campion travelled to the English College at Douai, then on to Rome and the Society of Jesus. No difficulty was made about Campion's reception into the Jesuit world and it was decided that he should join the Austrian set-up under Father Magius. This reminds me of Waugh going to British Guiana in search of Father Mather. I feel sure Waugh would have strongly identified with the ex-Oxford scholar's lonely travels across foreign lands to the home of a Jesuit he had never met. A few years later, in 1580, Campion was summoned to Rome. There he was instructed on what was to be his mission. He was to return to England and work towards the preservation of the Catholic faith. In other words, he was given a death sentence.

End of part two: party time for Evelyn? Well, at least a letter to Madders, surely. After which Evelyn may have pushed on with the third part – the 'Hero' section. Upon his return to England, Campion was encouraged by his supporters to put something in writing that could be printed and distributed. He came up with the document that is called *Campion's Brag*. Waugh describes the long letter as intoxicating, and suggests that it is impossible to read the statement even today without emotion. A bit like *A Handful of Dust*, then.

Campion went off around the country, introducing the zeal of the counter-Reformation. Waugh writes: 'The Government had taken away the traditional, simple priest. Here in his place came a new kind of Holy man – intellectual, committed, implacable.' Campion soon found he was travelling in a world that was tremulous with expectation for what he offered. His group travelled secretly through Berkshire, Oxfordshire and Northamptonshire. According to Waugh, the priest probably visited fifty or more Catholic houses in three months. Much of this parallels Waugh's own experience. Notably, his being encouraged to write something pro-Catholic on his return to England from abroad; his output being eagerly awaited by a general public; the generous hospitality that was made available to him by ancient Catholic families.

After returning to London, Campion was instructed to come up with a longer document that could be printed. This was a hugely risky operation as the authorities were determined that there be no repeat of the impact that *Campion's Brag* had made. Various people involved in the production were arrested. One man was racked to make him reveal the hiding-place of the printing press, without success. What a substitute for the old cliché of the pen being mightier than the sword: the printing press being mightier than the rack. All of which would have titillated Waugh's bibliophile instincts.

Only three copies of the first edition of *Ten Reasons* exist, Waugh tells his reader in the first edition of *Edmund Campion*. However, in later editions Waugh explains that a fourth copy was discovered in a second-hand bookshop in 1936 and gifted to Campion Hall. What Waugh doesn't say is that it was he who bought this copy and presented it to the Jesuits. Just as he made no public statement of the fact that all the royalties from *Edmund Campion*, the work of nine solid months, were to go to Campion Hall. This they have been doing since first publication. And they will continue to do so *in perpetuum*.

In fact, I saw this fourth copy when I was given a tour of Campion Hall some months ago. The book was in a glass case, so I couldn't get my hands on it. The Father who showed me around was in a hurry as he had a dental appointment. I was not left with the impression that I'd been accompanied by a modern embodiment of the spirit of Edmund Campion. But never mind, I saw right round the building, and noted Waugh's several contributions to the decoration of it, including a glorious Madonna and Child that he'd got hold of in Abyssinia.

Ten Reasons made its first appearance at Commencement, on 27 June. Copies were introduced into St Mary's, Oxford (whose bells Evelyn would clearly have heard from his rooms as an undergraduate at Hertford College). The polished style of the essay and the romantic manner of its appearance had a particular appeal to the university. But for Evelyn, *Ten Reasons* doesn't cut it like *Campion's Brag* does. And whether Waugh was spending the weekend with Sir Robert at Newton Ferrers, or with Lord Brownlow at Belton House, or with Katharine Asquith at Mells, it is to the *Brag* that I can imagine him turning for rhetorical flourishes.

In July 1581, having been in England for over a year, Campion resumed his travels. While he was preaching at Lyford Grange in Berkshire, a priest hunter got wind of what was going on. And although Campion and two fellow priests were hidden away in a secret room, the next day they were discovered when a chink of light in the well over the stairs was noticed. So that was that: the beginning of the end for Edmund Campion.

In the book, Waugh mentions that Lyford Grange still stands, reduced in size and importance, but still 'a house of poignant association to the Catholic visitor'. Waugh writes that the site of the priest's cell has long since disappeared and 'there is no good reason for identifying the long room in the house as the chapel. The moat and drawbridge posts can still be seen and a line of trees marks the avenue which once constituted the main approach.' What Waugh doesn't say is that Lyford Grange is another Catholic house that he himself knew at first hand, since his old Oxford chum, Douglas Woodruff, was its owner. A single sentence in the author's note to the first edition of *Edmund Campion* states: 'Mr Douglas Woodruff revised the proofs, advising me in several difficult points of accuracy and discretion.' This sentence amounts to the chink of light in the stairwell at Lyford Grange.

It also reminds me that in *Rossetti* Waugh wrote about the murals by Dante Gabriel Rossetti to be found in the library of the Union building in Oxford, without telling the reader that this was where he too was working. It seems that for Waugh to write a biography, there had to be strong personal links between the author and his subject, but that these links had to be kept hidden from the reader. The two biographies completed by Waugh by 1935 are autobiographies once-removed. The three travel books completed by then were written up matter-of-factly from diaries. And the four novels are personal experiences transformed into art. Indeed, solipsism seems to underlie almost everything that Evelyn Waugh wrote.

But where was I? Or rather where was Evelyn with his biography of Edmund Campion? Back to the Easton Court Hotel to begin the final section? Or on to Mells for the Martyrdom? If I'm in some doubt about Waugh's movements, Waugh is definite about Campion's. He was taken to the Tower of London and a royal warrant was signed authorising torture. He was put to the rack at least three times, though nothing of substance was obtained from this terrible process. As I reach this point in the story an image flies to mind. I don't know how seriously to take it. But take note of it I must: Evelyn is lying on the rack. And the rack master? There is only one candidate.

'Call me Evelyn, Evelyn.'

'Evelyn?'

'Evelyn *Heygate*,' says the rack mistress, checking that her prisoner is securely tied to the bed by his wrists and ankles.

'Now, Evelyn, darling. I want you to admit that you are a Protestant and that you are in love with John Heygate.'

'Never. On both ridiculous counts.'

'Now and for ever.'

'Never.'

She-Evelyn turns a ratchet handle.

'Ahhh . . . '

'Go on, say it! You know it makes sense. You are a Protestant who is in love with John Heygate, the man who makes love to me in his car, and on top of mountains, and on this bed that can become ever-so-much more comfortable than it must seem right now.'

'Ahhhhhhhhhhhh-h-h-h-h-h-h-h . . . '

That's enough: torture is a serious business. Although Waugh stated jauntily in a letter to Laura Herbert, whom he'd met at a house party at Pixton Park in Somerset, that he intended to arrest and rack Campion at Belton, then draw and quarter the priest at Mells. Actually, I like to think it would only have been when back in solitary confinement here at the Easton Court Hotel that he would have had the composure to come up with the sentiments with which he concludes his ostensibly restrained but truly passionate little book about human suffering. On the surface, it's not about Evelyn at all. But dig a bit, and the author's own inner workings are revealed.

Waugh wrote two books in a row concerning the long and winding road of an individual to his death. First, Tony Last. Second, Edmund Campion. And, if my analysis is correct, in both these books Evelyn takes a surrogate of himself to the point of death. Waugh, or a part of him, survives this bleak inner period and goes on to marry Laura Herbert and to raise a family with her. But an important part of Evelyn was at one with Edmund Campion on the day of his execution, when the priest's privates were cut off, and his entrails removed from his body and burnt in front of him.

'The End. Thank God.' There is no suggestion that Waugh wrote this at the end of the manuscript of *Edmund Campion*. But if he did, it would have had a different meaning from the same words written at the end of the *Rossetti* manuscript. That book concludes with the opinion that Rossetti lacked 'some essential rectitude that underlies the serenity of all really great art'. With Campion, Waugh felt he had found a human being who oozed essential rectitude from every pore, even as he lay stretched on the rack, with the remaining parts of his unfinished book, *The History of Ireland*, slipping beyond the reach of his suffering mind for good and all.

2

Kate arrives on schedule. Thank God. She announces her arrival with a squeal of brakes, a swish of gravel, and with the greeting: 'So this is where Evelyn used to bring his lady friends.'

That sounds promising. But before we go into it I must pass on to Kate the Waugh literature's only Pope joke. It goes like this. Late in life, Evelyn Waugh, ever more committed to his chosen religion, writes to the pontiff about the modern liturgy. The author is, shall we say, a little out of sorts with certain directions in which the Church of Rome is heading, preferring at all times the more traditional ways. The Pope writes back, pleading: 'But Evelyn, you've got to understand, I'm a Catholic too.'

Then I show Kate round the whole building, which she admires greatly. Like all Evelyn's bolt-holes, it's got class. In particular she takes a fancy to the sitting-room in which Waugh wrote *Brideshead*. It's a romantic setting, with a dark and ancient-looking table in the middle of the room and glamorous red ivy on the outside wall flitting round the window edge. The old visitors' book is still kept in the room, and inside it there is Evelyn's distinctive signature, on the 31 January 1944. Shame the visitors' book doesn't go back to pre-war years, it would have been interesting to see the signatures of Evelyn's female guests while in residence here. Or maybe he made sure that the names didn't appear in such a semi-public record.

I ask Kate where she's been on her travels, but apparently she's not

ready to tell me yet. She likes the gardens, which lead down to an attractive pond. I've been told that this wasn't part of the property in the thirties, but what does that matter in terms of us enjoying ourselves? It's on a bench by the pond that we sit down and discuss Waugh's time here. In August 1935, just three months after finishing *Edmund Campion*, Waugh went off to Abyssinia on behalf of the *Daily Mail* to cover the Italian invasion. But before he went, though he was courting Laura Herbert at the time – the nineteen-year-old, virgin, Catholic girl of impeccable pedigree – he was sexually involved with a couple of women. It's only the Selina Hastings biography that has much to say about this. Kate produces her own well-thumbed copy and takes up the story she seems primed to tell me.

'Selina doesn't date the affair with Clare Mackenzie, just states that she stayed with him at this hotel near Chagford. It seems that Evelyn walked out on Clare. We know this because she left him a note that reads: "Was it absolutely necessary to leave me when I needed you so desperately badly? One kind word last night would, I believe, have saved me from cracking so badly . . . My hand is so shaky this morning I can hardly hold the pencil steady." '

'What went on between the pair?'

'Selina gives no more details.'

'It's pretty obvious that Evelyn gave her a racking.'

'A racking?'

'The rack is an instrument of torture much used in the sixteenth century. Basically, the rack-master ties the hands and feet of the priest or girlfriend to a wooden contraption like a bed. He then ratchets up the tension of the ropes, and watches what happens to his victim's composure as the tendons that attach his or her limbs to his or her body are first stretched and then torn to shreds.'

Kate is not amused. She tells me that the letter from Clare Mackenzie to Evelyn goes on: 'But the doctor's given me some soothing medicine which may help. And God do I need it after your note this morning. I shan't stay here long now; what's the use, I should only be miserable without you. Please ignore a telegram in very bad taste if it reaches you – I hope it doesn't. I'm afraid I felt so ill I lost all sense of proportion and broke the rules.'

Kate wonders aloud what Evelyn's note might have said. Or Clare's telegram.

I don't know. But I can take a stab at both:

'Evelyn: "Let me know when you are ready for another racking."'

'Clare: "Being in bed with you at Chagford stop worse than the bloody rack stop stop stop." '

Kate thinks that, for once, I'm being hard on Evelyn. She takes this unusually sympathetic attitude towards my subject because there's another affair that shows him in an altogether different light. Kate explains: 'Although Waugh was clearly hoping to marry Laura Herbert by mid-1935, he may not have been confident of getting an annulment of his first marriage. So when he realised he would be out of the country on an Abyssinian jaunt for several months, he asked Joyce Gill if she would leave her husband and come with him. This she decided not to do, not least because she loved her husband, with whom she had two little boys. Two-and-a-half years later, in February

1938, she wrote to Evelyn, casting light on what had passed between them. Selina devotes a whole page to Joyce Gill's words.'

'I don't seem to remember them.'

Kate reminds me: ' "It's nearly 13 March which was the day you jokingly suggested that we might meet each year until I am seventy. And so I suppose that day will be for me a kind of agony for ever and ever . . . " '

Is this another racking I'm about to hear of? Well, let's just listen and see.

' "I do what you suggested and what – in my foolishness – I thought almost a crime. I think of you all the time when I am making love, until the word and Evelyn are almost synonymous! And in the darkness each night and in the greyness of each morning when I awake I remember your face – and your voice and your body and everything about you – so earnestly and intensely that you become almost tangibly beside me." '

'Who was this woman?' I ask.

'Joyce was the daughter of a vicar who left his wife and ran off to New Zealand with one of his parishioners. After that, Joyce was brought up by her mother in Birmingham, where she went to university. She dropped out of her course after a year to join a music-hall troupe. She gave up her stage career after eighteen months to come to London, where she got a job as secretary to the playwright Clifford Bax.'

'Cut to the chase. When did she get to know Evelyn?'

'Her history is just as important as his is. But all right, she'd met him at Oxford. She had been smuggled into an Oxford party dressed as a boy, and since then the pair had been friendly. Joyce was a couple of years older than Evelyn, and very different from him. She was musical, an active socialist, dismissive of religion and unconventional even in the bohemian world in which she moved. She was also impulsive and given to histrionics.'

'I like her.'

'She always admired Evelyn's work, but there was a side of him that she thought strait-laced.'

'You like her?'

'I'd like to know why she married Donald Gill, whom Selina describes as "an American businessman". She was clearly engaged with politics and the arts, but she may have had to make compromises in order to get by. Anyway, it was the flat in Canonbury Square, into which the Evelyns moved when they got married, that Joyce gave up in order to get married herself. When Evelyn used to visit Joyce there before their respective matches, she would tease him for being dapper. "A natty young man," she called him.'

'So did we, remember? Dapper Evelyn.'

'Joyce's friends were nearly all artists and writers. More so than Evelyn's were. So one has to wonder at the wisdom of her marrying a businessman. Apparently, in the years before her marriage she was introduced to the Bloomsbury Group, the Powyses, Edmund Gosse and Arthur Waugh. Through Arthur she met Alec Waugh. And through him, while dressed as a boy at that Oxford party, she came across Evelyn, her lover-to-be.'

'Is there more from that letter?' I want to know. 'Bearing in mind it's Joyce and Evelyn I want to know about. Not Joyce *per se*.'

Kate gives me a disapproving look and reads on.

' "After I am forty I won't want to see you. Then even the possibility of having your child will be gone. And I suppose that is at the root of this – this – I can't call it infatuation – because I know that that is an unworthy word for it; because I know, darling, that love is a juster description . . . " '

Kate continues: ' "I shall try most terribly hard to conform to the normal convention of 'decency' and not bombard you with love letters. And if ever I do write, darling, it is not a 'begging letter', only because I remember that once you said 'write to me if it helps' . . . Almost I could be contented if every night I could write and say, 'Evelyn, I love you,' and every morning I could say, 'Evelyn, God bless you,' But what nonsense! Of course I could not be content. I have only to remember your eyes – your mouth – and my heart aches as if it were a stone cut by a diamond." '

I am moved. So was Kate the first time she read it, she tells me.

But already I have my feelings under control. So much so that I risk another jest. I tell Kate that it is strange that Joyce Gill should have used the words about her heart aching as if it was a stone cut by a diamond, because that was exactly what Campion said to a visitor after a session with the rack-master.

Kate has had enough of my teasing references to *Edmund Campion*. Either I must explain them properly or shut up about it. So I explain who Edmund Campion was and how he fits into Evelyn-the-Unworthy's history.

3

After learning about Edmund Campion Kate feels the need for a walk on her own, leaving me still in the dark as to her recent travels. I'm beginning to fantasise that she's been to Boa Vista – after all there's an airport there these days – putting my own travels to shame. But I put that possibility out of my mind and return to the *Brideshead* room. Sitting there, looking out the window, the book that comes to mind is *Mr Loveday's Little Outing and Other Sad Stories*, and I go to our bedroom to fetch it, taking the steps on the external staircase two at a time.

The copy I have of Waugh's tenth book, in what I now see as a series of ten books (four novels, three travel books, two biographies and this collection of short stories) is not a beauty. The black-and-red snakeskin-pattern covers are faded and the gilt titling on the spine has all but disappeared. But it is a special book, being one of the first and only edition published by Chapman and Hall in 1936. The bookseller on AbeBooks had it listed as £30, but was happy to sell it to me for £25. I was disappointed when it arrived, as it isn't as well preserved as the matching volumes I have, the four novels. Then I noticed that the brightest gilt letters and the boldest red-black snakeskin belong to my copy of *Decline and Fall*. So all was right with the world.

Martin Stannard mentions in passing that Evelyn came to Chagford in February/March of 1936 to put together the collection of short stories that is proudly headed by 'Mr Loveday's Little Outing', a pissing-on-Arthur story, with 'Winner Takes All' coming up in the rear. According to the biographer it was an editing job that Evelyn enjoyed, partly because there were no new stories to write. Evelyn's edit was messed about with – some stories omitted in favour of new ones – when the collection was published again during the war as *Work Suspended and Other Stories*. But let's focus on the original collection as published in 1936. For me the best piece is the sublime 'Love in the Slump'. Intriguingly, much of it is set in this part of the world. Tom (one of Evelyn's favourite male names; the name for himself in 'Fidon's Confetion' and 'Winner Takes All') marries Angela. The wedding takes place at St Margaret's, Westminster, the same church in which Paul Pennyfeather was supposed to marry Margot Beste Chetwynde in *Decline and Fall*. Angela is twenty-five, pretty, good-natured, lively, intelligent and popular – just the sort of girl, Waugh remarks, who for some mysterious cause buried in the Anglo–Saxon psyche finds it most difficult to get satisfactorily married. Her basic reason for getting married is to escape prolonged residence in the house of her ancestors. She picks on Tom for no very good reason, but he has been mildly attentive to Angela since her first season. He is her male counterpart in about every particular, we are told. Waugh goes on to say that Tom took a third in History at Oxford. Could be almost anyone then! Pulling himself together, Evelyn tells us that Tom settles down to life in a firm of chartered accountants. Anyway, the point is that Tom and the angelic one get married and then catch a train from Paddington for the West of England. They are honeymooning at his Aunt Martha's house in Devon. Does it have any connection with the Easton Court Hotel? Well, possibly, given what happens, but the owner of the Easton Court was an American called Caroline Cobb.

The honeymooners wonder if they need to change trains, as it was someone else who bought the tickets for them. At Exeter, Tom gets out of the train to find out. He buys a West Country evening paper, learns that they need not change trains, and is returning to his carriage when he bumps into an old school chum from Eton, whose name he can't remember. The friend persuades Tom to have a drink in the station buffet before getting back to the train, as it has to halt at Exeter for twelve minutes. Tom makes a mistake at this point, a mistake that the reader knows he is going to pay for. He chooses to go with this mysterious, unidentified old friend instead of returning to his newly-wed wife. They have two whiskies together, man to man. Of course, when Tom gets back to the platform his train has gone without him. He supposes his bride will be all right. His cheery friend, who lives fifteen miles out of Exeter, assures him she will be ('Nothing can happen in England'), and invites him back to his place. I have checked, albeit on a small-scale map, and Chagford is about fifteen miles from Exeter.

The next day Tom wakes up, worried about not being with Angela, but despite this he is persuaded to spend the day hunting. The day's event ('over the worst hunting country in the British Isles') ends with him being thrown from his horse in the middle of an empty moor. He doesn't know where he is, nor the name or address of his host. After five hours walking across sodden Dartmoor, at eight o'clock at night, Tom trudges into the gas-lit parlour of the Royal George Hotel, Chagford. They provide him with a meal, and give him a room for the night. The next morning he makes enquiries about getting to his Aunt Martha's house and sends Angela a telegram. There is one train that day, and after three changes it leaves him in a village eight miles from his aunt's house. Tom, in for a bad cold, can't face the prospect of the long walk so spends another night at an inn. After three nights apart from his new bride, Tom finally makes it to their honeymoon venue only to find that Angela has legged it, apparently to the house of Tom's old school friend. Only Tom hasn't kept the telegram, so he still doesn't know the address. The fifth day passes in a stupor of misery for Tom. On the sixth day he rouses himself, and thanks to the name he finds on the inside pocket of the hunting coat he borrowed from his Eton connection, he tracks down the old school friend's address. He telegrams Angela there, asking if she's all right. She is quite all right but they have almost run out of honeymoon days, and so a meeting, she suggests, seems hardly worth it.

Evelyn!

When Tom and Angela do meet a couple of days later in London, they are still not really together. She is going out in the evening to see her mother, then on to meet 'your Devon friend'. In the last scene, a dialogue between Angela's parents, it's revealed that Angela has been offered the use of a house in Devon near to the home of Tom's bachelor chum. Somewhere she can go when she fancies a change. Nudge-nudge. After all the newlyweds can never get a proper holiday together because of Tom's work. Ah, yes, Tom's work . . .

I wonder why this story, which reads like a dream and has obvious resonance with the Waugh-Gardner-Heygate triangle, was dropped from the short-story collection in future editions. What do Waugh's biographers make of 'Love in the Slump'? Well, neither Martin Stannard nor Selina Hastings mentions it. And all Christopher Sykes, the first and official biographer, has to say, is that the story is based on the over-worked material of Waugh's early novels, and that it reads like a parody of his writing. Poor Sykes just doesn't – I mean, didn't – have an ounce of poetry in his Catholic soul. Well no, that's not fair. All three of Waugh's principle biographers have contributed compelling perspectives. Sykes's worst fault was the protective spirit that stopped him from going into personal areas, the sort of issues that subsequent biographers have got – or are getting – to grips with.

The story was first published in *Harper's Bazaar* in January 1932. That means it was probably written in November of 1931, when Evelyn was first in this area to write his third novel, *Black Mischief*. That might explain why so many of the locations in the story seem like ghostly variations of the same one: Easton Court. I get a strong sense of the Evelyn of autumn 1931 sitting here in this building, transforming experience into art. He sits here, putting the Evelyns of summer 1928 through the mincing machine of hindsight. It's as if the newlyweds were in the same place but were effectively apart. Yes, that's it. He-Evelyn and She-Evelyn actually spent their real honeymoon in the Abingdon Arms, Beckley. But were they ever truly together there? 'Love in the Slump' suggests not.

Simultaneously, or at least in the same story, the experienced Evelyn of autumn 1931 puts the Evelyns of summer 1929 through one-and-the-same mincer. At the back of his mind, he pictures the 1929 He-Evelyn in the Abingdon Arms, at work on *Vile Bodies*, and the 1929 She-Evelyn cavorting around London with John Heygate. How exactly does the telegram exchange in 'Love in the Slump' go? It goes like this:

'Are you all right? Awaiting you here. Tom.'

'Quite all right. Your friend divine. Why not join us here. Angela.'

'In bed severe cold. Tom.'

'So sorry darling. Will see you in London or shall I join you. Hardly worth it is it. Angela.'

The crunch of boots on gravel suggests Kate has got back from her own little outing. Has she popped off for a few hours to British Guiana? Has she enjoyed a few hours hacking over the worst hunting country in the British Isles? Has she got a cottage hideaway that I know nothing about, complete with the latest generation of Heygate? Or – the real fear – has she been motoring around the countryside in the manner of John Heygate, putting my own timid insights into the shade? These are all legitimate questions I might ask my elusive partner, but she beats me to it by skipping indoors and firing off questions of her own.

'Have you e-mailed the Pope yet? Is he going to let you into the Church of Evelyn? Or has he put you down for a session on the papal rack?'

'Actually, I did e-mail the Vatican,' I tell Kate. 'I may have over-egged it, though,' I say, frowning for effect.

'What makes you say that?' asks Kate, seriously.

'Because the Pope writes in his reply: ' *"But, Duncan, you've got to understand, I'm a cuckold too."* ' '

4

Over dinner, conversation passes smoothly enough from the old-Etonian in 'Love in the Slump' to John Heygate. Kate tells me that she has had a very odd experience. In a nutshell, she's read Heygate's novel *A House for Joanna* and she feels that it's full of significance for the Evelyn story.

Kate, who hints that she's been working even harder than me in the cause of our project, continues: 'Richard told me that the book was written about the house in Sussex, which his father bought and renovated with his second wife, Gwyneth. The book is very specific about time and place. John and 'Joanna' got married in the autumn of 1935, having known each other since summer 1934. Summer 1934 also being the time that John Heygate had his last fling with She-Evelyn at the top of the Stelvio in Italy.'

'OK, let me get that in perspective. By the time John Heygate and this new woman were house-hunting in Sussex at the end of 1935, Evelyn Waugh was in Abyssinia to cover the Italian invasion.'

Kate goes on: 'The couple first see the house together in November of 1935 and the whole book takes place over the next year; at its conclusion they're happily living in their farmhouse on a hill. It's a place called Kingsley Hill, in which Brian Epstein died of a drug overdose, decades later.'

'Did Richard tell you that?'

'Yes. But I haven't followed it up because we're not researching a book about the Beatles.'

'That's right, we're not.'

'But what I did follow up was Kingsley Hill itself. I went down to Sussex the same weekend you travelled to Bognor.'

'We could have gone together!'

'I liked the idea of going on a Heygate trip while you were on the trail of Evelyn. I had a lovely time reading the book in the village pub which was every bit as oldie worldie as the Abingdon Arms or the Barley Mow.'

I feel I've missed out. Both on a site visit and a secondary text.'

'There is no plot to *A House for Joanna*, I have to say. The house is bought, then renovated. No huge obstacles are put in the way at any stage. It is clear from the start that this is going to be a happy story. The book's feel-good factor is aided by the illustrations – line drawings that show the lovely old house on a hill with its own pond near by. However, there are some very odd things going on.'

'Oh, good,' I say, trying to forget about being left out of Kate's initiative.

'First, there are subtle references to Evelyn Waugh books. Remember the scene near the end of *Vile Bodies* where Nina has rejected Adam and taken up with Ginger Littlejohn?'

'Uh-huh. Little John Heygate.'

'On the way to their honeymoon in Monte Carlo, they are in a plane passing over the south-east corner of England and Ginger tries to remember a quote about '*This sceptred isle, this earth of majesty . . . this precious stone set in the silver sea*'. He forgets how it goes on. Nina tells him it's from a play but Ginger reckons it's from a blue poetry book. In the scene as written by Waugh, Ginger encourages Nina to look down at the land. She does this and she sees a nightmare vision of indistinguishable men and women marrying and shopping and making money and having children. The plane lurches and Nina announces to Ginger that she's going to be sick. Unconcerned, Ginger points out that that's what the paper bags are for.'

'I know the scene. "That's what the paper bags are for", is good.'

'Well, I think Heygate must have been annoyed by the implication that he would be ignorant about such a well-known Shakespeare quote, so in *A House for Joanna* he reprises the scene. John and Joanna are going on holiday and their plane's flight path should take them right over their own property on the hilltop in Sussex. John arranges for his gardener to build a bonfire and for a party of locals to be drinking the couple's health as they fly over in the evening. In fact the newlyweds miss their flight on the way over to France, so the locals toast is an empty gesture. But on the way back, they have another chance to look down on the house. John realises their seats are on the wrong side of the fuselage and, inventively using communication skills, gets a French couple to swop seats with him and Joanna. But then he realises he's got that wrong and they have to swop seats again. They see the house, and the remains of the bonfire, and are even able to make out the alterations that have been made in their absence, though that's hardly credible. Not that it matters. What comes over is John Heygate's commitment to his house, his country, his wife. It's maybe even a celebration of the idealistic way he's portrayed in the Waugh scene.'

I'm absorbed.

Kate goes on. 'Later in the book there is another weird Waugh reference. Heygate realises that Joanna is pregnant and that they will need a housekeeping couple to live with them. The couple who eventually accept the position have the surname of . . . guess?'

'I can't.'

'Todd!'

'"As in the nutter from *A Handful of Dust*?"'

'That's the one. But John Heygate doesn't make that much of it. He just lets the name leap from the page every time it crops up. It makes for a strange reading experience.'

'I wonder why he did that?'

'I'm not sure but . . . '

'It could have been a tit-for-tat thing.'

'How do you mean?'

'When John Heygate was forced to resign from the BBC, he started to work as a journalist using the byline: 'A Bachelor'. When Waugh's book, *Labels*, was published in America in autumn 1930, it came out under the title: *A Bachelor Abroad*. After all, Heygate wasn't a bachelor for long – he married She-Evelyn in August 1930. From earlier that month, when Waugh's divorce proceedings from the same woman had been completed, it was he who reverted to being a bachelor.'

'Anyway, I asked around Kingsley Hill to make sure Todd wasn't a local name. It's not. Then I sat down in the village pub, the Warbill-in-Tun, with a drink and calmly thought it through. Surely, the use of the name Todd is a subtle dig at Evelyn, who portrays John Heygate as John Beaver, social misfit and selfish oaf. At the end of *A Handful of Dust*, Mr Todd is going to make Tony Last's life a misery, having to read Dickens to the old man day after day. At the end of *A House for Joanna*, Mr and Mrs Todd are going to make the raising of John's son a doddle for the married pair.'

'Would that son have been your Richard chum?'

'I asked him about that. Sir Richard's older brother was born back in that year, in 1936. Richard has inherited the family title because the brother died when he was quite young. But the next really interesting thing about the book came out of that same e-mail exchange with Richard. He told me that when living at the house on the hill in Sussex, his father, who had a drinking problem, got very friendly with the Oxford Group, the originators of Alcoholics Anonymous. Apparently, he invited some of them to live in the house. Apparently, also, he threw his barrel of whisky into the village pond, as a sign of abstinence. The villagers soon fished out the barrel and drank it dry, but I suppose that was in the spirit of the thing. John Heygate was going to church regularly then as well, and the local priest asked why he never took communion. Heygate's answer was that he didn't feel he deserved it, because he had once hurt somebody very badly and he didn't feel he was entitled to communion.'

'Did he mean Evelyn?'

'Yes. The priest reported the case to his bishop who told Heygate that if he could get the forgiveness of the person he had wronged, then his sin would be extinguished in the eyes of the Church and he would be able to take communion. According to Richard, his father wrote a long, rambling letter to Waugh and got back a note, which said simply: "OK – E. W." '

'I know about that. It was written in 1936, according to the Waugh biographies.'

'That's what's strange,' says Kate, engrossed in her own analysis. '*A House for Joanna* was published in July 1937. The book must have been written in 1936 and there is no sign of any problems on the horizon. Admittedly, the protagonist doesn't miss any opportunity to have a drink to celebrate his marriage, or the housewarming, or the baby to be, or with the locals in their charming pub. But the drinking seems social. However, obviously the romance he was writing was not the full story of what was going on in his life in 1936. What he didn't record was his alcoholism, his relationship with Alcoholics Anonymous and with the Church.'

We need to take our time here. I need to make Kate slow right down at this juncture. 'I don't think the "OK – E. W." note is dated other than by year. So let's see what would make sense. At the start of 1936, Evelyn was still in Abyssinia, though he got back from there in January. He then spent a couple of weeks here at Chagford putting together *Mr Loveday's Little Outing and Other Sad Stories*.'

Kate doesn't look as if she's giving me her full attention. She has more to say from a Heygate perspective. But she'll just have to wait because I have to go through this stuff for the sake of my own analysis.

'By mid-April, Waugh was writing up his Abyssinian book. In May he was awarded the Hawthornden Prize for *Edmund Campion*. And in that same month he wrote a long letter proposing marriage to Laura, with the proviso that even if Laura were to look favourably on such a dicey proposal, Rome would have to come up with an annulment of his first marriage. Then, at last, on July 22 Rome *did* annul the marriage to Evelyn Gardner. Maybe the Pope had got round to reading *Edmund Campion*. Indeed, that may be the fundamental reason that Evelyn chose such a pro-Catholic subject in the first place. I can see him saying to himself: "If this doesn't get me an annulment, nothing will." That's what I can imagine Evelyn drafting as an Author's Note at the front of his manuscript. And at the end of his personal copy of the printed first edition, Evelyn could now write in his own flowing hand: *The End (of my first marriage). Thank Pope*.'

Shit, where was I? Oh, yes; I tell Kate: 'In August, Waugh had to go back to Abyssinia to do extra research in view of the way the war surprisingly ended. Then he came back to England to finish the book, *Waugh in Abyssinia*. I can imagine that the long letter from John

Heygate, provided it was received *after* he'd got his own blessing from on-high, would have elicited a generous response. Not a long response, Evelyn was not going to open up to John Heygate of all people. But to forgive, once his marriage to Evelyn Gardner was dissolved in the eyes of his church? Oh, yes, He-Evelyn could manage that. But I wonder – did getting the forgiveness of He-Evelyn help John Heygate?'

'According to Richard, from then on his father's instability grew more pronounced. He was discovered attempting to walk on the sea at Eastbourne after seeing a shining light beckoning him.'

'That would be the light of St Evelyn, Martyr.'

'Heygate was incarcerated in Ticehurst Towers, which Richard told me is still in existence and which I briefly visited. Heygate escaped from the place after going into a pub on an attended walk and climbing through the loo window. It was at this point that he managed to throw out the Oxford Group that had got such a hold on him. Richard reckons that Waugh also had an attack of the same alcoholic delusions in *The Ordeal of Gilbert Pinfold*. And that parallel got me thinking how close the biographies of Evelyn Waugh and John Heygate are.'

'Are they?'

'Both were born in 1903. Both wrote about their time at public school. Both chose Evelyn Gardner as their first wife. Both had novels published in 1930. Both were alcoholics for much of their adult lives. Both set up home when they married for a second time. Both had children with their second wives . . . '

'And there was me looking for a parallel between the lives of Waugh and Campion. How tunnel-visioned I am. But look, I want to get back to "OK – E. W.".'

'OK, Dunc,' says Kate.

'As I said, it might not have happened without the Vatican having annulled Evelyn's first marriage. But there's another thing that might have helped account for it. There's a scene in *Edmund Campion* that takes place a few days before the priest's execution, and in the aftermath of his torture. The condemned priest forgives and indeed protects the man who betrayed him to the authorities. Now, I just think that if Evelyn recalled writing that scene, as he surely would, then he would know how he had to respond when asked a small favour by the man that had betrayed him.'

'Pity it didn't help John Heygate in the long run.'

'How did things work out?'

'Richard told me that his father was in India during the war. He had an Indian mistress out there, and he wrote about their relationship in a book that was published in 1946.'

'In date terms, roughly the equivalent of *Brideshead*.'

'I don't think it was a success. It was the last book he published, and in *Debrett's Peerage* in the fifties, John Heygate, who'd been Sir John since 1940, described himself as a retired writer, which is an unusual thing to do. He kept drinking, I think that's what put paid to his creative spark.'

'It didn't in Waugh's case.'

'In the memoirs of Anthony Powell, Heygate's old friend refers to him as being in a terrible state at the end of the war, through drinking. It's the last mention he gets in Powell's autobiography. And Richard told me that his father's alcoholism just got worse over time. His third wife, an Irish woman, used to help him by hiding his booze and placing enticing bits of food about the house. When Sir John started eating he would lose his appetite for drink. And once he stopped drinking for a few hours he would be off it completely for weeks. Until the next binge.'

'How did it end?'

'He killed himself in 1976. His third wife had died by then. Apparently, what Sir John enjoyed most in his declining years was driving to see the villagers in the hills close to where he lived. When his eyes failed and he couldn't drive any more, he shot himself.'

'Shame.'

'There's a footnote about John Heygate by Alexander Waugh in *Fathers and Sons*.'

'You've got your own copy of that too, then?'

'Don't you remember? You off-loaded the paperback copy that you were given for your birthday.'

'By hook or by crook, she's got every Waugh book.'

Kate ignores this. She goes on: 'According to *Fathers and Sons*, John Heygate shot himself after suffering depression and syphilitic madness. The footnote goes on to say that shortly before his death John Heygate wrote to Evelyn's son.'

'Auberon?'

'Heygate told Auberon that several people had asked him to write down what he knew about his father, but that he never had done and he never would.'

'No rack-master would ever get such information out of him, no matter how severe the racking.'

'All John Heygate would say was that he retained feelings of love and admiration for Evelyn Waugh. He said that Auberon's father had been a great man and that he – John Heygate – would always feel proud to have known him.'

My feelings about John Heygate have turned full circle since Kate delved into his history. He's practically up there with Edmund Campion as a saint and a martyr. What I mean is, after three marriages and however many mistresses, his privates were cut off, his entrails boiled in a whisky barrel in front of him, and his eyes gouged out. Pain (rather than Party) Without End. At least that's how it must have felt for a while. God rest his tortured soul.

Kate is still speaking. She tells me that in a book that Richard Heygate has recently co-written, called *Endangered Species*, he writes of the death of his mother, the subject of *A House for Joanna*. After she suffered a bad stroke, Richard would sit beside her in the hospital and read aloud from *Brideshead Revisited*. Then, at her funeral service, Richard chose to read her favourite scene, the one where Charles and Sebastian have been enjoying a picnic with fine wine, on the way from Oxford to Brideshead. The scene where Sebastian says he would like to bury something precious in every place where he'd been happy, then when he was old and ugly and miserable, he would come back and dig it up and remember.

That's moving. It's all moving. I'd like to think that if ever Richard Heygate has cause to ask anything of Alexander Waugh, the answer might be along the lines of: 'OK – A. W.'.

5

Kate asks me why I'm lying awake in our double bed in the Easton Court Guest House.

'Because I've thought of something.'

'I know that. I can hear the brain cells hugging themselves.'

'It stems from that room downstairs. I mean the sitting-room where Waugh wrote *Brideshead*. I don't think I mentioned that a few months ago I ordered a microfilm copy of the novel from the University of Texas.'

'No, you didn't.'

'At the time I'd come across the statement in several of the biographies that Waugh used Alastair Graham's name instead of Sebastian's at various times in the manuscript. I wanted to know where exactly. But by the time the reel arrived I'd moved on. I did have a go at finding "Alastair", but I didn't manage to get all that far before boredom got the better of me. So I abandoned that and zoomed through the reel to pick up what else I could. At the end of the first draft come some insertions. And it's insertion C that Joyce Gill's letter has brought to mind.'

'Insertion C?'

'Charles has just been visited in his room by his cousin Jasper, who warns Charles that he's getting in with the wrong set. He's against Sebastian in particular. Charles's unspoken retort comes towards the end of the insertion and reads, "I could tell him that to know and love one other human being is the root of all wisdom." '

My turn to listen to Kate's brain cells getting into gear. Finally, she says: 'That's what Joyce had then, the root of all wisdom.'

'Evelyn too.'

'Who did Evelyn know and love?'

'First, Alastair.'

'Pity you didn't find out where his name crops up in *Brideshead*.'

'Oh, but I did. As I said, I couldn't face the prospect of going through the densely written manuscript, only to miss the Alastair references, then having to go through the bloody thing again. And again and again . . . '

'Oh *Brideshead*, will it never end!'

'Exactly. So I got in touch with a top *Brideshead* scholar, Professor Robert Murray Davis, who wrote books about *Brideshead* back in the eighties, and, though now semi-retired, still regularly gets himself to Austin, Texas, where most of the Waugh manuscripts are held. By return of e-mail he gave me exactly the information I'd asked him for.'

'Nice one, Bob.'

'The first occasion is a funny little scene that was deleted by Waugh, then slightly rewritten. It comes in Book One, after Charles had been out with Anthony Blanche, who has spent the evening buttering him up – praising his painting skills – and warning him against the influence of charm in general and Sebastian in particular. That night, Charles can't sleep. Waugh wrote these words for him: "I was dry-mouthed from the heavy mixture I had drunk, hot and cold by turns, with the excitement of thinking myself an artist, and Alastair the temptation to lure me from my lights." '

'Alastair the temptor!'

'The second mention is alcohol-related too. Again it's in Book One, but well into it, almost halfway through the book.'

'Oh, you can surely set the scene more vividly than that!'

'It's the Christmas holidays. Sebastian's back in England after being sent down from Oxford for a term – for drunkenness – a time spent abroad with the manipulative Mr Samgrass. Charles has chucked Oxford and is in the middle of his first year of studying art in Paris.'

'Better.'

'There's a family dinner taking place at Brideshead. Sebastian's in disgrace for having gone AWOL for a few days. Charles watches the champagne go around the table. Sebastian asks for whisky instead, his plan being to access more and stronger drink. But the butler checks with Lady Marchmain before placing before him a decanter with an unusually small amount in it. Sebastian raises the decanter very deliberately, tilts it, and then in silence pours the whisky into his glass where it covers two fingers. Waugh then writes via Charles . . . '

'Gosh, can you remember?'

'I think I can. "We all began talking at once, all except Alastair, so that for a moment Mr Samgrass found himself talking to no one, telling the candlesticks about the Maronites; but soon we fell silent again, and he had the table until Lady Marchmain and Julia left the room." '

'So, let's see. Alastair, not Sebastian, as Evelyn's temptation from art. And Alastair, not Sebastian, as addicted to alcohol. Quite appropriate slips of the pen, really.'

'Strangely enough, I'm thinking about Alastair right now because of John Heygate. Not that they played anything like the same roles in Waugh's life. Evelyn loved Alastair Graham, and he must have hated John Heygate, at least for a while.'

Silence while I sort out what I want to say.

'I was thinking what a strange life Alastair lived. He only worked for a few years in the diplomatic service, first in Athens, then Cairo, and after that he was forced to resign as a result of a sex scandal. I think he retired altogether and survived on whatever money his mother left him. He lived the life of a recluse somewhere in West Wales, and that's all I know.'

Silence. I wonder if Kate's still listening. 'Are you there?' I whisper.

'Yes. Just thinking about something.'

After a few moments more, I feel able to attempt some sort of overview: 'In 1981 *Brideshead Revisited* appeared on television in that incredibly successful dramatisation. Alastair may have had the satisfaction of watching Anthony Andrews playing Sebastian. Not a bad likeness judging by photographs of Alastair at Oxford. If he did see it, he must have enjoyed the spectacle, though he may have wondered why such a tall actor was playing the role of Charles Ryder.'

Silence again. Until I say: 'So what do we have? Oxford in the early twenties when Alastair was a young man. Then in 1944, middle-aged Evelyn brought that earlier era back to life again in his magnum opus. Then in 1981, a television company did its bit to immortalise Alastair and Evelyn's heyday . . . Oxford in 1922 . . . Oxford in 1944 . . . Oxford in 1981 . . . Young Alastair. Young Alastair. Young Alastair . . . '

'There was something timeless about his life?'

'That's what I'm thinking. I wish I knew more.'

'I know a lot more,' says Kate, stifling a laugh. 'I was going to leave it until tomorrow, but I might as well tell you now.'

'What are you on about?' I ask.

'I looked up Alastair Graham on the web and got very little, as you did. But one insignificant little mention led to something exciting.'

'Mmm?'

'Alastair is not only Lord Sebastian in *Brideshead Revisited*, he's also Lord Cut-Glass in *Under Milk Wood*.'

'How do you make that out?'

'In 1936, the year that John Heygate and Evelyn were in touch with each other, Alastair bought a mansion called Plas y Wern near Newquay, on the west coast of Wales. Dylan Thomas lived in the area for a year or so in the mid-forties, and was a frequent visitor to Alastair's mansion. Apparently, Alastair wasn't keen on the poet coming to his parties, because he had a tendency to drink too much and become boring, interfering with the hanky panky that was these get-togethers *raison d'être*. But on other occasions, Alastair, Dylan Thomas and the local vet met up just to drink in a pub and talk about books.'

'Where did you find this out?' I manage to ask.

'I'll tell you in a minute.'

Christ, why is it that today has turned out to be such a racking? So soon after reading about Campion, I felt the perspective on first Joyce Gill and then Heygate was stretching me too far. I felt that I'd had about as much as I could take from Kate for one night. But it seems that the rack-mistress is not finished with me yet.

'Back to this Lord Cut-Glass thing,' says she. 'Apparently, Alastair talked in a fastidious and well-bred – but not affected – way. Dylan Thomas referred to Alastair as "the thin-vowelled laird" and it's from a development of that that he came up with Lord Cut-Glass. He doesn't have a huge part in the play, but among the things that crop up in respect of him are fish-scraps and a fishy kitchen. Alastair was known in the area for his fish dishes and he published a pamphlet called "20 Different Ways to Cook Newquay Mackerel".'

'I wonder what Evelyn published the year that little gem came out.'

'The main thing about Lord Cut-Glass is his collection of clocks. Alastair was known to be obsessed with time-keeping while at Plas y Wern. He expected his bath water to be drawn at exactly the same time each morning. And locals could set their watch by the sight of his battered old car leaving the property every day for a local inn.'

'What about those parties though?'

'They were notorious. People came down from London for them. Lord Tredegar, the man over whom Alastair had to resign his post in the diplomatic service, used to turn up. So did writers and painters such as Compton Mackenzie and Augustus John. People from the intelligence services as well, plus the more presentable and open-minded locals. The house had no electricity. Holding a lamp, Alastair would lead the guests from the front door up to the library where in the dark there was much squealing as the women were touched up.'

'And the men, surely.'

'Alastair would supply his guests with glasses of rum, while there were jars of pickled herring on the side.'

'Pickled herring on the side! Over and above twenty different ways to cook your lover mackerel! And here's me believing that Alastair lived the life of a recluse in West Wales, as miserable as Evelyn had been while teaching in North Wales.'

'I think he succeeded very well in avoiding Waugh biographers, and journalists in general. His active interests in Newquay included books and literature, cooking, cheese-making, entertaining, sailing, playing the oboe, painting, embroidery, decorative knots and making deck shoes out of sail cloth and rope . . . '

'Making deck shoes?'

'Probably a throwback to his carefree days in Greece. In Newquay he was popular. He did have an evil temper though, and once stuck a fork through the hand of a local resident.'

'Lord Cut-Fork . . . '

'Lord Cut-Throat . . . '

It's hard to take all this in. That's the thing about being in the hands of a rack-mistress who knows her stuff, you never get a chance to get your thoughts straight.

'The reason I know all this . . . ' says Kate.

Oh good, the she-racker is going to relent.

' . . . is that a writer called David N. Thomas has written a book about Dylan Thomas showing how the poet's stay at Newquay was crucial to the development of *Under Milk Wood*. He shows that the village of Llareggub – which is Buggerall in reverse – is effectively Newquay. I know you would love this book because it takes geography and a sense of place very seriously. In fact, *Dylan Thomas* is subtitled *A Farm, Two Mansions and a Bungalow*.'

Kate has a point. My book may end up being called: *Evelyn Waugh: Two Colleges, Several Pubs and Innumerable Country Houses*. Though the truth is I don't know where tonight leaves me with my book. One thing has crystallised. I now have to credit Alastair with more gravitas – and with more literary influence over Evelyn – than I did before. He clearly had a passion for books and for artists, as well as parties and everyday things. And that must have contributed to the bond between them being so strong.

'I'm surprised you didn't hightail it over to Wales to follow up these findings on the ground.'

'No, I didn't go there. But what I did do yesterday was to break my journey at Barford.'

'Of course you did.'

'Barford House is surprisingly big, with six pillars built into the front façade and seven windows showing in both the ground and the first floor. However, there is an air of dilapidation about the place and I wondered if it had been divided into flats. Nobody was answering the bell, but I could see that the place was lived in.'

I suppose I should just lie back and enjoy Kate's narrative.

'I tried the bell again. This time a young woman answered, and as I was explaining my interest in the house an older woman drove up. This was the young woman's mother, friendly enough, but on seeing her husband arriving at the house on foot, she passed me over to him. For the third time I set about explaining why I'd disturbed the family's privacy. But as I felt him gradually relax, this encouraged me to relax too. Do you find it works like that?'

'It was a bit like that when I talked to the owners of Diana Cooper's old house.'

'Soon the owner was talking back. Alan Roberts is a builder and he knows a certain amount about Alastair Graham and Evelyn Waugh. When he bought the house in 1980 he tried to get in touch with Alastair, who had long been living in Wales by then. In fact, Alan does have somewhere a couple of letters answering the points he raised with Alastair about the original architecture. However, I was able to tell him something he didn't know – courtesy of Selina Hastings – by pointing out that the extension made to one side of the house, spoiling the symmetry of the façade, was a ballroom made by Mrs Graham for Alastair's coming-of-age party. An event that never took place due to Alastair's very definite views on what was and wasn't his idea of coming out.'

'Did the owner invite you in?'

'No, but he was OK about me going into the main part of the garden, behind the house. There is a long pond that Evelyn writes about in his *Diaries*. Beyond the pond, a broad path of paving stones leads farther down the garden to a gazebo or folly. I walked up the two broad stone steps and into the space surrounded by pillars. "Careful," said Alan. Well, I was being careful, because some chunks of stonework from the dome have recently fallen to the ground, though the lead canopy that tops the stone, echoing the cupola in the middle of the roof of the house itself, seems to be intact. As I stood looking past the pond back to the house, I felt Evelyn and Alastair must have stood precisely there. I pictured Evelyn and Alastair enjoying one of their "high-necked jumper evenings". Remember that bit in *Brideshead* when Sebastian and Charles have left the candlelight of the dining-room for the starlight outside and sit on the edge of the fountain, cooling their hands in the water and listening to it splash and gurgle over the rocks?'

'Yes, I do.'

'The next morning their exchange goes something like: "Ought we to be experiencing earthly joy every night, Charles?" "Yes, I think so." "I think so too." '

I don't say anything, so as not to interrupt the flow of Kate's story.

'I wonder if my thoughts became morbid because of the state of the gazebo. A pillar is missing, and the one nearest it is supported by a variety of props, poles and clamps. A scaffold consisting of rusty old poles has also been erected at some stage, but the structure is on the point of collapse at one side.'

'All things must pass.'

'I took photographs of the house from "the temple", as I think of it.'

'Waugh's lost novel, *The Temple at Thatch*, may have some connection with the place.'

'Perhaps. But in the end I was thinking about the wonderful novel that Evelyn eventually wrote in tribute to the love he'd both given and received in that place.'

'*Brideshead Revisited*.'

'What was that line from the manuscript you mentioned earlier? From insertion C?'

' "To know and love one other human being is the root of all wisdom." '

Silence.

'I want to know what happened to Alastair,' I say at last.

'His clock finally stopped in 1982. A morning's bath-water was run and never used. The people of Newquay had to learn to set their clocks by something other than his car departing for the pub in the evening.'

Let's leave it there. Another one bites the dust, but in a way of his own choosing, and after he'd got a chance to watch *Brideshead Revisited* on the telly. I can see him sitting at home pouring out a whisky in time with Anthony Andrews. And smiling with happy seraglio contentedness. That's what I want to think about Alastair Graham. God rest his eccentric soul.

6

It feels great still to be at the Easton Court. Kate's having a day's walking on Dartmoor and the last thing she said before driving off towards Chagford was that she looked forward to catching up with Evelyn and me this evening.

Now it's early afternoon and the September sun is lighting up the garden. Indeed, the light of day has regularly been drawing me out of this ground-floor study (it's the *Brideshead* room I'm working in). Just as the darkness of the solitude-promising study has kept drawing me back inside. Yes, I've been very comfortable occupying this space.

My original plan to take off with Kate for Pixton this morning and begin my research on Laura Herbert, Evelyn's second-wife-to-be. But if I'd done that, stepping back into the late 1930s, then I might have missed what I found staring me in the face when I sat down here first thing. Well, actually it was while waiting for the sausage-egg-tomato part of our breakfasts to arrive that I turned around to take a closer look at the collection of books in the shelves that line one wall of the dining-room at the Easton Court. I found that there were several books by Alec Waugh here. I slid one from its place and, suddenly, something came together in my mind. Something that has been a pleasure to follow through these last few hours. Evelyn's story once removed.

Alec Waugh wrote fifty-three books over the sixty-one years of his adult life. He was every bit as much of a writer as Evelyn was. He responded to the literary-salon atmosphere of Underhill – as well as to the encouragement and adoration of his publisher father – in such a way as to take to a writing career far more easily than Evelyn did. It's obvious from reading even a small amount of Alec Waugh's output that he was more at ease with himself as a writer and as a man. Does that make for a better writer? Of course not. He doesn't have his brother's spark, the spark that was ignited in Evelyn's imagination by conflict with the world. But, be that as it may, Alec's writing career throws shafts of light on all things Evelyn.

This morning I started by dipping into *A Year to Remember: A Reminiscence of 1931*, which was written by Alec in 1975, forty-four years in retrospect. Just as I've been reading the work thirty-two years after the writing of it. The book reveals that Alec found the Easton Court Hotel by chance in September 1931, when given a lift to Cornwall by two young ladies who were holidaying there. He told his brother about the qualities of this venue that made it suitable for a writer, and so it was that Evelyn came here in October to begin *Black Mischief*.

What else leapt out at me from Alec's book? One morning in June of 1931, Evelyn and Alec are sitting together on a terrace at Ville-franche in the South of France. A very slim and attractive woman comes into their sight. The brothers look at each other and know what each is thinking. 'Let's toss for it,' says Alec. 'Winner gets a three-day first-refusal,' suggests Evelyn. Alec wins the toss. This incident leads to Alec's main love affair in his *Year to Remember*. Oh, those unreconstructed, pre-feminist Waugh brothers!

But this incident reminded me that during childhood they were rivals for their father's affection. Evelyn lost out there too. It struck me – still strikes me – that the Evelyn-Arthur-Alec triangle fore-shadowed the Waugh-Gardner-Heygate one. Perhaps the earlier lost cause psychologically prepared Evelyn for the main defeat of his life. It would be funny if Evelyn Gardner's favourite novelist was Dickens too. I seem to remember she got on very well with Arthur. Selina Hastings quotes her as saying, 'Old Mr Waugh is a complete Pinkle-Wonk.' Tantamount to saying that her favourite novel was *Mr Pickwick's Papers*? Well, maybe not. For his part, Arthur liked She-Evelyn, finding her lively and warm. But he may have had reservations about her character, judging by that inscription he wrote in a copy of *Decline and Fall* doubting whether daughters were any less deplorable than sons these days.

I've dipped into another Alec Waugh book today. It's called *The Balliols* and was written by Alec in 1933. It's a family saga that begins with a man building himself a house in North End Road, Hampstead, in 1907. Edward Balliol has two sons, Hugh, his favourite, who serves in the First World War and who later works with Edward on the board of his company, and Francis, who is neglected. Alec and Evelyn, then. Francis is a minor character throughout, but on almost the last page of the book he is described in these terms:

> Francis was concentrating his attentions on the party. He was acting as secondary host. That is to say as barman. His face was flushed, accentuating a slight puffiness of cheek. He had given up football the previous year and was growing fat. He had asked himself whether he had ever really loved. He was nearly thirty. He was in the mood to fall or to imagine himself seriously in love. A great deal indeed depended on the type of woman by whom he was next attracted. He was one of those men, one of a smaller minority than is recognised, whose life is so centred around women that they can at a crucial point be broken by a love affair. If there was waiting for Francis the kind of marriage that subsides into a sympathetic comradeship, his life would continue on an even course of routine promotion . . . While again the demands and caprices of a flibbertigibbet might tantalise, exasperate his ambition into genuine achievement. It was a toss up. One way or another the outcome lay hidden in the next five years.

Quite cunning characterisation that. Alec is cutting things both ways. He knows that 'Francis' has already fallen for a flibbertigibbet and been broken by the experience, while at the same time the relationship has 'exasperated his brother into genuine achievement'. And as it happens, waiting for Evelyn *was* the kind of second marriage that subsides into sympathetic comradeship, and, one might say, it led to an even course of routine promotion in the literary world.

Did Evelyn read *The Balliols*? Well, I've just used Kate's laptop to log on to the University of Texas's website, as it's to the Harry Ransom Centre there that Evelyn's library went after his death. I can see that some of Alec's early books and some of his late ones were in Evelyn's collection. No titles between 1926 and 1948, though. With Evelyn having no base of his own for much of that time, I wouldn't expect him to have actively collected books in that period.

Evelyn: 'No, Alec, don't give me a copy of *The Balliols*, I've nowhere to put it. I'll read our father's copy when I'm next at home, if I can prise it out of his doting grasp.'

I'm pretty sure Evelyn read *The Balliols* because of what it says in the short story 'Winner Takes All', which was written following the completion of *Edmund Campion* in 1935, a year after *The Balliols* came out. When I was at Underhill, I reckoned I had worked out the key to that story, which was that the relationship of its characters, the brothers Gervase and Tom, closely echoed the history between Alec and Evelyn, particularly in the way that the older brother received preferential treatment from a parent. And I still think that is the crux of the matter. But I kind of glossed over the climax of the story on that occasion and I'm keen to revisit that.

OK, straight back in at the deep end of 'Winner Takes All' . . . Mrs Kent-Cumberland shares Tomb Hill with her beloved elder son, Gervase, who is making serious inroads into the family's fortune due to the expensive racehorses he keeps. The younger son, Tom, working as a manager on a sheep farm in Australia, has become engaged to his employer's daughter. He announces in a letter to his mother that he intends bringing Bessie MacDougal, and her father, Mr MacDougal, over to England to meet his own family. Mrs Kent-Cumberland is appalled at the prospect. And so she might be. For anyone familiar with Evelyn's correspondence with his Madresfield ladies will know that in his letters, one Tommy MacDougal, master of foxhounds at Malvern, is ridiculed as an idiot. The irony is that the MacDougals in 'Winner Takes All' turn out to be well-connected with upper-class English society, and *extremely* rich. Mrs Kent-Cumberland soon sees that Bessie would be much better suited to Gervase than his younger brother. So she arranges that Gervase is Bessie MacDougal's guide while she's in England and she digs out Gladys Crutwell for poor young Tom. Bessie and Gervase are married after just six weeks' engagement. Which completes the rout: older brother wins all.

Relevant here is that in 1932 Alec married an Australian heiress and that in 1934 she duly inherited a fortune. In a letter to Lady Mary Lygon, Evelyn tells her that his brother's wife, an Australian, has just inherited a fortune and that she is looking for a grand house to buy in England. In the same paragraph he makes another of his Tommy MacDougal jokes, and in so doing perhaps subconsciously makes a link between his brother's wife and the name MacDougal. It could have been simply the massive inheritance, which Alec would benefit from, that prompted an envious Evelyn to write 'Winner Takes All' when he did. But it might also have been a riposte to *The Balliols*, and in particular that summing-up of Evelyn's prospects near the end of the family saga, which the younger brother may well have found patronising.

I lean back on my chair in this cosiest of writing dens. I wonder if when conceiving 'Winner Takes All' Evelyn made a connection between his childhood experience of losing out to Alec and his adult experience of losing She-Evelyn to John Heygate. In other words is there a little bit of Heygate in Gervase? As well as the losing of Evelyn/ Tom's woman, I'm thinking of the time that Tom as a boy was supposed to get a child-size motor car for Christmas. His heart's desire. But Tom's mother thinks that the giver must have got the labels mixed up. And so Gervase gets the extravagant gift of the car and Tom receives a book. Yet another book. I don't suppose it's title was *Motor Tramp*, but that's what comes to mind now.

7

For the second night in a row I can't sleep. This time it's a single word that is keeping me up. A real name: Gervase.

I get out of bed without waking Kate, put on slippers, make my way down the external staircase and find myself in the dining-room of the Easton Court Guest House. I may be four hours early for breakfast, but a wall of books is available to me right now.

In post-war years, Waugh's novels were published in navy-blue covers by Chapman and Hall. There is a line of them here, and it is the book at the end of a shelf that I take hold of. That is *Unconditional Surrender*, Waugh's final novel, written – so an end-note tells me – at Combe Florey, from March 1960 to March 1961. After a quick flick through its pages, I realise I'm going to need to refer to the two earlier volumes as well. So I slide *Men at Arms* and *Officers and Gentlemen* from the shelf, and take all three books to a nearby table. Out of the corner of my eye I notice a covered jug of fruit juice standing on the breakfast bar next to some glasses. So I pour myself a measure of orange and it really does feel like the dawn of a new working day.

I remember that the trilogy closely follows the *Diaries* for the years 1939 to 1945. That is, the work is primarily a war memoir. What's relevant to me here is that the protagonist's personal life references the story of the Evelyns. And with that in mind, I scan *Men at Arms*.

The protagonist is Guy Crouchback, who comes from a long-established Catholic family. In August 1939, when the novel starts, he is approaching his thirty-sixth birthday, as was Evelyn Waugh. Guy was once married to Virginia – not a Catholic, but a bright, fashionable girl – and they settled in Kenya (where Evelyn spent a month of 1930 following his stay in Abyssinia). Guy and Virginia live 'in unruffled good humour'. Guy 'farmed assiduously and nearly made it pay'. Then, 'unaccountably', Virginia declared that she needed a year in England for her health. In one of her letters home, she informed Guy that she had fallen in love with an acquaintance of theirs called Tommy Blackhouse, and that she wanted a divorce. So that was that: end of marriage. Waugh then makes a big deal of the eight years that Guy has been on his own. 'Time had stood still for him during the last eight years.' The eight-year period representing the time from 1929, when She-Evelyn bolted, to 1937, when He-Evelyn married Laura.

When Guy and Virginia meet again on page 96 of *Men at Arms*, at Claridge's Hotel, Virginia, who has by then been through assorted husbands and lovers, says to him, 'But it can't be possible just to have done *nothing* for eight years.' So Evelyn has to make up a background for his protagonist. There is no mention of Madresfield, Bognor Regis, Fez, Brazil, Chagford, or a stream of successful books. Instead, the story is that Guy moved from Kenya to Santa Dulcina in Italy, where he tried to make wine, began a book, and contributed local guide-books to an up-market tourist agency that didn't get off the ground.

None of which rings true. But it's all dealt with in a single stylish paragraph, so Evelyn gets away with it.

Quick march through the next 50 pages of war manoeuvres, then Guy is back at Claridge's again. He tries to seduce his ex-wife. To begin with, Virginia is up for this. Here, Evelyn is perhaps drawing on his own experiences as recorded in his diary of January 1940. That is, of having a very pleasant evening of cocktails and reconciliation with Teresa Jungman, and of having the best forty-eight hours of his life with Laura. However, Guy and Virginia are interrupted by farcical phone calls from one of Guy's fellow recruits, and the romantic mood is spoilt. When Guy pushes his luck, Virginia retorts by referring to their honeymoon, saying: 'Not a particularly expert performance as I remember it.' The climax of the scene comes when Virginia realises that Guy is trying to get her to bed because she is still his wife in the eyes of the Catholic Church and therefore the only person that Guy can legitimately make love to. She doesn't take kindly to this perspective, accusing him of being a wet, smug, obscene, sexless, lunatic pig.

The portrayal of Virginia is detailed and convincing. And possibly the sympathy that Evelyn shows the ex-wife is born of the fact that his second marriage has been a success. Evelyn has loved Laura without being rejected (they'd been married thirteen years by the time Waugh wrote the scene between Guy and Virginia), which allows him to revisit the relationship that went wrong in 1929 with less bitterness than in his pre-war writings.

On to the second book in the trilogy, *Officers and Gentlemen*, which was published in 1955. In this volume, Evelyn has more to say about 'the other man'. Tommy Blackhouse is portrayed with more respect than John Beaver in *A Handful of Dust*. Waugh goes so far as to say: 'Men who have loved the same women are blood brothers even in enmity; if they laugh together, as Tommy and Guy laughed that night, orgiastically, they seal their friendship on a plane rarer and loftier than normal human intercourse.' Steady on, Evelyn. Still, it is good to know that Waugh really would seem to have reconciled himself to John Heygate.

Or had he? Because halfway through *Officers and Gentlemen*, Virginia takes a new lover, someone to whom Guy had taken an instant dislike in *Men at Arms*. His name is Trimmer, and his general worthlessness echoes Beaver of *A Handful of Dust*. Virginia has a fling with this Trimmer in Glasgow. But then, reluctantly and partly for financial reasons, embarks on a long affair with him when they meet again in London. She goes with the tedious Trimmer – who is being touted as a war hero, though he is nothing of the kind – on a tour of British towns that I'm guessing Waugh deliberately makes sound unappealing: Scunthorpe, Hull, Huddersfield, Halifax . . .

Guy does not meet Virginia throughout the whole of *Officers and Gentlemen*. And it's only in the final novel of the trilogy, *Unconditional Surrender,* that it becomes clear why Waugh introduced an obnoxious partner for Virginia. Trimmer is no longer on the scene, but he has left Virginia pregnant. Virginia is homeless and broke, and with Guy inheriting a fortune from his father, he suddenly becomes an attractive option for his ex-wife. This time it is he who turns down her advances. But when she explains about the baby, Guy realises that he represents Virginia and her child-to-be's best – if not only – hope of security. Despite how ridiculous this will make him look in the eyes of his friends, he decides that he *will* take her back as his wife. Is this Evelyn forgiving She-Evelyn and Heygate to the extent of offering a home to their hypothetical love-child? I think it is. And Waugh makes this all the more poignant by having a bomb drop on Virginia, so that the only thing that Guy gets out of the deal is responsibility for his rival's child.

In the epilogue of *Unconditional Surrender*, set in 1951, we learn that Guy has married for a second time, to Domenica, whose relative youthfulness, Catholic background and propensity for farming, make it clear that Evelyn has his own very precise choice of second wife, Laura, in mind. They have two children of their own, but the heir to Guy's fortune is the child that Virginia christened Gervase, in honour of Guy's grandfather, father and brother.

Winner takes all, then. The child of Virginia and Trimmer will inherit Guy's estate, not the legitimate children of Guy and Domenica.

Apparently, on hearing a critic's opinion that the irony of the ending was ambiguous, and that it would be clearer if Guy and Domenica did not have any children of their own, Evelyn decided he would make such a change for the Penguin edition. Well, the paperback came out in 1964 and – I've just checked – such a change wasn't made. Evelyn and Laura raised six children and perhaps Evelyn decided it would be a bit much to write them out of his life's work altogether.

As I walk back up to our bedroom, I ask myself what the 'unconditional surrender' of Evelyn's last novel's title refers to. Well, it has one meaning in a war context, but right now I see it as Evelyn's ego surrendering to the universe. All barriers between himself and John Heygate have collapsed. The spirit of He-Evelyn, She-Evelyn and Heygate are coming together in a cloud of dust that might as well be called Gervase.

Evelyn (unconditionally surrendering to his rack-mistress): 'I admit that I am a Protestant, deeply in love with John Heygate, and I pledge allegiance to the fruit of his loins.'

The birds are singing, I would like to tell Kate my latest quasi-religious joke, but she is still asleep. I open my suitcase and take a little blue envelope from its place of safe-keeping. The envelope contains the letter that Kate gave me for my fifteenth birthday. It is written on headed paper, dated 23 February 1953, and reads:

DEAR MR WOOD – I must write to thank you again for your great kindness this morning in searching for my little boy, Septimus, and for bringing him back to us in safety. It was a most neighbourly action and my wife and I shall always be most grateful to you.

Yours sincerely,

EVELYN WAUGH

I have read this many times since Kate presented it with a flourish a few weeks ago. There was a time when it seemed appropriate to substitute the name Aloysius for Septimus. But, right now, the name that seems to slot into place between the neat commas is Gervase. Heygate-Evelyn's little boy. Or, putting it facetiously, Hey-Evelyn's heir.

Evelyn is lying back on the rack, having unconditionally expired, it would seem. But when I look into the corner of his room, I see that a small boy is waving a flag back and forth. Let me read once again the semaphore signal: 'Life-force . . . life-force . . . life-force . . . '

RESURRECTION

English Gothic IX

When I wake up for the second time in our bed at the Easton Court, I think to myself that there's nowhere else in the world I'd rather be. I inform Kate of this blessed state of affairs.

She feels the need to test it out: 'Wouldn't you rather be lying in the night nursery at Underhill, overlooking the North End Road, with the sound of your father reciting Dickens floating up from the breakfast-room?'

'Nope.'

'Wouldn't you rather be lying in a room painted buttercup yellow high in Meadow Buildings, with a view from the window of Christ Church Meadow, OXFORD, to pull you out of bed?'

'Nope.'

'Wouldn't you rather be lying sweating buckets under a mosquito net in Boa Vista, a Boa Vista that hasn't changed from the one that nearly did for Evelyn all those years ago?'

'Shit, no. And while we're at it I wouldn't rather be stretched out on a rack in a dungeon in the Tower of London either.'

But the funny thing is, I *have* thought of a place I'd rather be. I wouldn't rather be there right now. But I would rather be there come lunchtime . . . So after a playful romp and a late breakfast, we set sail for Dorset. It's the Barley Mow we're headed for.

En route, after listening to my take on the *Sword of Honour* trilogy, Kate goes quiet for a few minutes. Then she starts talking about Waugh's 1947 trip to the United States: 'He was supposed to be in California to see film executives about a possible movie version of *Brideshead*. As it turned out, he got obsessed with a cemetery called

Forest Lawn. He told his agent that the people at MGM bored him, but that they had at least been of help in introducing him to morticians, the only people worth knowing in that part of the world.'

'Mmm. He wrote *The Loved One* when he came back from that trip. I haven't read it for a year or so. And then I didn't so much read the book as annotate a few copies. How does it go again?'

'I think you've missed something. *The Loved One* goes like this . . . Dennis Barlow is living in California as a Hollywood scriptwriter. That doesn't really work out, and instead he takes a job at a pet cemetery called the Happier Hunting Ground. After the suicide of an older English colleague, who'd been sacked from his job with the film studio, Barlow gets a chance to explore Whispering Glades, the equivalent of Forest Lawn, a totally tasteless – utterly kitsch – memorial park and undertaking facility. While soaking it all in, he attaches himself to Aimée Thanatogenos, a girl who works there making cosmetic improvements to the faces of the corpses.'

'Aimée Than . . . '

'Think Al-o-y-sius. Take it bit by bit. Than-a-tog-e-nos.'

'Thanatogenos. OK, what about her?'

'Well, first let's notice how much effort Evelyn has put into naming the character. Aimée means 'loved one' in French. In the process of writing the book, Ev changed her surname from Kraft, recognising her cosmetic skills, to Sprott, emphasising her polyglot Americanness, before settling for a surname made up of two Greek words: *thanatos*, meaning death, and *genos*, meaning type.'

'Okey, dokey.'

'Aimée is torn between admiration for Mr Joyboy, her senior colleague who does most of the work on the stiffs, and attraction to Dennis Barlow who tries to seduce her with poetry.'

'I remember. He pretends that he's written what are, in fact, well known poems by classical English poets.'

'Yes. Aimée is constantly wondering how to choose between horrible Joyboy and patronising Barlow. It's a funny but deeply un-PC work.'

'Actually, I loved certain aspects of it when I was a teenager. I remember that Joyboy's mother has a parrot called Sambo who is given some great lines.'

'The parrot doesn't talk.'

'Sorry, it's Joyboy's mother who has the great lines. She says at one point, in order to insult her son: *"If I hadn't Sambo to love me I might as well be dead."* '

'It's the parrot that dies. And Barlow deals with the cremation, following Joyboy's instruction to do so. Joyboy invites Aimée to the pet cemetery for the bird's funeral knowing that she will be unimpressed with the way they do things at the Happier Hunting Ground.'

'One up for old Joyboy.'

'Joyboy is another great name. But again Waugh took some time to get there. At first he was "Elmer" in the manuscript, then "Boyes", before inspiration came.'

'Every time the name crops up it gets a smile from me.'

'Of course, Barlow also gets opportunities to get his own back on Joyboy. A confused Aimée finally kills herself in Joyboy's workroom. And Joyboy – the basement boy once removed – is forced to ask Dennis to help get rid of the body.'

'Are you by any chance linking this up with the Evelyns' love triangle?'

'Of course! Joyboy is an obvious Heygate, while Barlow's anti-Americanism, his contempt for the film industry, his fascination with Whispering Glades, his status as a published writer in England, is pure Evelyn.'

'Dennis Barlow is clearly the nth in a sequence of surrogate Evelyns. What about Aimée as She-Evelyn. Is that a good fit?'

'Not bad. Aimée writes letters to a newspaper agony aunt called the Guru Brahmin, asking which of her two suitors she should plump for. This may be a reference to She-Evelyn writing letters to He-Evelyn in the summer of 1929 asking for advice on what she should do about the awkward fact that she'd fallen in love with their pal, John Heygate.'

'Mmm. Anything else?'

'Do you remember how the book ends?'

'Remind me.'

'It ends with Barlow and Joyboy manhandling their loved one to the crematorium and stowing her in the oven. Barlow turns on the gas and lights it. Flames shoot out from all sides of the brickwork. He closes the iron door and remarks to Joyboy that he reckons "she'll take an hour and a half".'

'An hour and a half to produce a handful of dust?'

'It passes through Barlow's mind that he must rake through the ashes of his loved one, pounding up the skull and pelvis to complete the work.'

'Poor Aimée. Reminds me of the death of the love interest in *Black Mischief*. Prudence gets boiled down in a pot. All that survived of her was a red beret.'

'To pass the time, while the loved one is burning up, Barlow recites a poem to his rival. Joyboy objects to the fact that it's one of Barlow's "phoney poems". I've looked it up, it's an Edgar Allan Poe, and Waugh quotes from it three times in *The Loved One*. The original is called "To Helen", but in *The Loved One*, Barlow addresses his words "To Aimée". However, I couldn't help but think along the lines of "To Evelyn".'

'How does it go?'

'Which version?'

'You choose.'

> 'Evelyn, thy beauty was to me
> Like those Nicean barks of yore
> That gently o'er a perfumed sea
> The weary way-worn wanderer bore
> To his own native shore.'

For a few minutes I think it's me that's the weary way-worn wanderer. Then I remember that Waugh wrote the *Sword of Honour* trilogy after he wrote *The Loved One*. Gervase is Waugh's last word on his first marriage. Not Joyboy. A further thought makes me buck up no end.

'Do you notice anything about the male protagonist's name in *The Loved One*?'

'Dennis Barlow? Dennis is possibly an update of Dionysius.'

'Barlow is certainly a contraction of Barley Mow. Chuck out the last two letters of "Barley" and the first of "Mow". Hey presto – Barlow!'

'Oh, that is one lucky coincidence.'

'You can be sure that as soon as Waugh reached England after his Hollywood venture he made straight for the pub that we're heading for now.'

The revelation has put me in such a good mood that I start to sing: 'Joyboy went to mow, went to mow a meadow. Do you know this ditty?'

'Not sure.'

'Course you do. Join in when you get the idea. 'Two men went to mow, went to mow their girlfriend. Two men, one man and Joyboy, went to mow their girlfriend.'

Kate joins in once we get to verse five. And by the final verse we seem to be singing from the same hymn sheet: 'Ten-Ev went to Mow, Barley Mow a meadow. Ten-Ev, Nine-Ev, Eight-Ev, Seven-Ev, Six-Ev, Five-Ev, Four-Ev, Three-Ev, Two-Ev, He-Ev and Joyboy . . . BARLEY MOW A MEADOW.'

With every mile we travel we're getting closer to Waugh's spiritual home. Accordingly, the grouping of Henry, Pansy and the Evelyns is brought out for another airing. Kate wants to tell me what happened to Pansy later in life. Good, I'm curious.

'Henry and Pansy raised three children. After he died, she moved to Rome, a place she loved, not least because of her conversion to Roman Catholicism. She had a thing about Pope John-Paul II and would give guided tours of the Vatican. She lived until she was ninety-five, a long and useful life, much loved to the end by a large family.'

'What about She-Evelyn?' I ask, suddenly curious. 'That is if she avoided being cremated by the combined testosterone of her first two husbands.'

'It's about time you asked that if you really are going to call your book *Evelyn, Evelyn.*'

'Perhaps I will. *Evelyn, Evelyn,* as in Evelyn Waugh, the writer, and Evelyn Gardner, the woman who had a huge impact on that writer. Er . . . Do you know what became of her?'

'She divorced John Heygate in 1935 and married Ronald Nightingale, whose name may have subtly inspired the name of Charles Ryder's first wife's second husband – Robin. The Nightingales also raised three children. She lived until she was ninety, another long and useful female life.'

'No pounding of her bones into dust while she was still in her prime, then. Indeed, Pansy and She-Evelyn seem to have done just as well in the longevity stakes as those old boys Harold Acton and Anthony Powell. Though Baby Jungman beats them all, still being alive at a hundred and one.'

'But it's another thought that really interests me: 'Did She-Evelyn ever get a chance to put over her side of the Evelyns' story? I've kind of lost track.'

'Christopher Sykes didn't consult her. Being a Catholic, and so taking a dim view of adultery, he was very much on He-Evelyn's side. I suppose it was only when Martin Stannard was researching his biography that She-Evelyn was asked to put on record her side of things.'

'When was that?'

'In 1986, when she was in her early eighties.'

'Nearly sixty years after the events of 1928 and 1929.'

'In reply to Stannard's initial enquiries, She-Evelyn wrote Stannard a couple of fairly short – friendly but formal – letters in January and February of that year. In these she did make the point that Christopher Sykes had never come to see her. Maybe that prompted Stannard to arrange a meeting. Anyway, they met in April and he no doubt delicately went over a whole range of matters concerning the break-up of the Evelyns. According to the professor, she was a delightful woman. It was painful for her to recall those years, and she was very brave, but also cautious. Not sure he got a great deal out of that interview, to tell you the truth. From the notes in his book it would seem that the written correspondence was of more use to him.'

'Stannard should have met her in the Barley Mow. Then he might have learned something about the upside of the Evelyns.'

Right on cue, we pull up at the pub's car park. The first thing we do is take a few pictures. The ones of Kate are of a relaxed and happy human being. The ones of me are of a distracted individual. We take a few more and get exactly the same result. All things considered, I feel I've still got a few rabbits to pull out of my hat before I can be satisfied with my year's work.

We walk into the pub and my face breaks into a smile. Too late for the camera but not too late for other purposes is what I'm hoping. I've bought myself a pint of Badger and at the first sip I feel my brain cells lining up in squadrons. Oh, this final chapter is going to be almost too easy – God's own essay!

I heard recently that Alexander Waugh is going to be general editor of a collected edition of Evelyn Waugh's writing that will run to about forty volumes, to be published by Oxford University Press over fifteen years, starting in March 2016, fifty years after Waugh's death. I think

Evelyn would have approved of the choice of publisher – his old alma mater. The OUP will probably insist on launching the books at a party held at an Oxford College, but they really ought to consider having the launch party for the critical edition of *Decline and Fall* right here. Alexander would sit at the very table his grandfather sat at before him, and the toast would be the same as it was then: 'To Fortune, a much-maligned lady!'

Kate soon sees the way the land lies. That is, in the face of my Waugh fixation, she suggests that she motors into Wimborne and books us in for the night at the Albion Inn, as She-Evelyn might have done in days of old. So what does that suggest we're in for? Another night lying awake listening to the inn sign swinging in the breeze? Well, that's fine, because it will give me time here on my own to nail this right now. I get out a notebook and make a start. It's to be an imagined scene for *Decline and Fall* in the light of having read *Motor Tramp*. Just as Evelyn effectively succeeded in writing John Heygate into his last imaginative work, *Unconditional Surrender*, so I'm intent on retrospectively reading Heygate into Waugh's first novel.

Kate asks what I mean. Oh, so she's hanging on in there is she? She's seeing this process through to the end? Well that's good. I mean that should be good for the work. I get out of my bag one of my most valued possessions. It's the red-and-black snakeskin-pattern hardcover edition of *Decline and Fall*, the original form of the book as published by Chapman and Hall. It's not one of the two thousand-odd books first published in September 1928, but one of the fifth impression that came out in May 1930, on the back of *Vile Bodies'* best-sellerdom. As I lay it open on the table, the snakeskin cover soaks up a little spilt Badger. The black and red blur together to form a purple patch, the size of an old penny, which only adds to the book's value as far as I'm concerned. Then I turn to the chapter in the last part of the book entitled 'Resurrection'.

I tell Kate: 'Three weeks after the bogus appendectomy operation that got him out of Egdon Heath Prison, Paul is sitting on the veranda of Margot's villa on Corfu, with his evening aperitif before him. Margot is not in residence. He is watching the sunset on the Albanian

Hills as Waugh himself did when he came back from a trip to Greece to see Alastair Graham. Later, Paul walks down to the quayside and bumps into Otto Silenus, the odd architect who turned Margot's country house, King's Thursday, into a Modernist monstrosity. Back at Margot's Mediterranean villa, Otto makes a big speech to Paul, in which he compares life to the big wheel at Luna Park.'

As I'm telling Kate this, the analogy makes sense to me for the first time. Because I realise that the wheel is not a vertical one, like the London Eye, but a great disc that revolves quickly in the middle of the floor. 'I must have read that carelessly on previous occasions. It makes much more sense now. Otto divides people into different groups. Group one: those who sit in rows of seats away from the wheel itself, minding their own business or watching what happens to those who try and sit on the wheel. Group two: those who try and sit on the wheel but who are continually having to resist being flung from it by centrifugal force. Or do I mean centripetal force?'

'I don't know. But I know what you mean.'

'And thirdly those rare individuals who have the ability to get to the middle of the circle, where the hub is hardly moving and where it is much easier to stay on the wheel. Otto reckons he is of this third kind. Grimes is the sort of person who loves holding on to the outer edge of the wheel, even though he regularly gets thrown off it. Margot manages to cling on to the wheel, never losing her poise even though its going round so quickly. Paul, however, is the common sort that isn't able to hold on to the whizzing wheel, and doesn't enjoy getting flung from it, therefore he should keep to the safety of the seats that are situated in rows away from the wheel itself. In other words, he is a passive type. Otto reckons that instead of dividing people absurdly into sexes, they should be divided into static and dynamic. Margot and Grimes being dynamic, Paul static.

'And Otto sitting at the centre of the wheel. Is he static or dynamic?'

'He had to get to the centre in the first place, so I suspect Waugh sees him as dynamic in a strictly limited way.'

Kate takes hold of the copy of *Decline and Fall* and opens it up at Waugh's drawing of Otto Silenus standing on a pile of rubble.

'He looks a bit like you,' says Kate. 'I think it's the glasses and the sideways look.'

I consider the picture as if for the first time. Otto is standing on rubble. A dwelling has been demolished by a crane, which has clearly been acting under his direction. I ask Kate to remind me what the caption says.

'*I do not think it is possible for domestic architecture to be beautiful, but I am doing my best,*' says Kate, in the voice of a Dalek.

Oh dear, Otto has knocked down the temple in the grounds of Barford House. At least, that's what the collapsed pillar and big blocks of stone make me think of. Surely, I can't be related to Otto! On the other hand, last night when I envisaged Evelyn and Alastair standing in the middle of that temple that was one of several occasions when I felt we had penetrated right to the heart of something – the still, silent centre of another human being's life.

'What about Evelyn himself as far as the wheel metaphor is concerned?' asks Kate.

'I think He-Evelyn is split between the various categories. Perhaps he started off as rather a static person, like Paul Pennyfeather. Later, beginning at Oxford, he tried to clamber on to the wheel of life. He was flung off that by She-Evelyn, one of the very people who helped him on to the wheel in the first place. However, the trips to Africa and South America were attempts to hold on for dear life to the wheel that he'd set spinning himself. And from time to time, perhaps while writing *A Handful of Dust*, he fancied himself right at the hub of the wheel. In fact, I think he regularly felt close to the centre of things when he was ensconced at the Easton Court, from as far back as his first visit in November 1931 when he wrote "Love in the Slump".'

'I quite like that analysis.'

'Funny, that wheel metaphor was the scene I was going to suggest I would omit from *Decline and Fall*, to make room for a Heygate-inspired scene. But I realise now it's much better to leave all Waugh's work intact, and to try and sneak in my own perspective between the wheel metaphor and the Epilogue.'

'You'd better watch out or you'll be flying off the wheel yourself!'

'I fancy I'm right at the centre now, in which case there's little danger of that. But I may be fooling myself.'

'Don't forget me. I'm here as well.'

'How could I forget? This whole project would dissolve without your she-male presence. The vague similarity of the words She-Kate to Heygate doesn't bother me one jot.'

Kate smiles. 'Remind me again – the Epilogue?'

'Paul finds himself back at Oxford.'

'Oh, yes. In his third year of uneventful residence at Scone.'

Kate has that clear enough. Now let me have a stab at sewing a new scene in her mind.

'Instead of going straight back to Oxford from the villa on Corfu, let's imagine Paul being driven in a Daimler, or an MG, to an inn at the top of the Stelvio, that mountain in the Alps where John Heygate spent some time with She-Evelyn.'

'Margot's waiting for him, I presume. Are they in bed together?'

'In the aftermath of making love they are indeed lying in bed listening to the car-climbing event, which has just started at the base of the mountain, forty-eight hairpin bends below them. Margot impresses Paul with her ability to tell the driver from the sound of his car engine.'

'I could do that,' says Kate.

'Be my guest.'

'The first car is driven by Ernest Vaughan. I can tell from the mad revving of the engine. He won't get past the first corner.'

'What is he doing in the event then?'

'Oh, it gives the other drivers a psychological lift to drive past his crashed car with Ernest's apparently lifeless body being carried from the wreck.'

'Nice one. Who's the driver of the next car?'

'Maltravers.'

'Which? Margot's old husband in *Vile Bodies* or Sarah's virile lover in *Agents and Patients*?'

'Can't you tell from the vibrant humming of the engine, darling? That's one car I'll never regret being in the passenger seat of.'

'I suppose you've been there with all the fast drivers?'

'Being with Grimes wasn't much fun. His wooden leg is not up to clutch control, so all that was down to me.'

'A bit like when Aloysius was in the car with you?'

'Oh, I don't like dear Aloysius being compared with Grimes! Leave Alo out of this, please.'

'OK, let's stick with Grimes.'

'You'd have thought it would be quite exciting being driven by such a life-force. Trouble was, his middle leg could only be really satisfied by something I couldn't provide. So I wasn't sorry to leave his car and jump into Nipper's. But being his passenger wasn't much better, darling. Dirty fingernails! And not too fussy about what he did with them, the filthy beast.'

I remind Kate what I'm trying to do here. Paul gets to sleep with Margot. But there is no point in him thinking that the glamorous woman behind the shades is his property. She will sleep with whomsoever she likes, just as she's always done. However, I realise this scenario isn't satisfying me as much as it did when I first thought of it on the first sip of Badger Ale. I've remembered that Waugh already acknowledges the inevitability of Margot's unfaithfulness in *Decline and Fall*. All Margot has done is sleep with Paul on one occasion, in silence and with the light off. It's hardly the basis for a lifetime of monogamy. She tells Pennyfeather she's going to marry Maltravers, and he knows that she also has Alastair Vaine-Trumpington on the side. So I'm not so sure that this is essentially a post-*Motor Tramp*, post-*Handful of Dust* reading of *Decline and Fall*. As Waugh wrote the sparkling comedy, he was already bearing infidelity in mind. He was with the incorrigible She-Evelyn, learning at first hand the power of a charming woman.

Suddenly I know what it is I'm really doing here. As soon as I realised – only the day before yesterday – that it does not make sense for me to chase Waugh all the way to his death, I've been looking to find or to define him at his zenith. Good.

Of course, 'zenith' depends on what criteria are used. As far as maturity is concerned, I think it was at about the time he finished *A Handful of Dust* while staying at the Easton Court Hotel. Or maybe that's too specific. Maturity might almost be expressed as 'closeness to the centre of the wheel'. And for me that would be when he was writing at the Easton Court on any of several occasions between 1931 and 1936.

But I'm here in the Barley Mow because I think this is where he was *happiest*, whatever unhappiness the sublime time directly led to later. That is, he was happiest in 1928, when he was romantically attached to the mesmerising Evelyn Gardner and intellectually absorbed in *Decline and Fall*, with all the Badger beer he could drink thrown in as a bonus.

'Wasn't he just as happy with Alastair? Drinking that bottle of fancy wine, the one that was *d-d-divine* with strawberries, the day they first drove to Barford?'

'He may have been. But he didn't capture those feelings in writing until twenty years after the event, when he wrote *Brideshead* at the Easton Court Hotel. And so there the happiness is tinged with melancholy and a sense of loss. After all it's the recollection of the thoughtless happiness of someone who is no longer as happy or even capable of being as happy. However, when Evelyn was in the Barley Mow, he was happy. He knew it and he was expressing it.'

'And you were happy when you first read *Decline and Fall*?'

'I was happy *while* I was reading the book, but I was seventeen and at secondary school, which is too young for fully cognisant happiness.'

'I'm happy right now,' says Kate.

'Me too.'

'Another drink?'

'Nope, I don't need it. I don't need any more after I finish this drop of Badger. Not a thing to supplement the last year's research. Dare I suggest that this year may have been as good a year for us as 1928 was for the Evelyns. Thanks to them, I feel we've found some centredness at the Easton Court, some happiness at the Barley Mow. And to celebrate I'm going to sit here simply breathing in and out.'

'Meditating?'

'Sort of. Only I don't suppose I'll be able to keep my mind completely empty. In fact I won't even try. In . . . '

'What a lovely time we had at the Abingdon Arms!'

'What about our walk up the river at Oxford?'

'Is that the day we ended up in the Ritz with Richard?'

'No, it's the day we ended up up the Amazon with Lewis Carroll.'

'Oh, yes. Up the Amazon! Would you like me to read some Dickens aloud to you?'

'Yeah, cheers, Margot. Make it *Motor Tramp*, if you don't mind. There are passages in that book I can never hear without the temptation to weep.'

Though to tell the truth, what I really want to hear, now that the afternoon is wearing on, is a particular track from *Heathen*, the album Bowie made a few years back. *Evelyn!* he might have called that collection. The lyric that I've been singing to Kate and myself, towards the end of the day, all through this year of Waugh wanderings, is dead simple, and goes like this:

> 'We should crawl
> Under the bracken.'

ACKNOWLEDGEMENTS

For a wide variety of reasons, my thanks go to Kate Clayton,
Ed Jaspers, Jeremy Beale, John Wilson, Alan Roberts,
John Howard Wilson, Richard Oram, Robert Murray Davis,
Martin Stannard, Chris Sheppard, Val Hennessy, Simon Petherick,
Ryan Davies, Luke Ingram, Jamie Keenan, Richard Heygate
and Alexander Waugh.

I am so sad that John Howard Wilson died between
the writing of this book and its publication.

I should point out that Kate has not corresponded
with or met Richard Heygate.

COPYRIGHT INFORMATION

293